Wine Education Made Easy:

Understanding the Grapes and the Wine We Love

By

BuyWine.com Wine Academy

Contributors:
Elliott Essmen, Zeke Quezada, Alma Callan, Joe Filutze

Wine Education Made Easy
By BuyWine.com

Copyright ©2018

For Miss Victoria,
Thank you for sharing your time with my Business for all these years. You are my treasure; God gave me you as the most precious thing ever!
"Stay Blessed Always"

Table of Contents

Chapter One

What Exactly Is Wine?

Wine is fermented fruit juice. Fermentation occurs when microorganisms called yeast metabolize the sugars in fruit juice, creating alcohol and flavor compounds.

The yeast may occur naturally in the environment, or the winemaker might add commercially produced yeast.

Of all the fruits used to make wine, the fruit of the **grape** is the most widespread and successful for several reasons.

Reason One: Grapes are among the **sweetest** of fruits. This means their sugar content is sufficient to generate the level of alcohol consumers expect in a wine. When trying to make wine using the juice of apples, for example, producers must often add sugar from another source, because the apple juice simply is not sweet enough. Ironically, many times the sweetener they use is concentrated white grape juice.

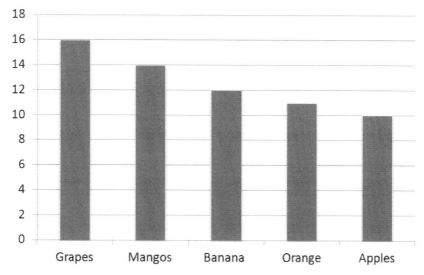

Sugar Content grams per 100 grams

Reason Two: Grapes have the right kind of **acid**. **Tartaric acid** maintains the chemical stability of the wine and contributes to its taste and color. You will notice from this chart of fruit acidity that grapes do not have the **most** acidity (there is more to a wine than acidity), but the **right kind**, tartaric acid.

Fruit Juice	Acidity g per 100ml	Type of Acid
Apple	0.36-0.80	Malic Acid
Cranberry	1.6-3.6	Citric Acid
Grapefruit	1.2-2.0	Citric Acid
Lemon	4.0-6.2	Citric Acid
Mango	0.34-0.84	Citric Acid
Orange	0.80-1.4	Citric Acid
Peach	0.24-0.94	Citric Acid
Pineapple	0.7-1.6	Citric Acid
Plum	0.94-1.64	Malic Acid
Strawberry	0.6-1.1	Citric Acid
Grape	0.4-0.9	Tartaric Acid
Tomato	0.34-1.0	Citric Acid

Reason Three: Grapes bring **flavor intensity**, on their own and when fermented with yeast.

Reason Four: Red (black) grape skins, seeds and stems add **tannin**s to wines. These are naturally occurring compounds that give the sensation of dryness or astringency in the mouth. We do not taste tannins – we feel them.

The right balance of tannins with alcohol, flavor and acidity makes for an enjoyable and balanced red wine.

Chapter Two

A Short History of Wine

The oldest evidence of winemaking comes to us from the Caucasus region and the Middle East (where the present-day countries of Georgia, Armenia, Azerbaijan, Turkey, Iran and Iraq intersect).

Map of Caucasus and Near East

Wild grapes grow in this region. Neolithic humans probably enjoyed eating the sweet fruit of these vines. Pottery containers appeared during the late Neolithic era, about 11,000 BC. The first wine probably fermented spontaneously when grapes were stored in a pottery vessel. The weight of the grapes broke some of the skins, juice collected at the bottom of the pot, and wild yeasts started to consume the sugars in the juice, creating a mildly alcoholic beverage. It did not take people long to figure out how to make this happy juice on purpose.

The oldest evidence of human winemaking comes to us from the country of Georgia and dates to about 6,000 BC. Eight thousand years later, Georgia has a healthy wine industry and claims to be "The Cradle of Wine." In neighboring Armenia, archaeological evidence of a complete winery dates to 4,100 BC. This winery includes both a wine press and fermentation vats. The Greeks were producing wine by 4,500 BC. There is widespread evidence that the Egyptian and Sumerian civilizations had domesticated grapes and created extensive winemaking industries by 3,000 BC.

"Egyptian winemaking about 1500 BC."

The Canaanites developed a strong wine culture in what is present-day Lebanon. During the Iron Age, they were succeeded by the energetic Phoenicians. The Phoenicians founded Carthage, which spread the wine trade throughout the region. Ships laden with amphorae of wine would occasionally sink, later to be found by modern-day archaeologists. The Carthaginians probably brought wine grape cultivation to the western Mediterranean lands of Spain and France well before the Romans colonized these areas. Significant evidence exists for their influence on the Etruscans in Italy, also before the Roman heyday. Crete certainly felt their effect, as well as mainland Greece.

Greece in fact probably acquired winemaking from several sources and directions. By whatever means it arrived, it flourished. By the classical era, Greek wine would come to set the standard for the Mediterranean world. Greeks introduced viticulture (grape growing) and winemaking to colonies in areas as diverse as Italy, Sicily, France and Spain. The Greeks even had a god specifically for wine (and partying): Dionysus, called Bacchus by the Romans. When Rome supplanted Greece as the definitive Mediterranean civilization, it further developed both viticulture and winemaking. Under the Romans, most of the present-day wine producing regions of Western Europe were established.

"A Roman wine shop sign from Herculaneum."

The accepted date for the "fall" of the Roman Empire is 476 AD. Although the so-called "Dark Ages" were to follow, European winemaking would flourish under the umbrella of the Catholic Church. The Church needed wine to celebrate mass. Monastic orders like the Benedictines and Cistercians expanded winemaking throughout France and Germany. Over the centuries, in many regions, monks carefully developed both viticulture and winemaking as a labor of love, keeping careful records of which plots of land, down to individual vineyard rows, produced the best grapes for the best wine. In the northern parts of France (like Burgundy) and in Germany, monks used meticulous care to produce quality wines in areas of marginal climate, creating the ancestors of today's cool-climate wines. The monastic wine culture continued for at least a thousand years.

A monk making sure the wine is just right.

For several reasons, by the modern era, France came to lead the world of wine.

- One reason has to do with climate. France straddles the Mediterranean and continental climates of Europe, resulting in a great variety of wine types and concomitant expertise.

- France s rivers supported an excellent wine transportation system, bridging Mediterranean and Atlantic Europe and giving wine access to international markets.

- France s rival and trading partner England also played a part in making France the leader. The marriage of England s Henry II and Eleanor of Aquitaine in 1158 brought vast areas of southwestern France, including Bordeaux, under English control, and gave the English a taste for French wine that persisted long beyond England s loss of its French territories in the Hundred Year s War (1337-1453). The light red Bordeaux wine that came to be called Claret became a part of British culture (and both red and white Burgundy would eventually follow).

- Champagne for one, would not exist without the British, whose glassmakers were the first to produce bottles that could withstand the pressure of all those bubbles. It s not just France we are fighting for, it s Champagne, Winston Churchill is reputed to have said.

- The French Revolution (1789-1799) saw great upheaval and the expropriation of monastic vineyards, but it also ushered in an age of standard setting, the metric system being a prime example. Although some of the first wine standards were put into place in Portugal, France was the first country to create a truly organized national wine place naming system, the controlled appellation system, which became the international model. French wine, and British enthusiasm for it, proved a powerful combination.

Let's look for a moment at those wine grapes we consider "international" varieties (they grow all over the world and are made into wine all over the world). Among red grapes, these are Cabernet Sauvignon, Merlot, Pinot Noir, and Syrah. These are all of French origin. The white grapes are Chardonnay, Sauvignon Blanc, Pinot Gris (or Grigio), and Riesling. Riesling is German; the other three are French. Sometimes you see Chenin Blanc and Sémillon, both French, on the list.

Wine producers all over the world are planting Tempranillo and Garnacha (from Spain), Sangiovese and Barbera (from Italy), and even Assyrtiko from Greece, but the French grapes are still the biggies. It's worth noting that Malbec, which thrives in Argentina, and Carménère, which is big in Chile, are both originally French. Ditto for Uruguay's Tannat. Australia's number one grape Shiraz is actually Syrah, originally French.

It is worth adding that British tastes and market also made the international market for fortified wines like Portugal's Port and Madeira, Spain's Sherry, and Sicily's Marsala (which was actually invented by Englishman John Woodhouse in 1773).

The wine world will undoubtedly evolve and generate competition for the Cabernets and Chardonnays, the Syrahs and Sauvignon Blancs, especially when you consider climate change and global warming. Even here, the Brits have a leg up—the warming climate is having the effect of transforming England into a country that not only buys wine, but that also produces it.

Chapter Three

Wine Grape Species

Like all plants, we classify grapevines according to the system of taxonomy laid out by Swedish botanist Carl Linnaeus in 1753. Grapevines belong to the order called Vitales, the family called Vitaceae and the genus Vitis. The genus Vitis has about sixty different species, but one species rules the world of wine: Vitis vinifera, the Old World wine grape.

All the international grape varieties are sub-species, cultivars, of Vitis vinifera: Cabernet Sauvignon, Merlot, Pinot Noir, Syrah, Chardonnay, Sauvignon Blanc, Pinot Gris, Riesling. Add to these some dozens of other important wine grapes: Zinfandel, Sangiovese, Tempranillo, Garnacha, Albariño, Barbera, Nebbiolo, Chenin Blanc, Gewurztraminer, Cabernet Franc, Mourvedre, Malbec, Viognier, and add to these literally thousands of others, some widely grown, others hanging on in a few vineyards somewhere.

"The Vitis vinifera grape species"

Many of these major wine grapes sub-species (or cultivars) have their own variants called "clones." Over 100 clones of Pinot Noir exist, as an example.

What about the other fifty-nine species of Vitis other than Vitis vinifera? A good many of these species are native to North America. A prominent example is the Vitis labrusca, which we know better as the Concord grape. The Concord is great for eating out of hand, making grape juice or grape jelly, but early European settlers found that wine produced from labrusca grapes had an off taste of strawberries and wet fur, an unpleasant taste they labeled "foxy."

"No problem," they said. "We will bring over vinifera vines and grow them in the New World." American founding father Thomas Jefferson was one of those people who tried. He imported Italian Sangiovese vines to grow on this Virginia estate Monticello. He also imported an Italian winemaker. No matter what Jefferson did (or ordered his slaves to do), none of these vines lived long enough to bear fruit.

In the eighteenth century, no one could figure out why non-vinifera vines thrived (but made poor quality wine) and vinifera vines didn't make it. The reason would become evident in the next century. The culprit was the North American vine pest called phylloxera. Phylloxera is a sap-sucking insect, akin to an aphid, which attacks grapevine roots. American vine species produce a kind of sticky sap that the aphids do not like. As a further defense, American vines form a layer of protective tissue to cover any cut the insect might cause and protect the root from dangerous fungal or bacterial infections. Vinifera vines, on the other hand, are helpless against this destroyer.

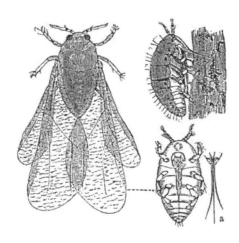

Phylloxera

During the 1850's, Victorian botanists imported American vines to England for their botanical gardens. The advent of the steamship shortened the ocean crossing dramatically, allowing phylloxera insects to survive among the vines. Within a few years, phylloxera destroyed every vineyard in England. It next hopped over to France. In 1863, the first French vines began to die. Over the next 25 years, phylloxera nearly wiped out French viticulture. It soon spread to the rest of Europe. Grape growers tried every method under the sun to combat the menace: copper solutions, flooding the fields, burying a live toad under each vine to "draw out the poison." Nothing worked.

It was phylloxera that spurred horticulturalists to create **hybrid** vines, crossing vinifera vines with phylloxera-resistant non-vinifera vines like Vitis labrusca. The resistance to phylloxera did not seem to come across in the newly created vine, but other attributes, like resistance to winter frosts, did replicate. Hybrid vines like Seyval Blanc are still used today in cold or humid climates where vinifera vines do not thrive, in parts of New York State, Canada, Japan, and England. Many make delightful wine, but they have an image problem and it is difficult for them to compete with the powerhouse international grapes on the market.

The horticulturalists kept at it, and a solution was eventually found. If crossing grape species doesn't work, why not graft the tops of vinifera vines (called scions) to non-vinifera roots? The DNA responsible for the actual grapes resides in the scion and not the root. Texas horticulturalist Thomas Volney Munson (1843-1913) was the great promoter of this technique (he used the wild mustang grape of north Texas for his roots). The technique worked, and the delighted French government awarded Munson the Legion d'Honneur.

Today, except in some isolated areas (particularly in Chile and Australia) where phylloxera does not reach, all commercial grapes are grafted to phylloxera resistant rootstock. Once grafting became the norm, rootstocks were developed to respond to a wide range of environmental challenges such as resistance to other diseases and pests, soil salinity, calcium content, soil acidity and alkalinity, too much water, too little water, cold resistance, heat stress, and so forth.

Chapter Four

Red Wine Grapes and Their Personalities

We use the terms "black grapes" and "red grapes" interchangeably. In either case, these grapes produce what is commonly termed "red" wine. Red grapes vary immensely as to the climates they prefer, the acidity they bring to the table, and their levels of tannins (the compounds in grape skins, seeds and stems that bring astringency, a drying sensation felt in the mouth). Like people, wine grapes seem to have different personalities. We take the liberty of giving them these human attributes.

Cabernet Sauvignon: The Hero

Robin Hood represents the heroic qualities of Cabernet.

Cabernet is relatively young, only appearing in its native Bordeaux region of France in the 17th century. The grape is a cross between the red Cabernet Franc and the White Sauvignon Blanc. It replaced Malbec as the most popular red grape in Bordeaux in the 18th century.

Buds and ripens later than most varieties.
Tough, thick-skinned, very small berries
Ratio of seeds and skins to pulp is very high
High level of tannins are extracted from skins and seeds during the maceration process

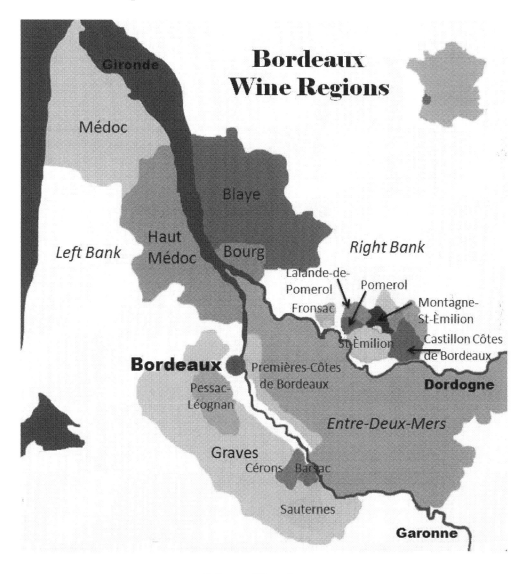

Map of Bordeaux

Classic Cabernet – full-bodied wines with high tannins and acidity, with great aging potential
Typical flavor profile:
    Black currant (cassis)
    Green bell pepper
        the result of chemical compounds called pyrazines, in grapes that have not been allowed to fully ripen
    Eucalyptus
    Tobacco

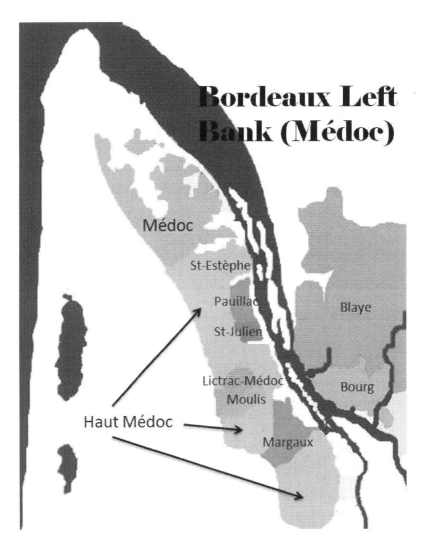

"The "left bank" of Bordeaux is home to the great Cabernet-led *grand cru* wines."

In Bordeaux, Cabernet Sauvignon is usually blended with Merlot and Cabernet Franc.

Cabernet Sauvignon provides structure, tannins and acids, dark-fruit flavors of blackcurrant and bell pepper.
Merlot is the juicer, "fatter" variety; has less structure, but good palate weight and fruit flavors.
Cabernet's robust structure is fattened out with Merlot's juicy fruit – a marriage with excellent long-term potential when assembled with care.

California Cabernet Sauvignon

Began to be produced in Napa and Sonoma in the 19th century
Buena Vista winery in Carneros grew Cabernet Sauvignon grapes as early as 1857
1976 "Judgment of Paris" – Stags Leap Napa Cabernet beat out Mouton-Rothschild and Haut-Brion in a blind taste test, with similar results in another test 30 years later

Napa Cabernet Sauvignon

Grapes picked not only on the basis of their sugar level (physiological ripeness), but also on tannin ripeness (phenolic ripeness)
Ripe tannins result in wines that can be uncorked and enjoyed at much younger ages and that do not need to be blended
New American oak was overused for aging for many years in Napa, but the trend now is to age in less aggressive French oak, often used.

Australian Cabernet Sauvignon

Cabernet is the number two red grape in Australia after Shiraz, with which it is often blended. It is produced all over Australia, but one distinctive region is Coonawarra in the state of South Australia, known for its "terra rossa," red earth soils.

The red earth of Coonawarra.

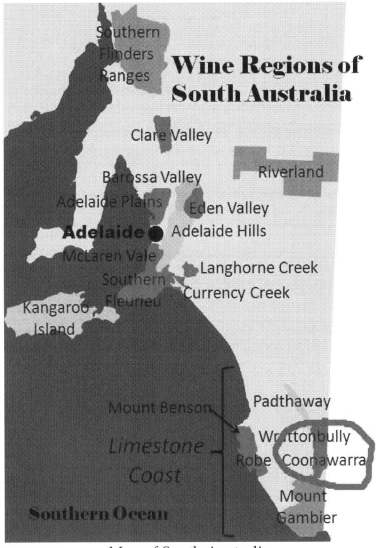

Wine Regions of South Australia

Southern Flinders Ranges

Clare Valley

Barossa Valley

Riverland

Adelaide Plains

Eden Valley

Adelaide

Adelaide Hills

McLaren Vale

Langhorne Creek

Southern Fleurieu

Currency Creek

Kangaroo Island

Mount Benson

Padthaway

Limestone Coast

Wrattonbully

Robe

Coonawarra

Mount Gambier

Southern Ocean

Map of South Australia

Italian Cabernet Sauvignon

Cabernet Sauvignon has been produced in Tuscany for over 250 years and is an important grape in "Super Tuscan" wines like Sassicaia.

Chilean Cabernet Sauvignon

    Maipo Valley is a leading region
    Cool Pacific breezes, warm days, cool nights
    Red fruit, green pepper, menthol, eucalyptus
    Does well in Bordeaux style blends

Merlot: The Team Player

We call Merlot the "Team Player" because it is such a good blending partner with other red wines, particularly Cabernet Sauvignon.

Merlot's home area is the Right Bank of the Bordeaux region of France.

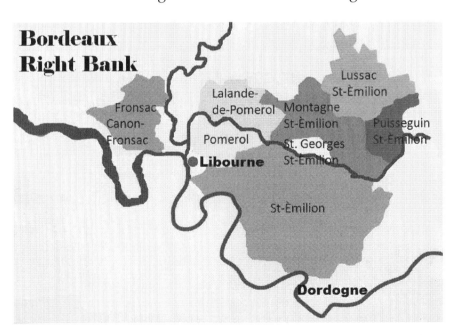

Mao of right bank Bordeaux

Merlot originally meant "young blackbird"– the grape has blue/black skin
Cool climate Merlot has flavors of plum, berries and tobacco
Warmer climate Merlot may have flavors of chocolate and fruitcake

Traditional Style of Merlot

Early harvest maintains acidity
Medium-bodied wines
Moderate alcohol levels
Fresh, red fruit flavors and leafy vegetal notes.

International Style of Merlot

Late harvest for deeper flavors
Inky, purple colored wines
Full body, high alcohol
Lush, velvety tannins
Intense, plum and blackberry fruit.

Worldwide Merlot Production

France, Italy, Switzerland, Romania, Croatia, Montenegro, Hungary, Bulgaria, Slovenia, Turkey, Australia, South Africa, Canada, Argentina

The Ups and Downs of Merlot

Merlot sales skyrocketed in 1991 when a feature on the television show "60 Minutes" linked red wine consumption to heart health. This was based on the so-called "French Paradox," the belief that the wine-consuming French have lower levels of heart problems even though they eat fatty foods.
    The logic:

Moderate consumption of red wine protects against cancer and heart issues by increasing HDL cholesterol and reducing LDL cholesterol
Red wines have high levels of antioxidants
        the darker the wine, the higher the antioxidant content
Red wines are also sources of resveratrol, linked to longevity and cancer prevention

Why Merlot?

Merlot has lower tannins and less acidity than Cabernet Sauvignon and so is considered smoother and "easier to drink"
Merlot is less expensive than Pinot Noir
Merlot is easy to pronounce
Merlot is easy to pair with a wide range of foods

Merlot Quality Declined

California Merlot acreage grew from a few thousand acres in 1985 to over 50,000 by the end of the century
Much Merlot was planted in unsuitable climates, usually too warm for the variety
Following the American rule that a wine labeled with a varietal needs to only have 75% of that grape, much wine labeled Merlot was plumped up with unsuitable blending grapes, which could be anything.

A reaction against Merlot set in. In the 2004 film *Sideways*, the wine-obsessed main character Miles exclaims, "If anyone orders Merlot, I'm leaving. I'm not drinking any ____ Merlot!"

But Merlot didn't sink **that** low…

The Merlot market declined, but stabilized a few years after *Sideways*
Higher-end Merlots are now holding their own
Example – some of the quality Merlots coming out of Washington State
Lower-end Merlots suffered (deservedly) from a reputation problem

Pinot Noir: The Spinster

We call Pinot Noir "The Spinster" because it should never be married with other red grapes. Blending compromises the delicate aromas, flavors, and mouthfeel of the grape.

Pinot Noir is over 1000 years older than Cabernet Sauvignon. During the middle ages, the church produced the best wine in France. Monks spent centuries developing Pinot Noir growing and winemaking techniques. Pinot Noir was favored for the sacraments, which helped its overall reputation.

Philip the Bold, powerful Duke of Burgundy, established Pinot Noir as Burgundy's preferred red grape in 1395 and gave the grape its present name based on its resemblance to a black pine cone.

"Philip the Bold"

Pinot Noir

Difficult to cultivate and transform into wine
Doesn't like hot, harsh windy climates
Genetically unstable – over 100 clones
Highly susceptible to vine diseases
Thin skins, make the wine…
    lightly colored
    medium bodied
    low in tannins
Unpredictable aging
Cherry, strawberry, raspberry, spice, earth flavors
Medium-bodied wine, with high acidity
Low to moderate tannins
Age-worthy, because of acidity and minerality
Transparent – really shows the character of a place. In Burgundy, varies from row to row
New World Pinots tend to have more fruit and less earthiness

Pinot Noir is nicknamed the "heartbreak" grape, because it is thin-skinned and susceptible to all sorts of disasters in the vineyards... and very difficult to ripen.

Pinot Noir requires **low yields** and is subject to numerous illness that can be brought on by wind, cold or hot weather, fungus or rot, due to its thin skin. The grape does best in **cool, dry climates** with well drained, stony, or chalky soils.

"The Côte de Nuits area of Burgundy is the home to the finest Pinot Noir."
Distinctive Pinot Noir Regions

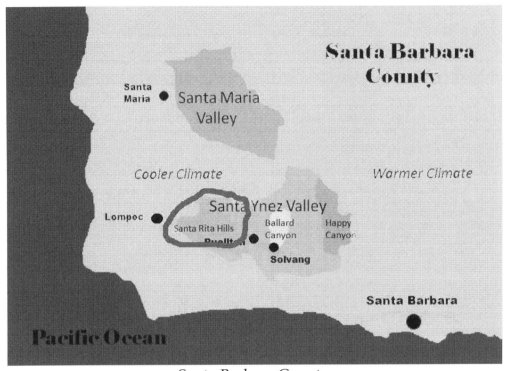

Santa Barbara County

Edna Valley, San Luis Obispo County, California. Photo by Elliot Essman

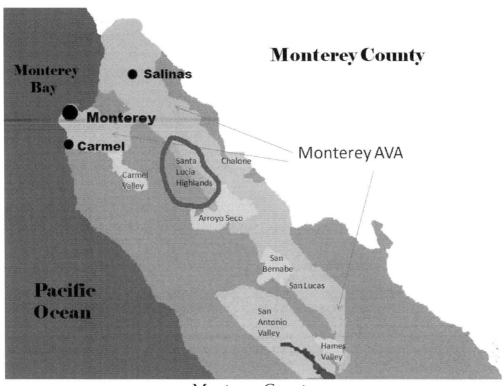

Monterey County

Sonoma's Russian River Valley

Oregon Wine Regions

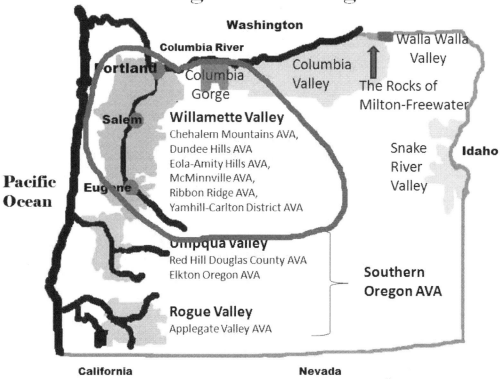

Oregon

Wine Regions of Victoria

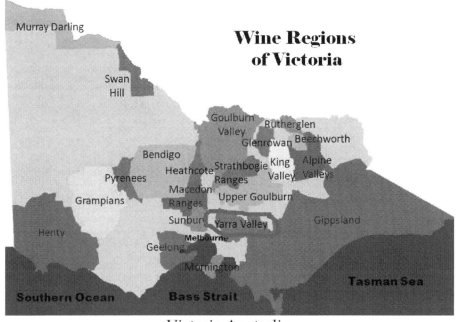

Victoria Australia

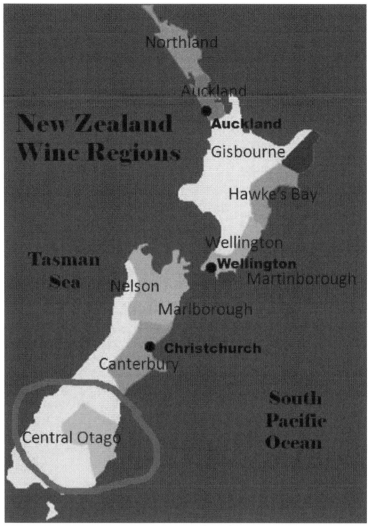

New Zealand

Pinot Noir – Important Grape in Champagne

The red grapes Pinot Noir and Pinot Meunier, along with the white grape Chardonnay, are used to produce base wines for Champagne Crushing the grapes without allowing skin contact assures a very lightly colored wine
Blanc de Noir ("white from black") Champagnes are made from Pinot Noir only
Blanc de Blanc is produced from Chardonnay

Pinot Noir and Chardonnay

Pinot Noir is one of the parent grapes of Chardonnay
Both are characteristic grapes of Burgundy, where each is almost always produced as a single varietal wine
Pinot Noir and Chardonnay prefer similar cool-climate growing regions, on a worldwide basis
The term "Burgundian varieties" refers to both

The Other Pinots

Pinot Gris (Pinot Grigio), Pinot Blanc, Pinot Meunier (used in Champagne) are probably not separate grape varieties
They are color mutations of Pinot Noir

Pinot Noir In Other Languages

Italy: Pinot Nero
Germany: Spätburgunder (late Burgundy)
Austria: Blauburgunder (blue Burgundy)
Hungary: Nagyburgund (great Burgundy)

Effect on Pinot Noir of the Film *Sideways*

Sideways promoted Pinot Noir
Pinot Noir demand skyrocketed
Finicky Pinot Noir is even harder to grow more of than Merlot, and quality suffered greatly
Unlike Merlot, Pinot Noir is best as an **unblended single varietal wine**
> Delicate aromas and flavors easily overwhelmed
> But it was plumped up with other varieties
The result was a lot of mediocre Pinot on the market, especially at lower price points

Syrah: The Gentleman

We call Syrah the "Gentleman" because it has natural elegance and strength, without being pushy.

The traditional home of Syrah is the northern Rhône region of France where the most prominent appellations are Côte-Rôtie and Hermitage.

Northern Rhône

Syrah is a small, dark skinned berry
     small bunches
     high acidity and tannins (less than Cabernet)
Ripens best in dry climates and soils that allow for deep root penetration
Lost ground and foreign attention in the first half of the twentieth century
Strong resurgence since 1970

Syrah Around the World

Moderate climates (northern Rhône Valley, Central Coast California)
     medium to full-bodied wines
     medium-plus to high levels of tannins
     flavors of blackberry, mint and black pepper

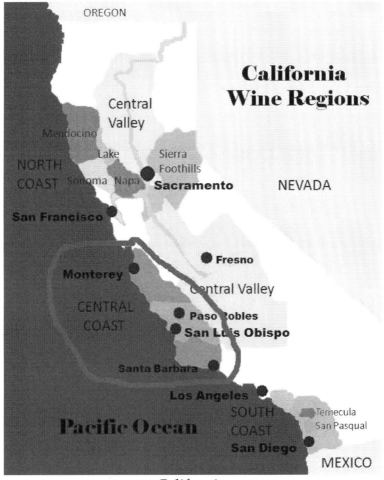

California

Warm Climates (The Shiraz of the Barossa Valley and McLaren Vale of South Australia)

  full-bodied with softer tannins

  jammier fruit and spice notes of licorice, anise and earthy leather.

.

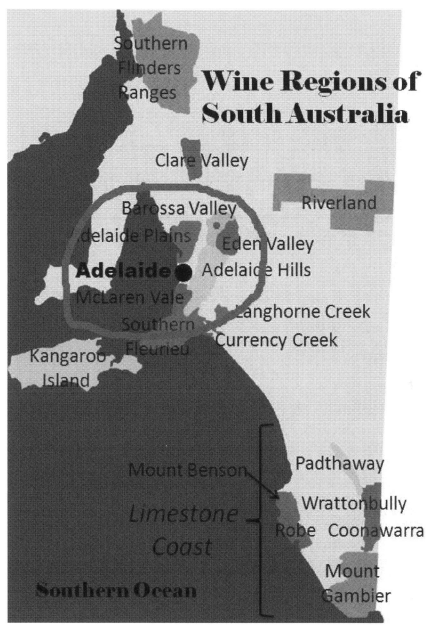

South Australia

Shiraz is Australia's flagship grape. It is often blended with Grenache and Mourvèdre to create distinctive GSM wines.

Grenache: The Poor Relation

We call Grenache the "Poor Relation" because it is so often needs to be blended with other wines

> Mediterranean grape, one of the most widely planted worldwide
> Garnacha in Spain, Cannonau in Sardinia
> Ripens late, likes hot climates
> Spicy, berry-flavored and soft on the palate
> Relatively high alcohol
> May lack acid, tannins, color – frequently blended with Syrah, Mourvèdre, Cinsault, Tempranillo
> France – lead grape in Châteauneuf-du-Pape, Rhône, Provence, Laguedoc-Roussillon
> Spain – Garnacha – Major role in Rioja and Priorat, Aragon, Navarra
> California – Central Coast and Mendocino in Rhône style blends
> Australia - varietal Grenache and GSM blends

Demand for single varietal Grenache and Garnacha is growing with the trend toward medium bodied wines.

Mourvèdre: The Sophisticate

We call Mourvèdre the "Sophisticate" because of the elegance it adds to blends.

    Small, thick-skin berries
    Tannic wines high in alcohol
    Major grape of Bandol in Provence
    Southern France and South Australia – adds flesh to GSM blends
    Widely used to create rosé
    Monastrell in Spain, Mataro in Australia

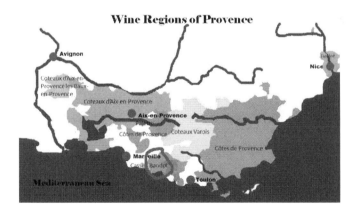

Wine map of Provence showing Bandol, one of the few French single-varietal wines made with Mourvèdre.

Mourvèdre does well in hot climates and should benefit from global warming

GSM Blends: A Distinctive Threesome

Grenache – Syrah/Shiraz – Mourvèdre

Grenache is the lightest of the three grapes, with pale red juice with soft berry scents and a bit of spiciness. It contributes alcohol, warmth and fruitiness.

Shiraz is full-bodied, with fleshy flavors of black fruits and pepper. It adds color, backbone and tannins.

Mourvèdre adds elegance, structure and acidity to the blend, flavors of sweet plums, roasted game and tobacco.

GSM Around the World

Châteauneuf-du-Pape from the southern Rhône is often similar to GSM, with a few additional blending partners.

Australia, especially the South Australia appellations of McLaren Vale and Barossa Valley.

Central Coast California.

Washington State

Priorat in northeastern Spain (Catalunia)

Tempranillo: The Spanish Gentleman

Spain's noble grape Tempranillo is indigenous to Spain and dates back to before the time of Christ. It has been grown on the Iberian Peninsula since the Phoenicians settled it in 1100 B.C.

thick skin
ripens early, hence the name (*temprano* means early in Spanish)
likes chalk
likes altitude (daytime heat, cool nights)
relatively neutral – blends well with other varieties (Garnacha, Graciano, Cabernet, Merlot) and takes on much character from aging in oak
varietal Tempranillo – plum and strawberry, tobacco, vanilla, leather and herb

medium plus tannins, medium minus acidity
Portugal, Mexico, New Zealand, California, Washington, South
Africa, Texas, Australia, Argentina, Portugal, Uruguay, Turkey,
Canada, and Arizona

Tempranillo is the lead grape in Spain's most famous wine, Rioja.   There it
is blended with Garnacha (which adds body and alcohol), Mazuelo (for
flavors), and Graciano (for additional aromas).

Tempranillo goes by more than a dozen different names around the world,
depending on where it is cultivated: Tinto Fino in Ribera del Duero, Tinta
de Toro in Toro, Ull de Llebre in Catalonia, Cencibel in La Mancha and
Tinto Roriz in Portugal.

Spanish Tempranillo (and Rioja) Aging Grades

> Vin Joven – usually unaged – drink young
> Crianza – two year aging, at least 6 months in oak – usually
> aggressive American oak
> Reserva – three year aging, at least one year in oak
> Gran Reserva – five year aging, at least two years in oak

Sangiovese: The Italian Prince

Sangiovese is Italy's most planted grape.

       Best in Tuscany
              sour red cherries, earthy aromas, tea leaf notes
              medium-plus tannins, high acidity
       Bulk, cheap wines elsewhere in Italy
       Plantings in California, Australia, Argentina

Sangiovese derives its name from the Latin *sanguis Jovis*, "the blood of Jove".

Sangiovese is known for its many genetic mutations, leading to a wide variety of wine types throughout Italy.

Two basic styles of Sangiovese:

- Fruit forward   red fruit like strawberries and cherries, tomato, spices like cinnamon and clove, less tannic, bright acidity.
- Rustic   dark chocolate and smoke with herbal notes like oregano and thyme, dried flowers, tomato, gripping tannins, highly acidic

Sangiovese Percentages

Brunello di Montalcino – 100%
Rosso di Montalcino – 85%
Vino Nobile di Montepulciano – 70%
Morellino di Scansano – 85%
Chianti – 80% (most are 100%)
Chianti Classico – 80% (most are 100%)

Nebbiolo: Italian Tradition

Botticelli's Venus

The Nebbiolo grape is native to Piemonte in Northwest Italy.

Barolo and Barbaresco are the most prominent Nebbiolo appellations. They are 100% Nebbiolo from individual villages south of Alba, and they cost a lot of money because they need to be aged for many years before they become drinkable.
Lightly colored red wines, highly tannic when young, often see long aging, which turns them brick orange at the rim of the glass, high acidity
With age, Nebbiolo takes on aromas and flavors of violets, tar, wild herbs, cherries, raspberries, roses, truffles, tobacco, and prunes
Nebbiolo doesn't travel well – Early efforts to plant it in California were eclipsed by Cabernet Sauvignon
The Langhe Nebbiolo DOC encompasses both the Barolo and Barbaresco areas, and allows up to 15% blending of local varieties like Barbera and Dolcetto, making a less expensive, earlier drinking wine
Ghemme DOCG – min. 75% Nebbiolo
Gattinara DOCG – 90% Nebbiolo
Other Nebbiolo appellations in Piemonte include Carema, Fara, Boca, Sizzano, Roero, and Nebbiolo d'Alba

Wine Regions of Piemonte

Boca●
Ghemme●
●Gattinara
Sizzano●
●Carema   Lessona   Fara●

Erbaluce di Caluso

Barbera del Monferrato

Turin ●

Barbera d'Asti

Asti

Freisa di Chieri

Colli Tortonesi

Roero

Nizza

Barbera d'Alba

Gavi

●Nebbiolo d'Alba

Brachetto d'Acqui

●Barbaresco

●Barolo

Diano d'Alba

Red dots indicate Piemonte's Nebbiolo appellations.

Italian feast

Third most planted grape in Italy. Used to be second, before the 1985 methanol scandal which killed at least 30 people and blinded many more
Medium-bodied, fruity wines
Deep color, high acidity, low tannins
Native to Piemonte region of north Italy, but grown all over Italy
Plantings in Australia, South Africa, California, Argentina, Mexico, Texas
Top international potential if well treated

Wine Regions of Piemonte

Boca

Ghemme

Gattinara

Sizzano

Carema   Lessona   Fara

Erbaluce
di Caluso

Barbera del
Monferrato

Turin   Barbera
d'Asti   **Asti**

Freisa di Chieri   Colli
Tortonesi

Roero   Nizza

Barbera   d'Alba   Gavi

Nebbiolo d'Alba   Brachetto
d'Acqui

Barolo   Barbaresco

Diano d'Alba

Red dots on the map indicate Barbera appellations in its home region of Italian Piemonte

Gamay: It's Beaujolais

Beaujolais Region

Gamay-based wines are typically light bodied and fruity.
Black currant, raspberry, violet, banana, earth.
The sole grape of Beaujolais.
A close cousin to Pinot Noir.
Likes granite and limestone soils.
Oak aging, if at all, is lightly done.
Tannins all over the place – wide variety
On the increase around the world in cool climate growing regions
> Loire Valley in France
> Patches in the Mâconnais, southern Burgundy
> Switzerland
> Canada – Niagara Peninsula
> New Zealand
> Australia
> Oregon

Quality Beaujolais compares favorably to its close cousin, Pinot Noir, but guess what…It costs less money

Malbec: The Tango Partner

Malbec is one of the Bordeaux blending grapes

Also called Côt and Auxerrois
Small grape with dark berries and thin skins
Needs more sun and heat than either Cabernet Sauvignon or Merlot
to ripen
Never truly succeeded in Bordeaux because of its susceptibility to
disease and rot, so only small amounts were planted for blends
Grown mainly in outlying areas of Bordeaux such as Bourg, Blaye
and Entre-Deux-Mers

Southwest France

The basis for the "Black Wine" of Cahors in the valley of the Lot River. Grows best in the arid limestone plateau of Cahors

Cahors wine must be 70% Malbec with possible addition of Tannat and Merlot. Tends to be basic and Rustic

A resurgence of Malbec in Cahors is occurring due to the success of Argentine Malbec

Cahors winemakers work with the Argentines to promote "World Malbec Day," April 17th

Malbec from Cahors is leathery and savory, with flavors of tart currant and black plum, black pepper and spice with high acidity, firm tannins, and a pleasant bitterness

Argentina

Malbec was brought to Argentina in 1868

Thrived in the dry high altitude climate of Mendoza

Rapidly became Argentina's number one wine grape

In the 21st century, made its name as an affordable alternative to Cabernet Sauvignon and Syrah

Malbec from Argentina is generally fruity, velvety, and high in alcohol, with flavors of pomegranate, blackberry, black cherry and plum. Oak aging can bring flavors of chocolate, cocoa and sweet tobacco

Big production with a wide variety of quality levels and oak aging practices

Brings a lot of the flavor and boldness of Cabernet and Syrah with much lower tannins

A very accessible food friendly red wine, a gateway red wine for white wine drinkers

And…yes…easy to pronounce

Cabernet Franc: The Companion

Cabernet Franc is one of the Bordeaux blending grapes
It is a partner of Merlot in right bank Bordeaux blends – Pomerol and
St. Emilion
Parent of Cabernet Sauvignon
Ripens earlier than Cabernet Sauvignon
Lighter in color than Cabernet Sauvignon
Aromas of tobacco, raspberry, bell pepper, cassis, violet – similar to
Cabernet Sauvignon
It is made into a single varietal wine in the central Loire valley
regions of Chinon and Bourgeuil

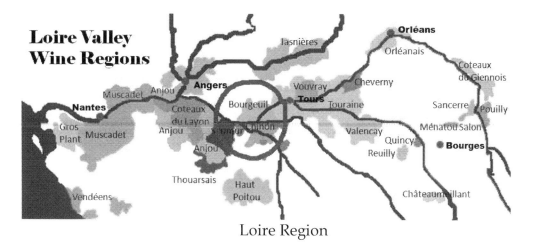

Loire Region

American single varietal Cabernet Franc

> California
> Missouri
> Michigan
> Long Island
> Finger Lakes
> Washington State
> Virginia (becoming the state's signature red grape)

Cabernet Franc – Cold Hardiness

> Washington State, New York State (Long Island and the Finger
> Lakes), Michigan, and Virginia have done well with Cabernet Franc
> The wood of the Cabernet Franc vine has a better ability to withstand
> **winter freezes** common in these areas than do Merlot or Cabernet
> Sauvignon
> A good example of using the appropriate grape for the growing
> environment

Carménère – The Immigrant

Welcome to Chile Sign

A little-used Bordeaux blending grape

Introduced to Chile in 1850s and has become Chilean signature grape as varietal

Late-ripening, does well with Chilean Central Valley's long growing season

Deep red wines, aromas of red berry, spice, smoky, chocolate, soft tannins

Best consumed young

When not fully ripened, herbaceous, with aromas and flavors of green bell pepper (result of pyrazines)

Ripeness brings out cherry notes and spice with leather and tobacco, smoke and cocoa, a savory wine that goes well with "umami" foods

Aging in wood tends to add a mushroom-like earthiness

Zinfandel: The Wanderer

The roads that brought Zinfandel to becoming California's "own" wine grape were long and convoluted, which is why we call Zin the "wanderer."

Zin has been on a long road and several times has almost disappeared

Zinfandel is a black grape. There is no white Zinfandel grape. White Zinfandel wine is made from the same black Zinfandel grape that makes red Zinfandel.
Most grape juice is actually clear. You make a lightly colored (pink) wine by giving the clear juice some brief contact with the grape skins.

We know now that California's Zinfandel is the genetic equivalent of the Croatian Dalmatian grape **Crljenak Kaštelanski**, as well as the **Primitivo** variety found in Italian Puglia across the Adriatic Sea from Dalmatia.

Researchers have only recently determined the genetic connection. The search for it is popularly called the "Zinquest."

So how did Zin get to California? It starts with a Napoleon.

Napoleon Battle

In the late 1700's, Napoleon conquers northern Italy, leading to the end of the 1100 year old Venetian Empire. In 1797, Austria takes over Venetian Dalmatia from the Republic of Venice

Cuttings of Crljenak Kaštelanski grape are brought to Schönbrunn Imperial Austrian horticultural collection in Vienna.

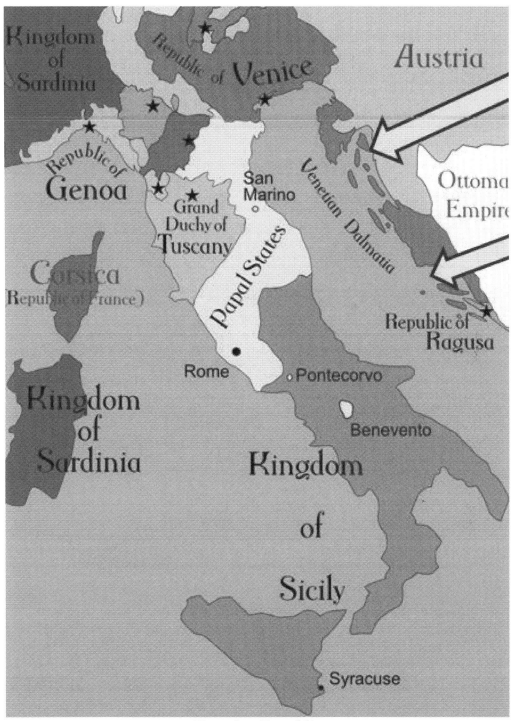

Venetian Republic

In 1829, Colonel George Gibbs, imports cuttings of the grape from Schönbrunn across the Atlantic to his property in Ravenswood, Queens. At the time, Ravenswood was entirely rural, although now it is in the middle of New York City.

Ravenswood Houses

Colonel Gibbs brings cuttings to Boston in 1830. The grape thrives in Boston **greenhouses**, but does not do well **outdoors** in the northeastern climate. Outdoor cultivation of the native Concord grape takes the focus and Zin is forgotten. Zinfandel almost disappears. What saves it? The California Gold Rush.

Gold Rush Poster

Boston nurserymen brought Zinfandel to California during the Gold Rush years. Zinfandel took well to the growing conditions in Napa, Sonoma, Lodi and the Sierra Foothills. It soon became California's most planted grape, meeting the demand of the growing population brought on by the Gold Rush.

The Italian Connection.

> Italian immigrant winemakers adopted Zinfandel as their own in the late 19th century.
> During Prohibition, many other wineries ripped out their vines and planted other profitable, predictable crops.
> Because of their deep culture of wine, many Italian families kept their vineyards going.
> Many of their old vines survive today.

Another threat makes Zinfandel almost disappear. Prohibition.

Prohibition

Many Zinfandel vines were abandoned with Prohibition.
After repeal, the concentration was on cheap, sweet, low quality
wines, which often used "borrowed" European place names.
The California fine wine business did not truly recover until the
1970s, and then it concentrated on French grape varieties like
Cabernet Sauvignon and Chardonnay.
But tough Zinfandel vines survived unattended in areas where it was
not worthwhile to dig them up and plant replacement crops.
We still could have lost Zinfandel in the 1970s as winemakers
discovered that good grape-producing land in areas such as the
Sierra Foothills was considerably cheaper than Sonoma and Napa.
Zinfandel vines might have been replaced by Cabernet Sauvignon,
which became California's number one red grape.

White Zinfandel comes to the rescue

The first Sutter Home White Zinfandel in 1972 was a standard dry
slightly pink wine.
In 1975 an accidental "stuck fermentation" resulted in a pink, sugary
wine.
The wine became immensely popular.

Today, white Zinfandel outsells red Zinfandel six to one, accounting for 10% of all the wine sold in the United States, by volume. Demand for white Zinfandel spurred winemakers to pay more attention to traditional red Zinfandel, especially the wine made from old vines.

Red Zinfandel has once again taken its rightful place as one of California's great red wines. Zinfandel is now second only to Cabernet Sauvignon among California red grape production.

Europe Jumps on the Bandwagon

In Croatia, Crljenak Kaštelanski was down to twenty-two vines just a few years ago, but has risen to 200,000 vines today.

In Puglia, Primitivo was better known and has only increased since the Zinfandel connection was made.

With the popularity of quality red Zinfandel, Croatian and Italian winemakers have begun to label their wines "Zinfandel," but the wine just isn't the same after nearly two centuries of genetic separation.

The difference is not just genetics.

Californians let Zinfandel ripen to high sugar levels, bringing high alcohol, low acid and riper, gentler tannins, for a smooth fruity wine.

The Italians pick the grapes earlier, at lower sugar levels, bringing lower alcohol, higher acidity and more expressive tannins, an entirely different wine style.

Chapter Five

White Wine Grapes and Their Personalities

What we call "white" wine grapes actually run from green to golden in color. We call these grapes and the wine they produce "white" for convenience. No prizes will be awarded for guessing which one we start with.

Chardonnay: The Lady

Audrey Hepburn

Chardonnay's original home is the Burgundy region of France, including the non-contiguous northern area known as Chablis.

 Chablis

Burgundy Wine Regions

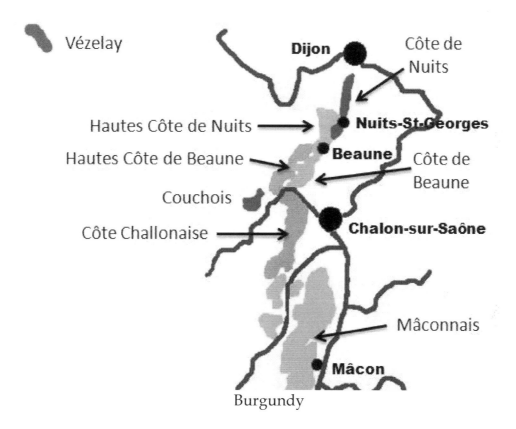

Chardonnay has a second home north of Burgundy in the Champagne region.

The Champagne Regions

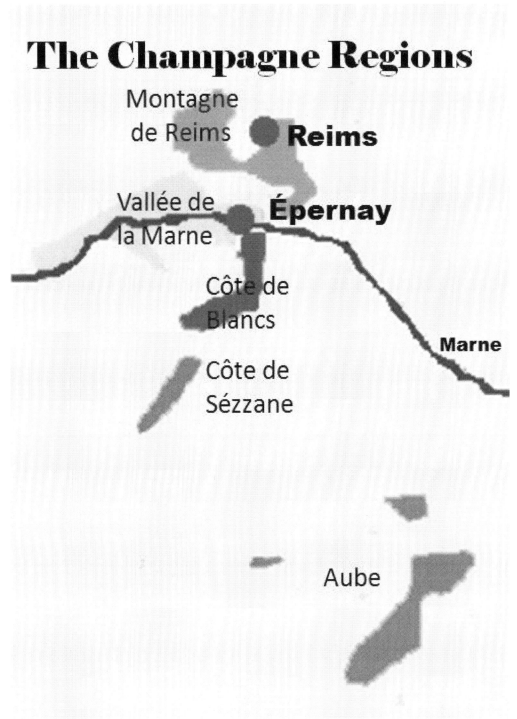

Montagne
de Reims

Reims

Vallée de
la Marne

Épernay

Côte de
Blancs

Côte de
Sézzane

Marne

Aube

Champagne

As to why Chardonnay came to be Burgundy's white grape, we have to go back to Holy Roman Emperor Charlemagne, or more precisely to his queen.

The Hill of Corton-Charlemagne

The land on which the Burgundy Grand Cru wine of Corton-Charlemagne is located was once the private vineyard of the emperor

Charlemagne is crowned Holy Roman Emperor in 800 AD

Apparently, Charlemagne's queen disliked the fact that Chuck's beard seems to be constantly stained from red wine. She forced him to switch cultivation to from red to white, and the rest is history.

The not-so-happy royal couple

Chardonnay:

Green-skinned grape variety.
Originated in Burgundy
Grown wherever wine is produced.
Very easy to cultivate in a wide variety of soils and climates.
A true international grape.
Tends to be neutral, and so affected by *terroir* (the character of the land) and winemaking techniques like barrel fermentation, malolactic fermentation and lees stirring

Barrel Fermentation

Most white wine ferments in stainless steel
Fermenting in small oak barrels highlights texture, body, and mouthfeel
Wines fermented in oak have less oak influence than wines aged in oak, with better integrated oak flavors and well-defined fruit
Chardonnay takes particularly well to barrel fermentation

Malolactic Fermentation

Lactobacillus bacteria consume harsh malic acid (the acid in apples) and turn it into softer lactic acid (the acid in milk).
Malolactic fermentation is encouraged for most red wines, and some white wines.
When done with Chardonnay, this process is what gives the wine its buttery character (although "malo" is often overdone).

Lees Aging

Fermentation creates enzymes which break down yeast cells in a process called autolysis
Cells release flavor and texture compounds such as mannoproteins, amino acids, esters, aldehydes, ketones, and others
These compounds add creaminess, richness and body to white and sparkling wines
Chardonnays may often be aged more than a year this way, possible with stirring

French Chardonnay – Styles

Lean crisp mineral wines of Chablis, un-oaked
Sensuous oak aged wines of Côte de Beaune. Fleshy apple, pear,
truffle and mushroom notes. Rich, sumptuous mouthfeel
A variety of Chardonnay styles in southern Burgundy, including the
Côte Challonaise and the Máconnais

International Chardonnay Styles

In cool climates, more acidity, green plum, apple and pear.
In warmer locations, citrus, peach and melon.
In very warm locations, fig and tropical fruit – banana and mango.

California Chardonnay

Most planted wine grape – 100,000+ acres
One-fifth of all table wine purchased in the US
Prohibition largely killed Chardonnay
Wente Vineyards developed a successful Chardonnay clone in the
1940s
Resurgence in 1970s
Napa Valley's Chateau Montelena Chardonnay beats white
Burgundies in blind test – 1976 (Judgment of Paris)

A California Style of Chardonnay Develops

Harvest at advanced degrees of ripeness and higher sugar levels in
the juice
Aggressive aging in new American oak
Big-bodied wines with big mouthfeel
High alcohol
Aromas and flavors of tropical fruit
Malolactic fermentation for butter flavor
Not particularly food friendly

ABC – "Anything But Chardonnay"

In the 2000s, heavy, over-oaked Chardonnay lost business to crisp,
lemony southern hemisphere Chardonnays and food friendly wines
like Pinot Grigio and Sauvignon Blanc
Trend is now to use less oak (or none at all), to pick grapes earlier to
preserve acidity
Ripe apple and citrus notes have taken over from tropical fruit

Cooler Heads Prevail

Chardonnay does best in cool climate regions with coastal fog that
slows ripening of the grapes and protect development of flavor and
acidity
Monterey County (number one county), Los Carneros in Sonoma
(number two county), Russian River Valley in Sonoma, Santa Maria
Valley in Santa Barbara County
Much cheap Chardonnay is produced in the hot climate Central
Valley of California. It has- little character

Sauvignon Blanc: The Pixie

Pixie

We call Sauvignon Blanc the "Pixie" because of its teasing, impish character.

Sauvignon Blanc's home territory is at the eastern edge of the Loire River region of France. Distinctive appellations are Sancerre and Pouilly-Fumé.

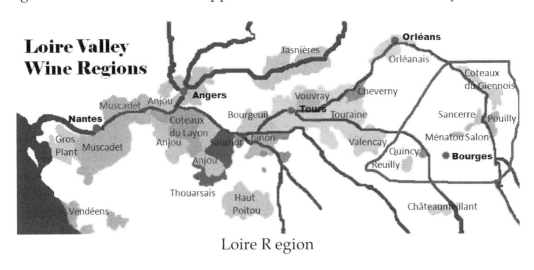

Loire Region

Under the local Loire Valley name of Fiers, Sauvignon Blanc is mentioned in Chapter 25 of François Rabelais' Gargantua in 1534.

Portrait of Rabelais

The term Sauvignon Blanc refers to the vine's resemblance to the leaves of wild grapes, from the French word *Sauvage*.

Sauvignon Blanc migrated to Bordeaux in the 17th century where it crossed spontaneously with Cabernet Franc to create Cabernet Sauvignon

Sauvignon Blanc is widely planted around the world.
Crisp, dry, and refreshing white varietal wine.
Some New World Sauvignon Blancs, particularly from California, may also be called "Fume Blanc" – some oak
Cooler climates bring noticeable acidity and "green flavors" of grass, green bell peppers, cat's pee, and nettles with some tropical fruit and floral.
Warmer climates bring on more tropical fruit notes but there is a risk of losing aromatics from over-ripeness, leaving only slight grapefruit and tree fruit (such as peach) notes, as well as a risk of losing acidity.

France – Three Regions for Sauvignon Blanc

Loire – Lime, grass, minerals. Best examples are medium-bodied, high alcohol, high acidity with white peach, grapefruit
Bordeaux – lighter bodied, lemony, grassy, high acidity, lemon curd, lemongrass and, if oak-aged, creamy nutty flavors and textures
Southwest France/Languedoc – light medium body and high acidity, citrus, often blended with Ugni Blanc or Colombard

New Zealand – Marlborough

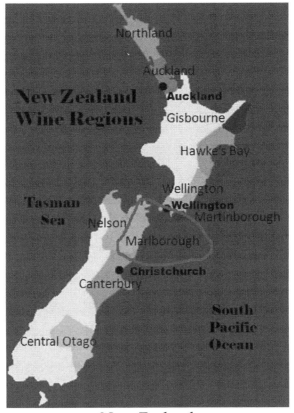

New Zealand

- Cool maritime climate
- Long steady growing season
- Grapes develop natural balance of acids and sugars.
- Brings out flavors and intensity.
- Asparagus, gooseberry, cat s pee and grassy, green flavor
- Methoxypyrazines become more pronounced and concentrated in wines from cooler climates.

In the South Australian regions of Adelaide Hills and Padthaway, Sauvignon Blanc is riper in flavor (than New Zealand Sauvignon Blanc), with white peach and lime notes.

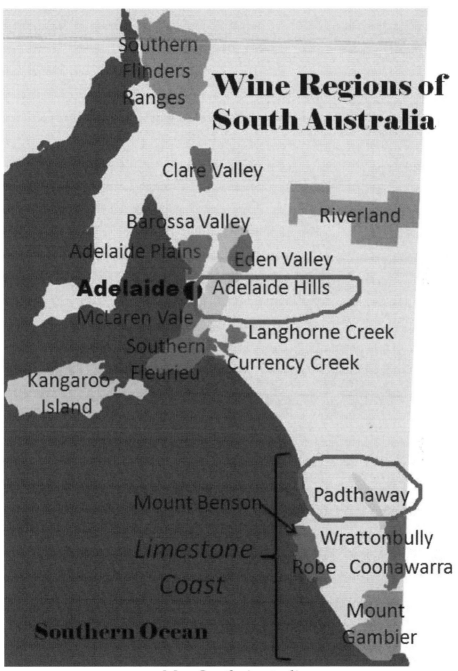

Map South Australia

Western Australia: Margaret River Sauvignon Blanc, often blended with Sémillon.

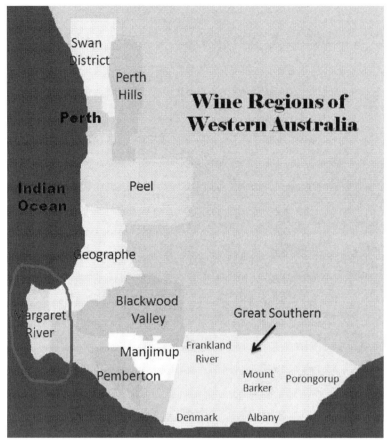

Western Australia

Sauvignon Blanc – Chile
Best examples from cooler coastal region. Notes of grass, lime juice, pineapple, green banana, high acidity and salinity

American Sauvignon Blanc

> Napa – warmer climate – white peach, grapefruit, and honeydew melon, medium body, medium acidity and moderate alcohol
> Sonoma – cooler climate – green apple, honeydew, pineapple – moderate alcohol, light to medium body, mid to high level acidity
> Washington State Columbia Valley – mineral, grapefruit, lime, light-bodied, high acidity
> Some examples have oak aging, lees stirring

Riesling: The German Prince

German Prince

Riesling is produced all over the world of wine, but in general, it thrives in cool climates. Its home is in Germany, where it represents more than half of all fine wine production. German Riesling is produced in a number of quality levels, based on the sugar content of the grape juice before fermentation. We cover this system in the section on Germany.

Map Germany

Rieslings from Germany and Alsace in France indicate Riesling on their labels

Aromatic grape with flowery, almost perfumed, aromas
High acidity
Makes dry, semi-sweet, sweet, and sparkling white wines.
Usually varietally pure and unoaked.
No malolactic fermentation
Highly terroir expressive

Riesling's naturally high acidity and pronounced fruit flavors give it great aging potential

Well-made examples from favorable vintages often develop smoky, honey notes
Aged German Rieslings may take on "petrol" character.

German Riesling's Reputation Problem

For many years, sickly sweet and cheap German wines were widely sold as "Rieslings," although most of the grapes used for these wines were Sylvaner and Müller Thurgau.
The fact that many quality Rieslings have sweetness to balance their high acidity puts off many buyers with bad memories of these forgettable wines.
The International Riesling Foundation has strict guidelines as to classifying sweetness levels of wines based on sugar vs. acidity (each in grams per liter) taking into consideration pH.
Grams per liter is a measure of the **amount** of acid or sugar in a wine while pH is a measure of the **strength** of acidity.
It is all about how sweet the wine **tastes** rather than the actual level of sugar in the wine – the **perception** of sweetness.
It is worth mentioning here that throughout the world of wine, makers of mediocre wine **add** sugar to cover up flaws and then **add** tartaric acid to reduce the perception of sweetness.
In good Riesling, by contrast, both the sweetness and the acidity are largely the result of the sweetness and acidity levels of the grapes themselves.

South Australia – Riesling from Clare Valley and Eden Valley. Crisp and dry with characteristic lime notes.

South Australia

Riesling from cool climate Margaret River in Western Australia may be bone dry with lemon, lime and floral notes

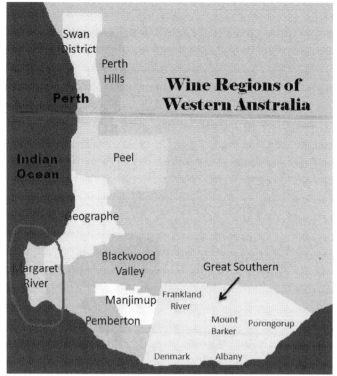

Western Australia

The very cool climate Finger Lakes region in New York State is making a reputation for dry Riesling.

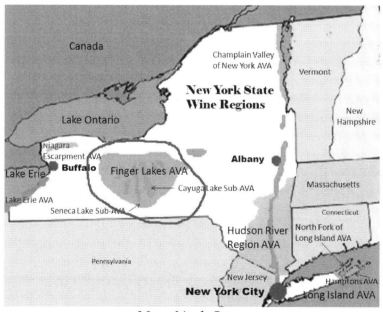

New York State

Pinot Gris: The Two Faces

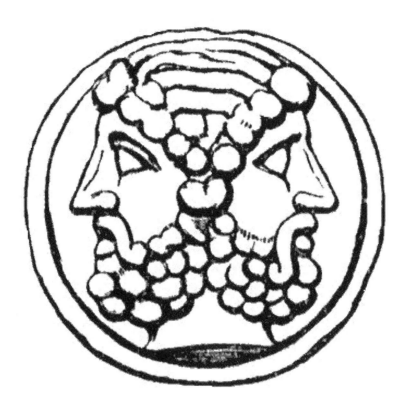

We call Pinot Gris the "Two Faces" because the styles of Pinot Gris and Pinot Grigio (the same grape), are so very different.

Pinot Gris originated in Burgundy, but is no longer produced there. Its present French home is the eastern region of Alsace.

Wines called Pinot Gris

Spicy full-bodied Alsatian style
    some sweetness in Alsace versions
New World wine regions
    Marlborough, New Zealand
    Tasmania and Victoria, Australia
    Oregon and Washington
Apple, pear, melon notes
Moderate to low acidity and higher alcohol
Oily texture – full-bodied

Wines called Pinot Grigio

Lighter-bodied, acidic Italian style Pinot Grigio
Lombardy, Veneto, Friuli, Trentino, Alto Adige
Northeastern Italian Pinot Grigio is the most popular imported white
wine in the United States
Some California wines are produced in this style and may be called
Pinot Grigio instead of Pinot Gris
Easy drinking, undemanding, goes well with food

Viognier: The Countess

The great elegance and class of Viognier gives it its nickname.

Viognier's origin is in the northern section of the Rhône Valley of France, especially in the far northern appellation of Condrieu.

Northern Rhône

Viognier around the world.

> Full-bodied, lush white wines
> > Usually meant to drink young
>
> Peach, pear, violet, floral, minerality
>
> Likes long warm growing season
> > But not too hot, otherwise the is the risk the wine will have too much alcohol and too-low acidity
>
> Central Coast California, Argentina, Chile, Australia, New Zealand

Viognier has become Virginia's signature grape. Its thick skin and loose clusters
make it more reliable in the state's humid climate than Chardonnay.

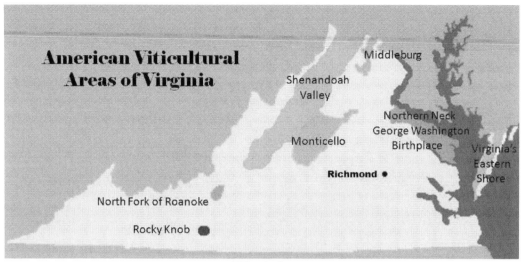

Virginia

Viognier almost disappeared

> Viognier is difficult to grow and is susceptible to numerous vine
> diseases
> By the mid-1960s, only 35 acres of vines grew in the northern Rhône
> in and around Condrieu
> In the 1980s, however international winemakers "discovered"
> Viognier
> Highly fashionable today, it thrives around the world (including
> 11,000 acres in France alone)

And how do you pronounce it?

> The "i" is like the "i" in "onion"
> The "gn" is like the "gn" in "lasagna"
> The "er" at the end rhymes with "yay"
> You stress the final syllable

Chenin Blanc: The Jack of All Trades

The title is a reference to Chenin's versatility.

Chenin Blanc's original home is the Loire Valley of France, especially the Anjou and Touraine regions.

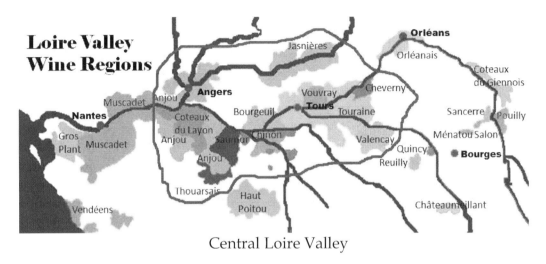

Central Loire Valley

Chenin Blanc's high natural acidity makes it suitable for a wide range of wines – dry, sweet, still and sparkling

When picked at optimum ripeness and when kept to a low yield, it exhibits floral and honeyed aromas and flavors, also green gage plums

A great quantity of high yield low quality Chenin Blanc is produced for blending purposes in California's warm climate Central Valley.

The cooler climate Clarksburg, California area is producing age-worthy varietal Chenin Blancs with musky melon aromas

South Africa is the world's largest producer of Chenin Blanc

Introduced into the South Africa by the Dutch in the 17th century

For centuries South Africa produced inexpensive, relatively neutral off-dry white wines

With the re-integration of the country into the wine world after the fall of apartheid, there has been a move towards quality

South African varieties designed to drink young often have notes of guava, banana, pineapple and pear

The Loire town of Vouvray produces Chenin Blanc wines in all levels of sweetness, still and sparkling. Photo by Elliot Essman

Sémillon: The Courtesan

Sémillon gets its title because when lovingly produced it is downright sexy.

    Dry and sweet wines
    France, Sauternes, Bordeaux Blanc
    Australia, Hunter Valley, Adelaide Hills
    Washington State
    Easy to cultivate
    Low in acidity
    Note that the Aussies spell Semillon without the accent.

Sémillon, blended with some Sauvignon Blanc, is the grape used for the exquisite sweet Sauternes from Château d'Yquem in the Graves region of Bordeaux.

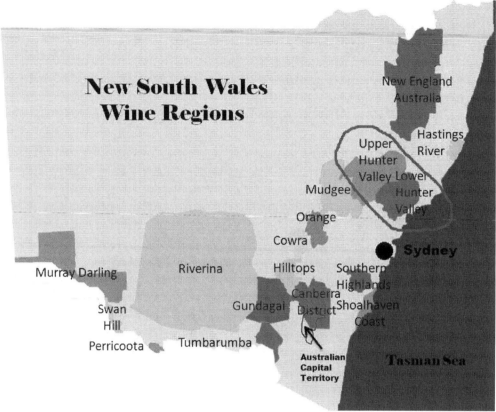

Australia's Hunter Valley has made a reputation for carefully produced single varietal Sémillon

Gewurztraminer: The Spice Box

Very aromatic, spicy
        lychee, floral, rose, passion fruit, savory finish
High natural sugar, results in…
        Off-dry and/or
        High alcohol
Cool climate
Germany, Northeast Italy, New Zealand, Switzerland, USA, Canada,
Southern Australia

Muscat Blanc à Petits Grains: The Sweetheart

Sugar Coated Lips

Small round berries
Ripens early
One of the world's oldest grapes
One of the few wines that tastes like grapes
Makes formidable sweet wines in southern France and Greece
As Moscato in Italy, the basis for Asti and Moscato d'Asti sparkling
wines

Albariño: The Mermaid

Native to Galicia in northwest Spain and northwest Portugal.
Plantings in cooler areas of California, New Zealand, Uruguay,
Argentina.
Distinct botanical aromas of apricot and peach
May be a light crisp wine, or fuller body.
Better examples have good complexity with mineral notes and
sometimes a slight salinity that goes well with seafood.

Rias Baixas in Northwest Spain is renowned for its Albariño.

Torrontés – The Mountain Goat

Argentina – White Torrontés

--Thrives in northern Salta province of Argentina
--Extremely high altitude (highest vineyards in the world at 8000 feet plus)
--Makes up for low latitude closer to the equator 25°S.
--Aromatic wines with moderate acidity, smooth texture, peach and apricot aromas and favors

High altitude winery in Salta, Argentina

Roussanne: The Redhead

Native to Rhône region of France
Unusual russet color when ripe
Warm climates – rich wines – flavors of honey and pear, and full body
Cool climates – floral and delicate, herbal tea
Plantings in California, Texas, Washington and Australia, Crete, Tuscany, Spain
Late ripening and poor yielding, susceptible to vine diseases
Rounds out both white and red blends, makes then fuller and sweeter tasting, mellower
Often blended with Marsanne and sometimes Viognier
Can be a component of red Hermitage and Châteauneuf-du-Pape

Verdejo: The Spanish Knight

Spanish Knight

Native to the Rueda region of Spain
High altitude vineyards with calcareous soils and wide diurnal swings
Extremely aromatic grape, soft and full-bodied
Normally harvested at night, to prevent oxidation and browning of the grape juice
Obscure for centuries, but modern winemakers have established Verdejo as the finest white wine in Spain
Rueda wine must be at least 50% Verdejo
Often blended with Sauvignon Blanc or Macabeo to add body and richness
Single varietal Verdejo is produced
Typically Verdejo-dominated wines are crisp with soft, creamy, nutty overtones, and sometimes accompanied by notes of honey
Typically mineral and highly acidic

Grüner Veltliner: Jewel of the Danube

Most widely planted grape in Austria, concentrated in northeast along the Danube

Large plantings in nearby areas of Moravia (Czech Republic), Slovakia, and Hungary

Herbaceous notes: green pepper, radish, dill, celery, lentil; citrus: lemon, lime, grapefruit; spice: white pepper, ginger; honey; minerality

Generally dry and crisp

Assyrtiko: Greek Treasure

Greek Vase With Vines

Native to Greek island of Santorini

Expresses nature of island's volcanic soil

Maintains its acidity as it ripens

Bone dry with citrus and minerality

Spreading all over Greece where it produces milder and more fruity wines

Blended with aromatic Aidani and Athiri grapes for Vinsanto, noted sweet wine

Slowly beginning to be grown in the New World (Australia)

Assyrtiko vines coiled for wind protection on the island of Santorini

Chapter Six

Wine Environments

Grapevines Need Temperate Climates

Vines need long, warm periods during crucial flowering, fruit set and ripening periods

After harvest, vines need to go dormant over the winter, so they can regenerate and marshal their nutrients for the next season

Too cold a winter is not good, however, because freezing can actually kill the vines

Vinifera vines may die if the temperature falls below about 5°F

Some vinifera vines, like Cabernet Franc, can withstand colder winters

Many North American varieties are hardier and can withstand even lower temperatures

Most productive wine growing regions are situated between 30 degrees and 50 degrees latitude, either north or south of the equator.

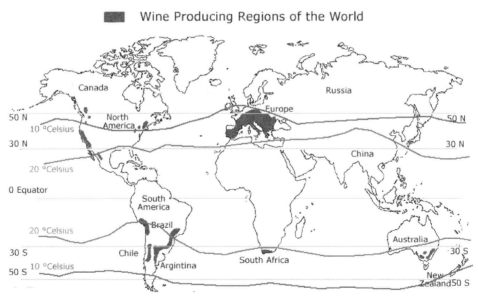

World map showing wine producing regions in temperate zones

Within these temperate zones, three primary types of climates affect wine grape production.

Continental Climates

Hot temperatures during the summer and winters cold enough for ice and snow.

During the growing season, wide day/night temperature swings. Frost and hail problems.

Vintage variation due to weather.

Examples – Burgundy, Rioja, north Italy, Mendoza Argentina, Loire Valley, Finger Lakes, Texas High Plains, Columbia Valley of Washington/Oregon

Mediterranean Climates

Long moderate to warm growing seasons

Little seasonal change – temperatures in winter are warmer than in maritime or continental climates.

During growing season, **little rainfall**. Drought an issue, irrigation may be needed

Examples – California, Tuscany, Southern Rhône, Provence, Languedoc, Catalonia, South Australia, Western Australia, Chile Central Valley

Maritime Climates

Close proximity to large bodies of water that moderate their temperatures.

Often excessive rain and humidity may promote grape diseases, such as mold and mildew

Distinct seasonal changes, but with warm, rather than hot, summers and cool, not cold, winters.

Examples – Bordeaux, Willamette Valley Oregon, Rias Baixas Spain, New Zealand, Southern Chile, Alsace, Southern Oregon

It is often handy to classify climates as either warm or cool.

Warm Climate Classification

Consistent temperatures throughout the season.
The slow drop off from summer into fall gives grapes ample opportunity to become fully ripe but more natural acidity in the grapes is lost.
Inland California, Argentina, Australia, Southern Italy, Greek Islands, Central and Southern Spain, Central and Southern Portugal, most of South Africa, Southern France, Southern Italy

Cool Climate Classification

Cool climate regions get just as hot as warm climates in the peak of the season.
However, temperatures drop off quickly towards harvest, which make the wines taste different. Lower temperatures preserve acidity but they also make it difficult for grapes to ripen.
Coastal California, Northern France, Washington State, Oregon, New York, Southern Chile, Northern Italy, New Zealand, Germany, Western Cape South Africa

Some Other Climate Terms

Macroclimate – the climate of a broad area – Dry Creek Valley in Sonoma, Pomerol in Bordeaux, Asti in Italy
Mesoclimate – the climate of a particular vineyard site
Microclimate – the specific environment in a small restricted space- such as a row of vines

The term "microclimate" is often misused to refer to a vineyard site or even a small wine region.

Vines Need Water

On average, a grapevine needs around 710 mm (28 in) of water during growing season.
Mediterranean and continental climates may be quite dry and require additional irrigation.

Maritime climates often have too much rainfall during the growing season.

Bodies of Water

Bodies of water affect climate and hence wine producing conditions in many ways. The proximity of wine producing regions to bodies of water is a major theme in wine geography.

In a cold climate region like the New York Finger Lakes, the lakes store summer heat during the day and release it to warm up cooler evenings.

In the warm climate region of California's Lake County, warm air from land rises in the afternoon and is replaced by cooler air from the lake, which cools the land.

Major ocean currents are also responsible for cooling coastal lands, which otherwise would be too hot for viticulture. The Cape Region of South Africa would be too hot but for the Benguela Current that brings in cool water from the Antarctic. The Humboldt Current in the Pacific does the same thing for Chile. The California Current swoops down from Alaska, cooling the entire Pacific Coast of North America from British Columbia down to Baja California in Mexico.

Note how the Benguela current cools South Africa's Western Cape region

Cooling fog is an important phenomenon. In Monterey County, California, fog from Monterey Bay pushes in and down the Salinas Valley, bringing cool climate conditions to appellations like the Santa Lucia Highlands.

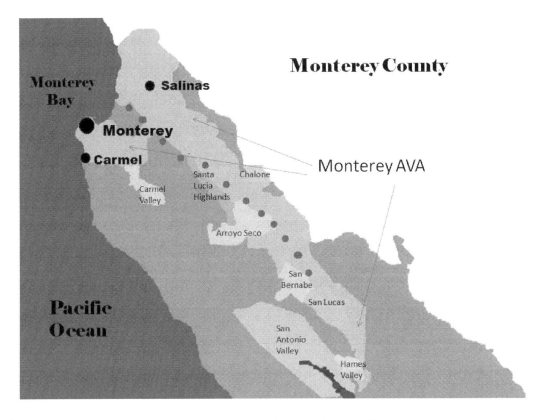

Blue dots represent the cooling Pacific fog that makes Monterey County ideal for delicate Pinot Noir.

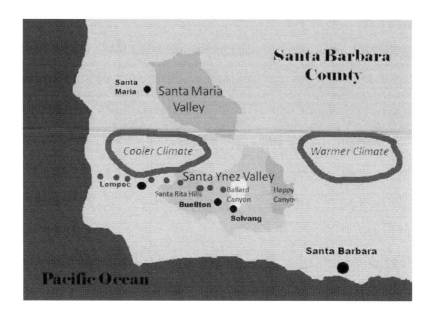

Note how the climate of Santa Barbara County gets warmer as you travel east and away from the cooling Pacific fog. The fog shrouds the Santa Rita Hills on a daily basis. The result is exquisite Pinot Noir.

Rivers have long been wine producing areas. Rivers tend to retain the sun's heat and reflect it out or up to warm adjacent vineyard areas that would otherwise be too cold.

Most major wine producing areas in Germany hug the country's rivers, modifying a climate that would otherwise be too cold.

Vineyard in Trittenheim, Germany overlooking the Mosel River. Steep slopes capture reflections of sun's rays off the river. Photo by Phillip Capper.

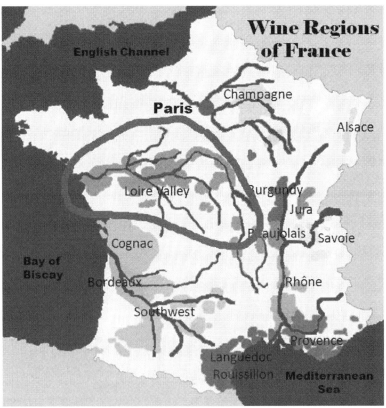

In northern France, the Loire River makes the temperature of the river valley significantly warmer than parallel areas either to the north or to the south.

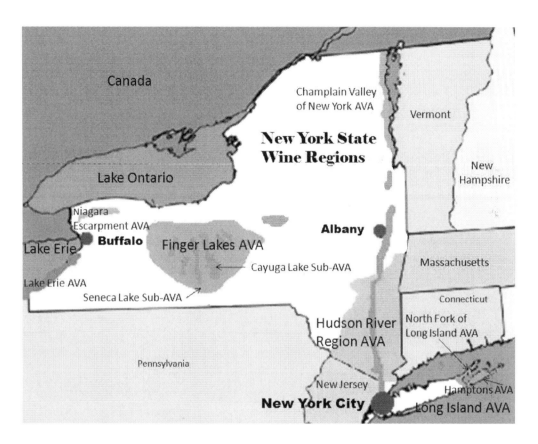

Note how all six of New York State's quite varied wine regions have one thing in common: the title of each has something to do with a body of water: Lake Erie, Niagara, the Finger Lakes, Lake Champlain, the Hudson River, and Long Island.

Global Warming

With global warming, established wine producing regions become hotter. The risk is that the grapes will become too sweet. The yeast used in winemaking converts grape sugars into alcohol, but beyond a certain level the alcohol will kill the yeast and stop fermentation, leaving unfermented sugar. You risk too much sugar, too much alcohol, or both.

Sooner or later, what were once cool climate regions become too hot, forcing growers to change the grapes they grow, which is a problem in Europe's highly traditional winegrowing regions. Cool climate viticulture will inexorably move to higher latitudes, north in the northern hemisphere and south in the southern. In the northern hemisphere, there is plenty of land to the north available to colonize. England, as one example, is benefiting. In the southern hemisphere, Chile and Argentina have breathing space to the south, but Australia and South Africa do not.

Diurnal (Day/Night) Temperature Variation

This is an important factor as the wine grower gauges ripening vs. acid retention. Wine grapes start off with high acidity and no sugar. As the grapes ripen, sugar increases as acidity decreases, and flavors develop. Ideally, vines will enjoy warmth and sunshine during the day, allowing them to develop their sugars and flavors through the ripening process, and then benefit from cool nights to prevent the grape from respiring too much of the valuable acidity and flavor compounds. In an ideal scenario, sugars will increase to just the right amount necessary to ferment the juice into a wine of appropriate alcohol content, acidity will decrease to a level that gives the juice a satisfying acidic pucker without burning the mouth, and flavor compounds will be optimal — all at the same time. This is the ideal time to harvest, providing that it does not rain during harvest, and factoring in the availability of labor.

We have already discussed cooling ocean fogs, but there are other factors that cool off vineyard nights.

High altitude vineyards absorb more solar radiation during the day and then cool off rapidly at night to maintain acidity. This allows the vineyards of Salta in Argentine, at 8000 feet above sea level, the world's highest, to produce wines even though, at 25 degrees south, the region is outside of the usual 30-50 degree temperate zone. The same phenomenon favors Israel's Golan Heights vineyards, 4000 feet in elevation.

High latitude growing areas have longer ripening days and yet greater temperature drops at night. The vineyards in Washington State, for example, see summer ripening days that are two hours longer that those of Napa or Sonoma in more southerly California. A problem in higher latitudes of course is that winter can be so cold that the vines die, an ongoing issue in Washington State.

Arid wine regions have temperature drops at night due to lack of warming humidity. Again, interior Washington State, as in Walla Walla, is an example.

Because high diurnal temperature swings are absent in the vast Central Valley of California, it is known for low quality, bulk production of wine grapes, as well as table and raisin grapes (not to mention a veritable cornucopia of other kinds of produce that do well in warm climates). In the center of the valley, the northward running San Joaquin River and the southward running Sacramento River converge into an inland delta system that significantly cools evenings, resulting in productive fine wine regions like Clarkesville and Lodi. West of this area, the Sierra Foothills counties benefit both from higher altitude and from the effect of these cooling river systems.

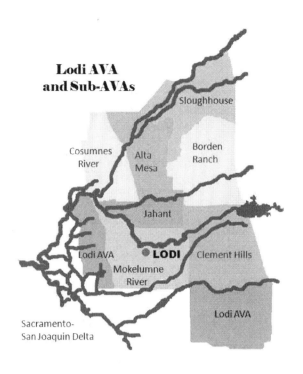

Lodi AVA and Sub-AVAs

Sloughhouse

Cosumnes River

Alta Mesa

Borden Ranch

Jahant

Lodi AVA

LODI

Clement Hills

Mokelumne River

Sacramento-San Joaquin Delta

Lodi AVA

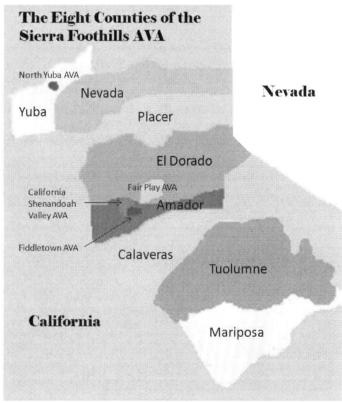

The Eight Counties of the Sierra Foothills AVA

North Yuba AVA

Nevada

Nevada

Yuba

Placer

El Dorado

California Shenandoah Valley AVA

Fair Play AVA

Amador

Fiddletown AVA

Calaveras

Tuolumne

California

Mariposa

Map of Sierra Foothills

Weather and Wine

Weather in spring shapes **quantity** of harvest because of presence or absence of spring frosts, and their intensity

Weather at the end of summer is crucial to **quality** since this is the major ripening period

Choice – harvest sooner (no rains yet) or wait for the absolute best conditions and get higher quality grapes (if labor available)

Winemakers use commercial weather services to monitor weather conditions both at the macro and micro level: using weather satellites for a larger picture and vineyard-specific sensors

Vineyard Elevation

Planting a vineyard on or near the highest point on any given location will promote better air and water drainage.

Air drainage is essential in frost and freeze events. Cold air is heavier than warm air, so it settles in low areas.

Water drainage is also important because standing water will limit the oxygen available to the vine root system.

Vineyard Aspect – angle toward the sun

In the northern hemisphere, in cool climates, southern, southeastern, and southwestern slopes allow maximum heat accumulation to grow and ripen grapes.

In climates with warm or hot summers and cold winters, eastern, northern, and northeastern slopes moderate the heat.

The reverse is true in the southern hemisphere.

Vineyard Soil

Ideal soil is deep, **well-drained**, with some water-holding capacity (so vines don't suffer in heat).

Grapevines like infertile ground. Roots spread far and deep in search for water and nutrients.

Reflective and re-radiation effects of the soil are important in cooler growing regions where every heat unit is needed to ripen the grapes.

Growing Season

Growing season – number of days between last frost (28°F) in spring and first frost in fall.

Season must be long enough to let both the fruit (grapes) and vegetative parts (leaves) of the vine mature.

Look for the coolest possible site that can fully ripen any variety on a consistent basis.

Chapter Seven

Vine Diseases and Pests

We have already covered phylloxera. Phylloxera might be the worst scourge ever to hit wine grapes, but it is by no means the only one. Vines are subject to attack from pests that range from deer to birds. We cover here the major fungal vine disease, several bacterial diseases, and common insect pests. Sometimes these appear together as in the cases where insects damage parts of the plant encouraging either fungal or bacterial infection.

There is no cure for some scourges of the vine. Sometimes winegrowers need to remove affected vines, or parts of vines. Other problems respond to chemical spraying. There is an increasing trend toward using natural means of pest control, such as encouraging beneficial insects who prey on the bad guys. Often the best defense against some problems is simply to plant the appropriate grape for the environment. Growers in humid Virginia, as one example, have had good results propagating Viognier. Viognier's loose bunches allow air circulation and inhibit fungal problems that are less widespread in largely arid California. In southern California, on the other hand, growers have had little success in combating insect-borne Pierce's disease, regardless of the grape variety they plant.

Fungal Vine Diseases

Powdery Mildew shows itself as powder-like splotches on grapes, stems and leaves. It can kill leaves, leaving the vines defoliated, which interferes with photosynthesis and eventually kills the plant. Copper based fungicides have been the traditional response.

Downy Mildew appears as greasy yellow or green spots on leaves. Leaf infection by bacteria can result.

Black Rot, as the name implies, consists of dark circular lesions on grape leaves. This has the potential to destroy an entire crop. Removal of affected areas and fungicides are the response.

Bunch Rot gives grape berries a soft and watery appearance as they become covered in fungal growth. Bunch rot is most likely to affect grape varieties with tight clusters of berries.

Gray Rot is caused by an unwanted invasion of the grapes by the *Botrytis cinerea* fungus. The fungus enters the grapes and shrivels them by removing the water inside. Under certain circumstances, the same Botrytis fungus can be responsible for what is called **Noble Rot**, a desirable effect of the fungus in which it adds a distinctive flavor and concentrates the grape sugars and flavors, forming the basis for rare and super-expensive sweet wines.

Desirable Noble Rot on Riesling grapes.

Undesirable Gray Rot on Green Grapes.

Anthracnose (bird's eye rot) is caused by the *Elsinoe ampelina* fungus and consists of small round spots that progress to small round shotgun pellet type holes. It affects all parts of the vine and is exacerbated by moisture contact. The copper based Bordeaux mixture is a possible treatment.

Leaf Spot is caused by the *phomopsis viticola* fungus. The grape leaves yellow at the edges.

Eutypa Dieback (dead-arm disease) is a fungal infection that enters vines through pruning wounds, especially in wet conditions, and results in the internal rot and death of entire sections of the vine. It is almost impossible to control without chemical fungicides.

Esca (Black Measles or Spanish Measles) consists of a fungal infection on nearly any part of the vine. Esca leaves black stripes, akin to tiger stripes, and often affects relatively young vineyards. Removal and destruction of the infected areas is about the only response.

Bacterial Vine Diseases

Crown Gall is caused by *Agrobacterium tumefaciens*, and consists of growths on vine roots, trunks and cordons. It usually attacks areas that have been injured, by pruning or even as a result of freezing winter temperatures.

Pierce's Disease is caused by *Xylella fastidiosa* bacteria, which is spread by leaf-hopping insects called sharpshooters, which feed on the plant's xylem. It causes scorching of vine leaves and eventually kills the plant. It is primarily a problem in hotter regions of the US like Texas and Southern California. Chemicals are the usual response.

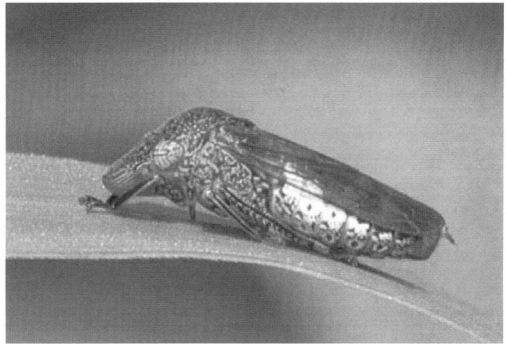

The glassy-winged sharpshooter insect responsible for spreading Pierce's Disease.

Insect Hazards

Japanese Beetles consume grape leaves and buds. These are best controlled using insect-killing soaps or neem oil.

Grape Mealybugs secrete a sugary substance that collects on grape berries and encourages growth of mold. These can be controlled either by spraying or by encouraging populations of natural predators.

The **Black Vine Weevil** feeds on leaves, buds and flowers and reduces vine vigor. Its larvae live in the soil and feeds on grape roots.

The **Grape Cane Girdler** encircles and punctures vine canes. Pruning out infested shoots is about the only control method short of spraying.

Chapter Eight

Viticulture

The term "viticulture" refers to the art and science of growing grapes. Viticulture is a branch of horticulture. We use the term more specifically to refer to the agricultural production of wine grapes.

Left to its own devices, a grapevine will snake its tendrils around any vertical or horizontal support it can find: a tree, a wall, a fence. The vine prefers to head upwards, towards the enriching light of the sun. Its aim is to use the energy of the sun to produce leaves. To the vine itself, the leaves are the gist of the plant. The tendrils of the vine from which the leaves spring have an impulsion to take over as wide an area as possible. The vine, however, is not content to take over a limited geographical area. It wants to colonize non-contiguous areas. For this purpose, it creates sweet and tasty grape berries which contain seeds. Its hope is that animals will eat the desirable fruit, and spread the durable seeds elsewhere in their droppings, in the process perpetuating the species.

This is how nature wants it the story to play out, but humans are in charge of viticulture. For humans, the entire process revolves around the sweet grape. Humans know that some attention must be paid to the sunlight-absorbing leaves, but only in a proper balance with the grapes. The aim is to expose the foliage to the sun for sufficient photosynthesis without excessive shading of the grapes. Shading has the potential to impede the ripening of the grapes. Shading can also promote grape diseases, particularly those caused by fungal attack. The grower will use "canopy management:" manipulating shoots, leaves, and fruit for the betterment of vine and fruit quality.

If any of this seems contrary to nature, well…it is. Grapevines are among the least natural of all agricultural products. One reason we have already discussed: most vines are grafted to custom-engineered rootstock. Further, commercial grapevines do not reproduce sexually through the promulgation of their seeds. As with humans, sexual reproduction gives unpredictable results. Cloning may be the stuff of science fictions with humans, but it is standard procedure with grapevines: asexual reproduction through vine cuttings is the norm. If the desired new vine will be reasonably close to the original vine, the grower may use a process called "layering," which requires bending a vine and burying the ends into the soil. The vine will eventually grow upwards out of the soil, using the nutrition system of the original root while it gradually develops its own root system.

The grower wants to use cloning to create the most efficient and profitable vineyard possible. He or she has two choices. In **clonal selection**, the grower identifies the ideal base plant from an existing vineyard or from a nursery and uses that single plant for all cuttings. In **massal selection** the grower takes cuttings from several different vines in a vineyard that has shown desirable traits. Massal selection is the traditional system. Many critics of clonal selection believe it discourages genetic diversity and results in wines that are predictably dull.

After drastic pruning in winter, vines are precisely trained and groomed throughout the growing season. It is all human action. The only "natural" option the grower has is to use sustainable systems of pest and disease control, but even here the human manipulates nature.

Vine Training Systems

Scores, perhaps hundreds of vine training systems are used in the world of wine, depending on climate, soil, vineyard aspect, grape variety, and, in many areas, tradition. Vines are tamed using stakes, posts and wires collectively called "trellises."

A simple stake vine management system in Italy. Photo by Franco Folini.

This style of trellising in Napa, California is a type of Lyre spur training that creates essentially a "U-shape" with the vines, keeping the grapes high off the ground. Photo by John Morgan.

A cane-trained vineyard using vertical trellising.

The Lenz Moser vine training system. Photo by Karl Bauer.

New vine growth tied to a trellis for support.

Overhead trellis in Puglia, Italy.

Trellised vines, McLaren Vale South Australia.

The Annual Cycle of the Vineyard

The months used here are for vineyards in the northern hemisphere. Southern hemisphere vineyards are six months ahead. We say "ahead" because harvests in the southern hemisphere take place early in the year, in February, March or April, making a southern hemisphere vintage in any given year approximately six months older than the corresponding northern hemisphere vintage of the same year.

January and February is the time for winter pruning. Pruning in winter gives the means of maintaining a training system, allowing the grower to select which wood (canes) of the vine will produce fruit. Grapes are primarily produced from one-year-old canes. This necessitates removing the previous year's two-year-old fruiting canes or spurs. Some one-year-old canes are also removed to reduce yields and amp up quality. The grower wants to favor the growth of the most promising canes. The grower thinks ahead, striving to produce healthy shoots for the coming growing season as well as promising canes for the next fruiting season.

Winter Pruning

In **spur pruning**, vines keep one or two pairs of long canes (a permanent cordon) that run along a trellis. Each winter, the grower cuts back new canes that have grown along the permanent cordon to small shoots containing two buds, known as a spur. Come spring, the buds on the spur develop new growth.

In **cane pruning**, the grower selects two to four shoots (canes) from the previous season to train over the length of the trellis, removing all the other canes. In spring, new shoots sprout on the surviving canes.

In **March**, new vines may be planted from grafted cuttings.

Grafted vines from a nursery ready to plant.

A grafted Vine.

March may also see the beginning of **bud break**. The tiny buds on the vine begin to enlarge and bleed out liquids that rise from the roots. Soon after, the buds push out shoots, For the energy to do this, the vine uses reserves of carbohydrates (stored in the roots and trunk of the vine) that have been created the previous growing season. The buds will then sprout leaves that will commence the process of photosynthesis, producing energy to facilitate further growth.

Bud Break

May is the time the environment warms up enough to facilitate **flowering**. Most grapevines are hermaphroditic, meaning they self-pollinate, just around this time. The result is a tiny grape berry, the result of a process called **fruit set**. The process of fruit set does not always go well. If **coulure** occurs, berries fail to form properly and may prematurely fall off the vine. In **millerandage** berries form with uneven sizes, leading to problems later with uneven ripening and unpredictable grape juice quality. Malbec and Grenache have a particular sensitivity to coulure, Gewürztraminer and some Chardonnay clones to millerandage.

Grape flowers

Despite the name **fruit set**, the grape berries at this stage are tiny, green, hard, high in acid, and have very little sugar. The grower hopes now that spring will bring weather that is warm enough to promote fruit growth. An unfortunate spring frost at this time can ruin the fruit. Growers use many methods of frost protection: everything from smudge heaters to helicopters designed to circulate air. If all goes well, within forty to fifty days after fruit set the berries will have doubled in size and will go through a process call (from the French) **veraison** sometime in July or August. English speakers pronounce the word "ver-AY-zon." It is important not to confuse this with Verizon, which is a telephone company.

Veraison signals the beginning of the grape ripening process. At this stage, the grapes take on their expected color. The biological color change works like this: chlorophyll in the skin of the grape berries is replaced by anthocyanins in the case of red or black grapes or by carotenoids in the case of the green or golden grapes that make white wine. The color change does not occur uniformly in all grapes on the bunch, resulting in brief multicolored effects. In the case of grapes of all colors, the berries start to become softer, the grapes become sweeter as they build up fructose and glucose, and the acidity in the grapes begins to decrease.

Grapes at the veraison stage

Once the bunches of grapes have fully changed color, the grower might want to thin out less promising looking bunches to reduce the yield and allow a greater proportion of vine resources to go to fewer bunches. This quality move is called **green harvesting**.

The period of tension now begins for the grower: determining when to harvest. Harvest usually occurs in September or October, depending on climate (but global warming seems to be pushing harvest, and in fact all warmth-related vineyard processes, earlier and earlier). Electronic equipment can measure acidity and sugar level in a grape, but ultimately the determination of harvesting time is a judgment call. In an ideal scenario, the grower will harvest when the grape sugars have increased to an optimal level and the grape acidity has decreased also to an optimal level. Flavor compounds and phenolic compounds like tannins must also be considered. And yet, even if the grower gets all these factors spot on, two great uncertainties loom. One is the possibility of autumn rains, which can compromise a harvest and promote fungal diseases. The second is the availability of labor. Grape picking, like all vineyard and winery work, is *skilled* labor, usually furnished by teams of migrants from other countries (in the case of both the United States and Europe). It is ironic, perhaps, that many of those who issue blanket criticism of immigrants continue to purchase and enjoy wine—perhaps, for consistency's sake, they ought to favor other beverages.

After harvest, the grapes are gone but the vine leaves remain. These green leaves continue the process of photosynthesis, creating reserves of carbohydrates that the vine stores in its roots and trunks. October is a prime period for this process, which will continue until enough fuel has been put into storage to get the vine through next year's bud break and flowering stages. Once the storage process is complete, November perhaps, the grape leaves turn yellow and fall off, preparing the vine for its coming period of winter dormancy. The grower will leave the vineyard alone for a time, but then the pruning shears will come out and the cycle will begin all over again.

Chapter Nine

Winemaking

Wine is not all one thing. Winemaking processes different from grape to grape, from region to region, from high-end to low-end, certainly from style to style. To break down this complicated subject at least a little bit, we will cover winemaking by dividing it into five general areas:

- Red wines
- White wines
- Rosé wines
- Sparkling wines
- Fortified wines

Red Wine Making

The process of making red wine begins with the harvest. Since the skins of red wine grapes contribute to the wine's color and flavor, the careful harvester tries to keep the bunches of grape whole. Individual plastic boxes are used to avoid a situation in which grape skins will break from the weight of grapes above (if the grapes were, for example, shoveled into a large hopper). The careful winemaker will put together a sorting line, so that quality grapes can be separated from shriveled or diseased grapes and also to avoid getting any matter other than grapes (MOG) into the fermentation vessel. The grapes may then be sent through a de-stemming machine or be de-stemmed by hand. Some red winemakers choose not to de-stem, and send the stems into the fermentation vessel with the grapes. The stems can add tannins.

A grape sorting line.

The next step is to **crush** the grapes. This was traditionally done with an implement that seemed perfectly designed for crushing grapes without crushing the seeds inside: the human foot. Crushed seeds can add bitterness to the mix. Modern crushing machines now use rollers or paddles to do the same thing. Some are combination crusher-de-stemmers.

The crushed grapes and the juice they exude next go into a **fermentation** vessel. The winemaker at this point will either add commercial yeast or depend on local ambient yeast
to begin the fermentation process. During fermentation, yeast converts the grape sugars into alcohol. This alcohol acts on the skins of the grapes to extract anthocyanin pigments, flavor elements, and phenolic compounds, particularly tannins. The seeds also contribute tannins. This alcoholic extraction is generally not enough to produce a deep colored red wine, however.

The wine requires an additional soaking, or maceration period, to bring out all its potential color and flavor. A low-end, mass-produced red wine might see a fermentation period of only several days. A big red wine designed to age might undergo a fermentation of a week followed by an extended maceration of several weeks. In order to extract color, red wine is usually fermented at a higher temperature than white wine. In addition, exposure to oxygen is more prevalent in red wine making than in white. This is because phenolic compounds in red grape skins, stems and seeds slowly react with the oxygen to form pigmented tannins, which contribute positively to the red wine's eventual texture.

The crushed skins, seeds and stems, if any, in red wine fermentation tend to float to the top of the fermentation vessel and form a "cap" that tends to prevent contact between the skins and the juice. Two methods come into play to integrate the cap materials with the juice in order to assure maximum extraction. In **punching down** (*pigeage* in French), a winery worker will use a spade-like tool to break the cap and push it down to the bottom of the fermenter, allowing the juice to rise to the top. This procedure, still done primarily by hand, must be done several times a day over the fermentation and maceration period. In **pumping over**, a hose is placed deep into the fermenter to allow wine from the bottom of the fermenter to be pumped over and onto the top of the cap, thus breaking the cap and circulating its contents among the wine. This is often accomplished using automatic devices.

A wine worker punching down the cap.

An automatic process of pumping over red wine.

After the wine goes through its alcoholic fermentation it might undergo an additional pressing operation. The free-run wine from the initial crushing is collected in a tank. The skins and seeds that remain are then sent through a wine press, creating what is known as press wine. The free run wine is often of a better quality than the press wine. Since the majority of the grape's acidity is lodged in the grape pulp, free run juice is more acidic, press wine more tannic (the tannins come from the skins).

The two types of wine may be processed into separate batches of wine, or they might be combined. With a traditional basket press, the winemaker turns a large screw device that serves to press the grapes so that the press wine runs out at the bottom. Modern wine presses, which are often computer controlled, can exert a specified amount of pressure on the grapes, and have the ability to generate multiple press runs of different pressure levels. This is a way to arrive at just the right level of tannin in the press wine so that the combined wine has the balance of tannin and acidity the winemaker is looking for. At this point (or further down the line during the barrel aging process), the red wine might be racked: pumped from one container to another so that sediment may be removed in successive stages.

A modern pneumatic wine press

Most red wine undergoes a process of **malolactic fermentation** at some point after the primary fermentation is completed. In "malo," lactic acid bacteria (which may already be present in the wine or may be added) metabolize harsh tasting malic acid in the wine and replace it with softer lactic acid. This operation must be carefully monitored because it tends to reduce the total acidity in the wine. Acidity, especially in warm climate regions, is a precious commodity.

Not all red wine sees contact with oak, but in general red wine is matured in oak barrels or casks much more frequently than is white.

In barrel maturation, substance like phenolic tannins already in the wine combine with phenolic compounds from the wood for additional level of flavors. As with any process in winemaking, oak contact must be accomplished with skill and some restraint. Serious red wines age eighteen months or longer. The winemaker must choose between new oak, oak used one or more times, and among types of oak (French or American, for example) before determining the final blend. The size of the barrel also makes as a difference—the smaller the barrel, the greater the oak contact. In less expensive wines, oak chips, staves, and even oak juice are often used to add oak elements more quickly. In some parts of Europe, woods other than oak, like acacia or chestnut, are sometimes used.

Before blending and final bottling, wines may go through a process called **fining**. The winemaker adds a fining agent to the wine that attracts and clumps up fine particles, yeast cells (alive and dead), and tannins the winemaker wishes to remove from the wine. The now-heavier particles sink to the bottom where they can be racked out. Many fining agents are based on animal products: blood and bone marrow, casein (milk protein), chitin (fiber from crustacean shells), egg albumen (derived from egg whites), fish oil, gelatin (protein from boiling animal parts), isinglass (gelatin from fish bladder membranes), diatomaceous earth (remains of ancient sea creatures). To make a wine vegan, non-animal alternatives are bentonite clay, kaolin clay, plant casein, silica gel, vegetable plaques, and limestone (although as to the last, it seems to this writer than a strict vegan would take limestone off the list, since, although it is a rock, it is derived from the remains of ancient sea creatures).

Nearly all wines get doses of sulfur dioxide to act as an anti-microbial agent and antioxidant to prevent spoilage. Filtering, which is controversial because many believed it detracts from flavor and liveliness in a wine, can remove some microbes, but only preservatives like sulfites can keep the microorganisms down over the long term. The alternative, in a sulfite free wine, is the keep the wine refrigerated at all times from bottling to consumption (and, even so, it should not be kept for long before enjoying). For a wine to keep long term, it needs chemical protection.

In fine wines, the various phenolic and other compounds continue to interact and gain layers of sophistication when aged in their bottles. At least this is the potential, but so much depends on how the wine is shipped and stored, and the intangibles of organic chemistry.

White Wine Making

The term "white" loosely describes wines that range from nearly without color to ranges of straw, yellow, and gold.

Color in wine comes largely from contact between the grape juice and the grape skin. Hence, it is possible to make a white wine from the juice of a red grape if the winemaker prevents or minimizes skin contact. We will look into this phenomenon in the coming sections on rosé wines and sparkling wines, but for now, when we speak of white wines we mean white wines made from white grapes.

You cannot make a red wine from a white grape, but you can make a deeply colored "orange" wine from white grapes if you macerate the juice on the skins for a long period to extract whatever pigments are available in the skins of the light-colored grapes. When we speak of white wines we mean white wines made without this kind of maceration.

It is useful to highlight some of the general differences between the process that produces white wine and the process used to produce red wine that we have just covered.

- White wine usually ferments at cooler temperatures than red wine.
- We ferment white wine almost always in closed fermentation vessels while we may use open vessels for red wine.
- White wine is less likely to see oak aging that red wine, and if it is aged in oak, the aging is for a shorter period and with less aggressive oak.
- Nearly all red wines undergo malolactic fermentation to soften their acidity, but this is only done with some white wines.
- Most crucially, we press white wines to separate the juice and the grape solids before alcoholic fermentation but press red wines after alcoholic fermentation.

We begin in the vineyard. As with red wine, our goal is not to damage the grapes, so we use stackable plastic boxes to protect the grapes from being crushed by their own weight. It is also important to keep the grapes as cool as possible through the entire winemaking process, and so we might harvest at night under lights (which increases operational costs).

Next, as with red wine, we sort, de-stem, and crush the grapes. Unlike the red wine process, we then press the sweet pomace that remains to separate the juice from the solids. We want to avoid further contact between these solids and the juice to prevent phenolic compounds (so essential to the red wine process) from promoting oxidation in the more delicate white wine or adding unwanted astringency, unwanted amber or brown coloring, and other effects. Oxidation, which is widely tolerated by red wines, causes acetaldehydes to be produced which can compromise the aromas of the white wine. At this stage, also to prevent oxidation, we add sulfur dioxide (sulfites). Because white wines lack the antioxidants found in red wines (tannins, proteins, phenolic compounds), they generally require a higher level of sulfur dioxide than do red wines.

Some optional steps at this point involve:

- Chilling the juice
- Allowing the sediment to settle out of the juice
- Racking
- Clarification. In this step, the wine is bulk chilled in stainless steel to precipitate out tartrate crystals, which, though harmless, give the appearance of shards of glass when the wine is bottled.

Tartrate crystals clinging to the bottom of a bottle of white wine.

Next comes the alcoholic fermentation process using ambient or cultured yeast. Most white wines are fermented in closed stainless steel vessels, often mechanically chilled, but an option, often chosen for high-end Chardonnay (the most popular of the white wine grapes) is to ferment in an oak barrel to add texture body and mouthfeel. It is important to distinguish barrel fermentation from barrel aging (a wine could be subject to both). Wines fermented in oak have less oak influence than wines aged in oak, with better integrated oak flavors and well-defined fruit. Since the juice is totally separated from the solids, the cap so prevalent in red winemaking does not exist, and so there is no need to punch down or pump over during fermentation (and there is no maceration step in the first place).

The next option is malolactic fermentation. In "malo," lactic acid bacteria (which may already be present in the wine or may be added) metabolize harsh tasting malic acid in the wine and replace it with softer lactic acid. It is this process that creates the buttery taste evident in some Chardonnays.

The white wine may now be aged in oak barrels or casks, but the vast proportion of white wines see no oak. In some wines, oak flavors and aromas are accomplished by macerating oak chips or staves, or by adding liquid oak extract.

A further option now is lees aging, with or without lees stirring. Fermentation creates enzymes which break down yeast cells in a process called autolysis. Cells release flavor and texture compounds such as mannoproteins, amino acids, esters, aldehydes, ketones, and others. These compounds add creaminess, richness and body to white wines. Lees aging may go on for more than a year in some cases. Obviously, this step adds to the cost of the wine.

Because of color issues, the fining process, in which a fining agent attracts yeast cells (alive or dead) and other particles so that they can clump up and sink to the bottom of the tank, is important in white wine production. Subsequent filtration to remove bacterial and superfine particles is another option. The white wine is ready to be bottled, and sometimes aged in bottle.

An orange wine produced by macerating white grape skins

Rosé Winemaking

As we have already discussed, you can make a white wine from red grapes by preventing *any* contact between the grape skins and the juice, since the color comes from the skins. If you allow *some* skin contact by briefly macerating the red grape skins in the juice (say, 24 hours), you arrive at a lightly colored, pinkish wine. The term "blush" wine applies to some very pale colored wines. Some lightly colored wines made by slight skin contact are termed "white" wines as in "white Zinfandel."

Another method is the saignée process, a component in red winemaking (saignée means bleed). The winemaker bleeds off some of the lightly colored juice so the skins, seeds, and stems that remain contribute to a more concentrated color, flavor and tannins in the remaining red wine. Rather than waste the runoff, the winemaker produces it as a rosé.

In the vin gris (gray wine) process, the wine is made from certain red grapes. The solids and the juice are immediately separated after pressing without any maceration. The wine is not actually gray but a very pale pink. French law requires that this method use lightly tinted red grapes like Gamay (the grape of Beaujolais).

Another way to produce a pink wine is to subject the wine to a de-colorization process using activated carbon. This process is avoided by fine wine makers since flavors and aromas tend to also be stripped along with the color.

The actual blending of finished white and red wines is not permitted in France, but there is an exception: pink Champagne may be produced by blending.

Sparkling Winemaking

In its broadest sense, the term "sparkling wine" indicates any wine in which bubbles rise to the surface after opening. Beyond this general definition, the category is broad. We can categorize these wines by country of origin, by base-grapes used, and certainly by method of production.

The European Union defines a wine as "sparkling" if it contains at least three atmospheres of pressure. Wines fitting in this category include French Champagne (usually six atmospheres), mousseux and crémant (also French), spumante (Italian for fully sparking), sekt (German). Semi-sparkling covers 1 to 2.5 atmospheres, using terms such as frizzante, pearl, pétillant and spritzig.

In fermentation of grape juice, we say for convenience that the yeast metabolizes the grape sugar and creates alcohol, but in actuality the process also generates carbon dioxide. In still winemaking, we vent off the carbon dioxide (taking care that it does not collect in pockets around the winery where the odorless gas has the potential to quickly kill winery workers). In sparkling winemaking, we use a number of methods to carbonate the wine. We may generate the carbon dioxide in a sealed bottle, in a large sealed tank, or we may simply inject it into the wine.

The **traditional method** of sparkling wine production used to be called the *méthode champenoise*, but the French have put a lid on this term in their ongoing effort to assure that the term Champagne and any variation thereof applies only to wines produced in the region of Champaign in northeast France. No other EU country may use the term Champagne or *méthode champenoise*. Some American winemakers still use the term, but this disallows their wines from being sold legally in the EU. The best American sparkling wine producers, a number of which are owned by French Champagne houses, label their top of the line products "Traditional Method sparkling wine." Of course, no one can legally limit the "look" of the standard dark green Champagne bottle with its gold-foil covered neck. The traditional method is used for Champagne in Champagne, for high end sparkling wines in other regions of France (where the term used for the wine is often crémant), and for sparkling wines elsewhere. In the northern Italian region of Piemonte, you can find traditional method gems that are rarely known outside the region.

A California sparkling wine labeled Champagne and showing the complete look of a Champagne bottle. The French do not like this

In the traditional method, the grape juice first ferments into a still wine that is specifically constituted to undergo further steps. This wine will be sharp and highly acidic, and not very appetizing to drink. The different Champagne houses take great pains to blend these base wines so that they consistently reflect the "house" styles. The wine then undergoes a second fermentation in the bottle. The winemaker adds yeast and a *tirage* of sugar into each bottle, seals the bottle with a crown cap, and patiently waits for the second fermentation to occur, on a bottle by bottle basis. You might be starting to think here that the final result will be expensive, and you would be right. This second fermentation in a sealed environment creates the bubbles as the carbon dioxide is trapped and forced to integrate with the wine. It also creates sediment, called lees, which must eventually be removed. To accomplish this, the bottles are stored necks slanting down in racks so that gravity will coax the lees down to the neck area. The bottles will then be put through *remuage* (riddling) in which each day the individual bottles are turned and adjusted slightly so the lees slide gradually into the neck without roiling the delicate wine. Experts used to do this laborious task by hand, but many wineries today have large machines called gyropalettes for this task. Non-vintage Champagne must be stored this way on the lees for a minimum of fifteen months, vintage Champagne at least three years.

Once the in-bottle fermentation and lees storage is complete and the sediment is safely ensconced in the necks of the individual downward-facing wine bottles, the wine must be disgorged. The winemaker chills the necks of the bottles so they freeze into a chunk of ice, turns the bottle upright, flips off the crown cap and watches the pressure in the now carbonated wine push out the precipitate. There is now a quantity of wine missing. The winemaker will fill each bottle with still wine and also add a precise amount of sugar, the *dosage*. The wine added is called the *liqeur d'expedition*. The level of sugar added will affect the sweetness level of the final wine. The wine is bottled for the last time with a special cork and a protective wire cage.

Gyropalettes allow Champagne producers to pass the savings in labor costs on to you, the consumer (but they do not – they keep the money).

The **ancestral method** is older than the traditional method. It may also be called the *méthode rurale*, or *méthode artisanale*. Here the wine undergoes a first alcoholic fermentation and then is bottled before the fermentation is complete, continuing to ferment in the bottle and creating carbon dioxide bubbles one the bottle is sealed. There is neither disgorging nor dosage, hence the final wines may be cloudy in appearance. It takes a great deal of skill to produce sparkling wines using this ancestral method. The wines tend to be rural and somewhat obscure.

The **transfer method** is something of a hybrid between methods. The wine undergoes its first fermentation, is bottled to accomplish the second fermentation, and then bottles are emptied into a tank, giving the maker a chance to adjust the blend. This method reduces the chance of bottle variation inherent in the traditional method. The wine is rebottled, with a dosage added. This method is used often for sparkling wines that eventually go into unusually small or unusually large bottles, and is popular in Australia and New Zealand.

The **charmat method**, of Italian invention, is also called the **tank method** or **Martinotti method**. It is used in Asti and Prosecco wines to give a much lighter effervescence than Champagne, and to preserve delicate fruit flavors. The wine is fermented in a stainless steel pressure tank. Once the juice ferments properly, the wine is filtered to remove the yeast, and then it is bottled. The longer the fermentation time, the more delicate the bubbles and aromatic qualities.

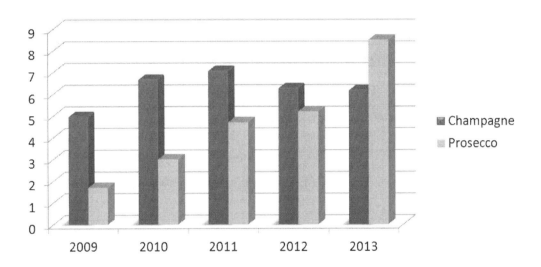

Annual Sales, Millions of Liters

The less expensive, less fussy Prosecco is successfully competing against Champagne in the sparkling wine market.

The **soda method** is an industrial process that injects carbonation into still wines. Bubbles here are large and lack the delicate beading of sparkling wines produced using any of the above methods. These wines quickly go flat.

Fortified Wines

A fortified wine is a wine to which brandy or some other type of sprit is added at some point in the production process. The result is a wine that is higher in alcohol than a standard still wine. Depending on production process and wine style, the fortified wine might or might not be also sweet. Port, Sherry, Madeira and Marsala are the best known fortified wines. Fortification of wine originally started as a means to preserve wine over long sea voyages. Consumers eventually came to appreciate the subtleties of flavor and texture created in these wines (often by the sea voyage itself), and industries developed to produce them for the public, often under British leadership.

Although widely imitated around the world, true **Port** can only be produced in the Oporto region of Portugal from grapes that grow on difficult terraced slopes in the Douro valley in Portugal's north. The wine is fermented but prior to complete fermentation the producer adds a neutral grape spirit called aguardiente to stop the fermentation **before** all the sugar has been metabolized by the yeast into alcohol. This leaves sweetness in the wine and also adds alcohol to a total of about 20%. Contrast Spanish Sherry where spirit is added only **after** the wine has completely ferment to dryness. Any sweetness in Sherry comes from the addition of sweetener later on. Hence Port is always sweet, but Sherry may or may not be sweet.

Rabelos, a type of boat traditionally used to transport barrels of port down the River Douro for storage and aging in caves at Vila Nova de Gaia near Porto. Photo by Thomas Istvan Seibel.

Tawny Ports are aged in wooden barrels that allow oxidation to promote gradual evaporation. The wine turns golden brown during this process and takes on a nutty character. The official age categories, as stated on the label, are 10, 20, 30 and over 40 years. Aging in bottle is irrelevant.

A **Colheita Port** is a single vintage aged in tawny style for at least seven years. This wine shows the actual vintage on the label instead of the usual Tawny Port indication of age. Even though Colheita Port shows the vintage on the label, it is *not* Vintage Port, which ages primarily in the bottle.

Ruby Port is the inexpensive, mass-produced variety. It is not aged.

Vintage Port is the wine all the fuss is about. Only every few years, perhaps three times a decade, individual port producers (called shippers) feel their base wines are good enough to declare a vintage. A vintage port will go through its first aging process in barrels or stainless steel for a maximum of two and a half years. Because of this short aging period, the Vintage Port retains its deep ruby color and deep fruit flavors. The important aging process goes on in the bottle and is often measured in decades, or even centuries. Because bottle aging develops a crusty sediment, Vintage Port must often be decanted before serving. A **Single Quinta Vintage Port** is a wine whose grapes have been sourced on an individual estate, or quinta.

Late Bottled Vintage (LBV) Port is a relatively new Port product, created from wine originally slated for vintage production, but one that did not succeed in reaching vintage Port status   due to lack of consumer demand or other reasons. The LBV will go through a longer barrel or container aging period than standard vintage port, perhaps four to six years. The wine may be filtered before bottling, which removes the sediment and obviates the need to decant the wine before serving. Typically, LBV Ports will not improve with age in the bottle.

Sherry

The first thing you need to know about Sherry is that it has an image problem. While certainly makers outside of Sherry's original home in southern Spain can and do produce credible Sherry-like wines, others have been responsible for spewing out highly sweetened, poor quality wines labeled Sherry. The sweetness here often serves the purpose, as it does so often in corner-cutting wines, of masking winemaking defects.

Real Sherry-from Spain is not always sweet. The types called Fino, Manzanilla, Amontillado,
Palo Cortado and Oloroso are most commonly completely dry, with a maximum of 5 grams of sugar per liter. Sherry labeled "dry," however may be much sweeter, as well as Sherry labeled "medium" and "cream."

Because of that image problem, many wine commentators consider good Sherries some of the best values on the wine market today.

The name Sherry derives from the Spanish town of Jerez de la Frontera in the province of Cadiz, part of the Andalusia region on the southern coast. Most Sherry is produced from the Palomino grape, although some sweet dessert Sherries have components of Moscatel and Pedro Ximenez grapes.

Let us take a moment to distinguish Sherry from that other Iberian fortified wine, Port. Port is fortified with spirits **before** fermentation is complete, leaving unfermented grape sugars in the wine, so Port is **always** sweet. Sherry is fortified **after** the grape sugars have been fermented to dryness. Sweetness in Sherry, if any, is added in a subsequent step, so **some** Sherries are sweet.

Also unlike Port, Sherries do not generally have specific vintage years. This is because Sherry is aged in what is known as a fractional solera system. The finished Sherry ends up a mixture of ages, the average age increasing the solera, a collection of stacked barrels, gets older. *Solera* means "on the ground" in Spanish, literally the lowest level of barrels. Sherry is bottled from these oldest barrels, the second level is used to refill the lowest level, the third level the second level, and so on. Newly fermented wine is put in the highest level. The barrels are not always actually stacked in the Sherry aging house, which can be immense; someone just keeps careful track of which is which.

A Sherry aging Solera.

Fino Sherry is the palest and driest. When Fino ages, a covering of a yeast called *flor* (which is derived from the local environment) develops, preventing contact with the air. A variety of Fino that ages in the sea air of the town of Sanlúcar de Barramedia is called **Manzanilla.**

Amontillado is initially aged under flor but is then exposed to oxygen, producing a darker sherry than Fino but one still lighter than Oloroso.

Oloroso is aged with oxygen contact longer than Fino or Amontillado, producing a dark, rich wine with alcohol as high as 20%., as opposed to 15-17% for the others.

Amontillados and Olorosos are naturally dry. Sometimes they are sweetened, but if so they must be labeled using a variation of the term Cream Sherry, which always connotes sweetness, and the term Amontillado or Oloroso may not be used.

Palo Cortado starts out as an apparent Fino, but then either the flor dies on its own or is killed by filtration. The result is more like an Oloroso than a Fino or Amontillado.

Jerez Dulce (sweet Sherry) is made either by fermenting dried Moscatel and/or Pedro Ximenez grapes or by starting with a dry Sherry and adding sweet unfermented grape must. The wine is syrupy thick and nearly black.

Cream Sherry is a sweet blend of several sherries, commonly Oloroso and Pedro Ximenez.

A Sherry fermenting barrel cut away to show the layer of flor.

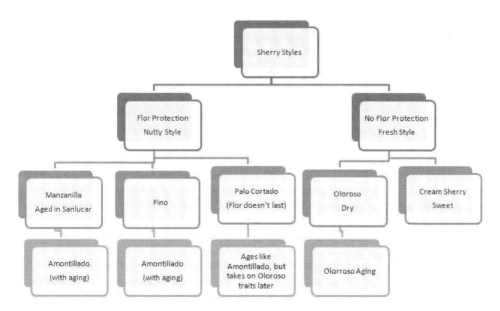

This hierarchical chart shows how the major styles of Sherry relate to each other.

Madeira

Portugal's Madeira islands west of Morocco have for hundreds of years been a stopping place for sea traffic between Europe and the Americas and between Europe and the East Indies. Madeira wine dates back to the early age of exploration when the islands supplied wine for ships. Wine would spoil on long voyages, and so mariners and producers would add distilled alcohol as a preservative, following the example of Port. The taste caught on. George Washington was enormously fond of Madeira.

Wine that made the trip through the hot tropics and back went through a taste transformation that drinkers found desirable. After a period during which casks of Madeira were sent on voyages not to transport them but for adding the benefit of this slow heating process, the winemakers developed techniques to heat process the wine right on the islands in warehouses. Madeira is now made in several different styles.

The red grape Negro Mole accounts for 85% of Madeira today. The four white varieties, which are identical to the present-day names of Madeira wine varieties, are Malvasia, Bual, Verdelho, and Sercial. Bual and Malvasia, which go into the sweeter wines, commonly ferment on their skins to extract phenolic compounds to balance the sweetness. The others are separated from their skins before fermentation. As with Port, fortification with neutral grape spirits is used to stop fermentation before all the yeast can metabolize sugar in the grape juice into alcohol. The earlier in the fermentation process this fortification is accomplished, the sweeter the resulting wine.

The artificial heating is called the *estufagem* process, and it makes Madeira unique. Three main *estufagem* techniques are employed.

- In the *Cuba de Calor* method, used for the cheapest wines, wine is bulk aged for a minimum of ninety days in heated stainless steel or concrete troughs at approximately 115 degrees Fahrenheit.

- The *Armazém de Calor* method calls for storing casks of wine in a dedicated steam heated room for up to a year.

- *Canteiro* is used for the most expensive wines. Barrels are stored in rooms that are naturally heated by the sun for up to a century.

During the *estufagem* process, especially those that take longer periods of time, the wine slowly oxidizes, bringing on a characteristic tawny color and the taste that is distinct to Madeira. This taste cannot be described. Buy a bottle. It will keep.

Madeira wine maturing. Photo by Paula Fernandes.

Madeira Styles (from dry to sweet):

- Sercial is very dry, with hints of almonds and high acidity.
- Verdelho is off-dry, with smoky aromas and flavors and high acidity. The style called Rainwater is a particularly light version of Verdelho.
- Bual gets sweeter. This wine is dark, full-bodied, with raisin notes.
- Malvasia (Malmsey) is decidedly sweet, with coffee and caramel flavors, but as with all Madeira the sweetness is greatly balanced by compensating acidity.

Wines made from the above four "noble grapes" commonly carry age statements on their labels. "Finest" Madeira is aged at least three years. It is usually used for cooking. "Reserve" is aged five years, "Special Reserve," ten years, and "Extra Reserve" at least fifteen years. "Frasqueira" Madeira is wine of a specific year, aged at least nineteen years in cask and a year in bottle. The Madeira winemakers may not used the term "Vintage" since the Port people have exclusive rights to the term.

Marsala

Marsala is an Italian fortified wine from western Sicily. It was created by English wine merchant John Woodhouse in 1773 who adapted some of the indigenous Sicilian techniques to create a fortified wine to compete with Port. The wine became extremely popular, and the British navy ordered huge quantities of it. Unfortunately, in modern times, Italian wine authorities were quite lax about regulating Marsala quality and a great number of mediocre Marsalas flooded the international market. For years, Marsala was best known as a cooking wine, but quality is now on the rise.

Because Marsala comes up so often in restaurant menus, it pays to stress that it should not be confused with the Indian culinary term "Masala," with no "r,' connoting a mixture of hot spices. Chicken Tikka Masala and Chicken Marsala are dramatically different dishes, although reach for the wrong spice and you could conceivable merge the two.

Marsala is fortified with distilled alcohol either during or after fermentation depending on style desired. There are three styles (colors) – Ambra, Oro, Rubino. Ambra and Oro are made from white grapes, a blend of Grillo, Cataratto, Inzolia (Ansonia) and Damaschino. Rubino wines are produced from Perricone, Calabrese (Nero d'Avola), and Nerello Mascalese.

> Sugar level:
> > Secco – maximum 40 g/l residual sugar
> > Semi-Secco – 41 g/l – 100 g/l
> > Dolce – minimum 100 g/l
> Aging requirements
> > Fine - 1 year in cask (17%abv)
> > Superiore - 2 years in cask (18%abv)
> > Superiore Riserva - 4 years in cask (18%abv)
> > Vergine - 5 years in cask (18%abv)
> > Vergine Stravecchio/Soleras Riserva – minimum of 10 years in cask

Vins Doux Naturels

The French have their own styles of lightly fortified wines called *vins doux naturel*. The production of these wines is centered in Languedoc-Roussillon in the south of France. VDNs are produced in a manner similar to Port. Neutral grain spirit (up to 10% at 90 proof) stops yeast action before fermentation is complete, leaving residual sweetness in the unfermented juice. Alcohol level varies depends on the regulations of each individual appellation but it is usually at least 15% abv.

VDNs Muscat de Beaumes-de-Venise, Muscat de Rivesaltes, and Muscat de Frontignan are all made from the white Muscat grape. Banyuls and Maury are made from Grenache Noir. The Grenache VDNs are produced in both oxidized and un-oxidized styles. The Muscat versions are kept from oxidizing to maintain their delicate aromas and flavors.

Chapter Ten

Wine Chemistry

Oxidation

Oxidation occurs when a chemical compound loses electrons. Oxidation is considered beneficial in some winemaking circumstances, but excessive exposure to oxygen under the wrong circumstances can cause a wine to spoil. Oxidation sets in as soon as grape crushing takes place. This is one of the reasons grapes are handled so carefully in their transit from the vineyard to the winery (placement in stackable shallow plastic boxes, as one technique). Oxygen reacts with chemical compounds in the newly liberated grape juice. A grape enzyme called polyphenol oxidase starts to work on the grape's phenolic compounds and starts to turn the juice brown, not a good thing for a beverage so dependent on color for its visual appeal. Natural molds that reside on the grape skins get into the act, accelerating the browning. The necessary solution to this problem is the addition of small amounts of sulfur dioxide to the juice to deactivate the enzymes. Later in the winemaking process, additional SO2 will be added to act as a preservative.

Acetaldehyde is a substance that occurs naturally in grapes. When acetaldehyde gets out of hand, unpleasant odors result. A key part of the process of alcoholic fermentation involves the opposite of oxygenation: the **reduction** of acetaldehyde to alcohol. Acetobacter bacteria sometimes can react with oxygen to reverse the conversion, converting the alcohol to acetaldehyde. Things can go downhill from this point. Fresh fruity flavors and aromas in the wine become casualties in this chemical battle. Acetaldehyde reacting further with oxygen converts into acetic acid. The result is vinegar instead of wine, activating every winemaker's worst nightmare.

The various steps involved in producing red wines often occur in the presence of some oxygen, in open top fermentation vessels, as one example. Punching down, pumping over, racking and other procedures provide measured oxygen contact. Red wines have high levels of phenolic compounds like anthocyanins and pigmented tannins, which not only protect against oxygenation, they also promote flavor and texture complexity. White wines differ profoundly on this issue. The phenolic compounds in white wine are incidental to the intended end result, but like acetobacter, they can react with oxygen to convert alcohol into even more acetaldehyde, seriously compromising color, aromas, flavor and freshness. For this reason, most white wines are fermented in closed fermentation vessels, keeping oxygen contact to a minimum.

Acids in Wine

Acidity in wine is one of its core characteristics. A wine that pleases has a good balance of acidity to other components like sweetness and tannin, and also has the right kind of acidity.

We measure acidity in two ways: the amount and the strength. The total acidity, or "titratable acidity," is measured in grams per liter of wine. We measure the strength in pH, the lower, the more acidic. On the pH scale, 7 is neutral, 0 is extremely acidic, 14 the highest base reading. Most wine has a pH somewhere in the middle of the 2.9 to 3.9 range.

Two organic acids play important roles in wine grapes and hence in the wine it produces: **malic acid** and **tartaric acid** (citric acid, also from the grape, plays only a minor role). Malic acid is present in most berries and fruits, in green apples above all. The term "malic" is derived from the Latin *malum*, meaning apple. In the growing grape, malic acid enhances enzymatic reactions that are essential to the growth of the vine. Malic acid, however, is less desirable in the ultimate wine. It lends a harsh taste, like green apples. Tartaric acid is found primarily in grapes, but its positive effects are found primarily in the wine. It helps maintain the chemical balance and stability of the wine, helps the wine keep its color, and, most important, has a stimulating taste.

Both malic and tartaric acids inhibit bacterial growth, with two important exceptions. The acetobacter that can turn wine into vinegar is one of them. Lactic bacteria is another. This lactic bacteria, existing in the wine or added at a certain point in the winemaking process, drives the process called **malolactic fermentation** (or malolactic conversion) which converts harsh-tasting malic acid into softer lactic acid, rounding out mouthfeel, and in the case of some white wines like Chardonnay, adding that buttery taste. Malolactic fermentation is promoted for nearly all red wines, but for only some whites.

Acetic acid is not resident in the grapes. Fermentation creates small amounts of this harsh-tasting unwelcome guest. If conditions and oxygen exposure are not carefully monitored and controlled, acetobacter can react with oxygen to turn alcohol into larger quantities of acetic acid, as we have already discussed in the section on oxygenation. Wine begins to taste bad, and rapidly turns to vinegar (and not the balanced pleasant kind we use for our salad dressings). The term "volatile acidity" refers to acetic acid as it constitutes a wine fault.

Finally, during the primary (alcoholic) fermentation, yeast metabolizes nitrogen to create small amounts of **succinic acid**, which creates a taste that is a combination of saltiness, bitterness and acidity, the basic taste of fermentation, also present in beer.

Esters

Esters are aromatic compounds that form during winemaking when an acid combines with an alcohol. The two components, acid and alcohol, have no aroma. When they combine during the esterification process, an often wonderful array of aromas results.

We classify esters into two groups. Biochemical esters are created through yeast action. Chemical esters do not depend on yeast action, but occur as a result of wine maturation.

When acids meet alcohol and esterize, the perception of acidity decreases even if the total acidity remain constant. This is a flavor and aroma phenomenon. Esters may also be quite delicate, breaking down when wine is moved around. Chemical esters may eventually reconstitute, but biochemical esters can be permanently lost (as the yeast that creates them is long dead). This is why it is best not to move or shake a complex wine.

Sugars

Grapes are among the sweetest of fruits, containing between 15 and 28 percent sugar. Glucose and fructose are the fermentable sugars. Arbinose, rhamnose, and xylose are unfermentable sugars that find their way into the ultimate wine in small amounts. Some of the fermentable sugar may also inhabit the wine, either by winemaking choice or by failure of yeast action. With global warming, depending on grape type, sugar content of grape juice is often so high that the yeast dies because of too much alcohol in its environment before it gets a chance to metabolize all the sugar into more alcohol. In high acid wines like Riesling, leaving in some natural grape sugar is a legitimate means of reducing the perception of acidity. In poor quality wines, leaving in residual sugar can be an attempt to mask winemaking defects.

Winemakers have three basic ways to arrest fermentation in order to leave residual sugar. One means is to fortify the wine by adding grape or grain spirits. This, of course, increases the alcohol level, which may not be desirable. The winemaker may also arrest fermentation by using a centrifuge to remove all yeast from the wine. A third way is to chill the wine to deactivate the yeasts and then filter them out.

The other option is to *add* sweetness to a wine that is already fermented by using unfermented grape juice. This option actually adds *less* sweetness than does arresting fermentation because of the difference in sweetness between glucose and fructose. Fructose is sweeter. In fermentation, yeast first ferments the glucose, so if fermentation is arrested the sugar left in the wine is more likely to be sweeter fructose. If unfermented grape juice is added, fructose and glucose will be about equal.

Phenolics

One of the major differences between red and white wine resides in the fact that red grapes have a higher level of phenolic compounds. Phenolics (also called polyphenols) include tannins, flavor precursors, pigments, and substances like resveratrol (which, some claim, has health benefits) and vanillin (which brings the characteristic flavor and aroma of vanilla to some wines). Phenolics come to the wine from the skins, stems and seed of the grape. The term "phenolic ripening" refers to the concept that exposure to sunlight over the ripening period increases phenolics (as opposed to "physiological ripening," which refers to grape sugar creation). Once the juice ferments into wine, a process we call polymerization occurs. Pigments, tannins and other phenolics form long molecule chains that ultimately fall to the bottom as sediment and result in a lighter, friendlier, less astringent wine.

Wine color comes from the grape skin alone. It is a function of the level of anthocyanins in the skins. More acidic wines (meaning wines with lower pH values) are redder than wines with higher pH value (less acidic), which tend to have bluer tones. White wines have different types of pigments called flavones. Low pH acidic wines are paler while high pH less acidic wines congregate around the golden edge of the color spectrum.

Chapter Eleven

Wine and Health

Moderate consumption of wine is widely thought to be "good for you," decreasing the risk of heart problems, strokes, diabetes and cancer. Drink more than this and, so the conventional wisdom goes, the alcohol in the wine will have deleterious effects. Notice that we have not defined "moderate" drinking. Governments in a range of countries have not come to any agreement as to what a moderate level of alcohol consumption actually is. Many persist in changing the recommendations, and most do not agree with each other. Such a problem could drive a person to drink.

In 1991, the investigative television programs "60 Minutes" did a feature on the "French Paradox:" the inference of which was that the French, who supposedly consume great quantities of fat, have decidedly lower incidence of heart disease, supposedly because they concurrently consume a great deal of red wine. Sales of the easy-to-pronounce easy-to-drink Merlot went through the roof. The logic:

> Moderate consumption of red wine protects against cancer and heart issues by increasing HDL cholesterol and reducing LDL cholesterol
> Red wines have high levels of antioxidants
> > the darker the wine, the higher the antioxidant content
> Red wines are also sources of resveratrol, linked to longevity and cancer prevention

The problem is that the logic behind this panacea does not take certain other French lifestyle factors into account.

- The French diet is rich in heart-healthy vitamin K2
- The French diet is rich in short-chain saturated fatty acids and poor in trans fats
- The French get most of the fats from dairy and vegetables
- The French eat much more fish than Americans
- The French eat smaller portions, more slowly
- The French eat much less sugar
- The French rarely snack between meals
- The French eat fewer convenience foods
- The French already speak French, and hence do not have to go through the emotional stress of trying to pronounce the language without seeming like an uneducated idiot

More recently, studies have appeared claiming that people who drink moderately have a longer life expectancy than people who do not drink at all. One obvious implication is that non-drinkers do not enjoy the relaxation and stress–reducing benefit of a now-and-then drink and hence worry themselves to death. The fallacy here is in the statistical base used. The cohort of non-drinkers includes reformed alcoholics and people who have been forbidden by their doctors from drinking because of various health issues. Both groups have lowered life expectancies because of variables unrelated to their abstinence. To arrive at a usable finding, the researchers would have to compare otherwise completely healthy non-drinkers against a similar group of moderate drinkers.

We know that excessive drinking causes heart and liver issues, cognitive problems like dementia, as well as social issues like aggressive behavior and drunk driving, but there is no substantial proof that heavy drinkers are more likely to suffer from cancer. Again there is a confounding factor in the statistical base. Heavy drinkers are much more likely to have poor diets and other lifestyle stresses. A greater proportion of them smoke, a carcinogenic factor that is impossible to pass over.

A person can become an alcoholic, or express alcoholic behavior, through the medium of any alcoholic beverage: wine, beer or spirits. Despite this, on a general basis, alcohol abuse is less widely associated with wine than it is with beer or spirits.

Now what about those red wine headaches? In the United States, many people believe they are caused by the sulfites that are necessary in wine to prevent spoilage. One reason for this is the fact that wine sold in the United States must be labeled "contains sulfites." The actual reason this labeling exists is to protect a small group of people who have allergies to sulfites that can be potentially fatal. A little known fact is that red wine requires a much lower level of sulfites than white wine. This is because the phenolic compounds in red wine are antioxidants and tend to protect the wine from oxidation. White wine lacks these phenolics and hence requires more SO_2. These very phenolic compounds combined with histamines (and alcohol) are the actual culprits. On the other hand, these are the same antioxidant substances that carry the supposed health benefits. This author believes that the real culprit in red wine headaches is not red wine *per se*, but *cheap* red wine. Red wine that undergoes the (more expensive) aging process will undergo polymerization, smoothing out the rough phenolic edges, and softening out the wine in all respects. This is the kind of claim you might want to investigate for yourself next time somebody else pays for your wine.

Chapter Twelve

World Wine Regions
North America

The United States

Prohibition of alcoholic beverages was repealed in the United States in 1933, but the effects are still felt—in federal wine labeling laws, in the marketplace, in the convoluted system of state and local regulations. We will start with wine labeling regulations.

> If only wine were labeled according to the rules of the Food and Drug Administration
> The FDA is a part of the Department of Health and Human Services
> The FDA's purpose is to protect the public from unhealthy or adulterated foods
> Wine labels would have content information like this useful food label

Nutrition Facts Label

Notice how we have highlighted the enormous amount of sugar in this product, which happens to be grape juice (but not the type of grape juice that makes good quality wine). You might want to enjoy this hyper-sweet product in moderation, but if you want to chug down the whole bottle, at least you know what you are putting into your body. If this were wine, the label would tell you *nothing* about the sugar level.

Wine labeling is regulated by the Department of the **Treasury**, Alcohol and Tobacco **Tax** & Trade Bureau
The all-powerful TTB
A good understanding of the limitations of this system will come in handy next time you visit the wine store

The TTB runs the American Appellation (Wine Place Name) System. The design and content of every label that goes on American wine must be submitted to the TTB for approved.

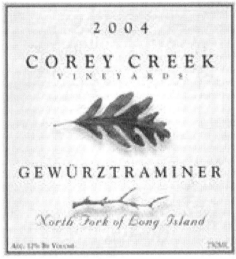

This label gives just basic wine information in a visually attractive format, but all the same it had to be approved by the TTB

Despite the genuine artistic value of this label, the TTB banned it. We cannot quite figure why.

Each American **state** automatically qualifies as an appellation that may be indicated on a wine label. Here are three examples.

California is a big place, and the label doesn't get any more specific. These grapes could be from anywhere in California.

Here's one from Texas.

Another from Virginia

We could give 47 further examples. Not all states produce wine grapes, but there are wineries in all 50 states.

Within each state, each **county** automatically qualifies as an appellation. This has its greatest significance in wine powerhouse California.

Monterey County

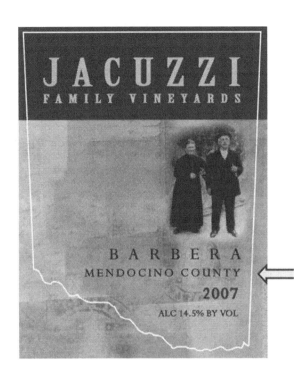

Mendocino County

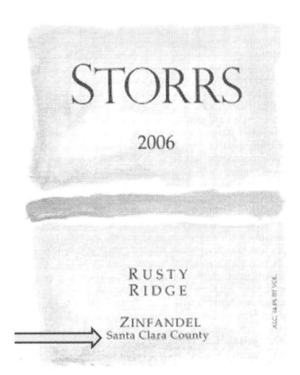

The other type of appellation other than a state or a county is an **American Viticultural Area** (AVA). This is pronounced "A-V-A. "

AVA status is awarded by the TTB based on petitions from an area's winemakers
The winemakers try to convince the TTB that their proposed AVA has unique climate, soil or other attributes that set it off for special status
The process of approval is difficult
The TTB puts out 35 pages of instructions on how to apply for an AVA
AVAs can overlap or nest
AVAs vary greatly in size
AVAs can encompass parts of more than one county or state
As a general rule, a wine producer can command a higher price for wines labeled with an AVA name rather than with a county or state name
When smaller AVAs are nested into larger ones, the smaller AVA usually commands the higher price
AVAs function, essentially, as brand names, tending to indicate quality

U.S. appellations, state, county or AVA, relate *only* to place. Compare this to France, where appellations describe a place, of course, but so much more:

grape or grapes allowed
pruning and vineyard management rules
whether irrigation is permitted
harvesting rules and maximum vineyard yields
type of yeast allowed in the winery
minimum and maximum alcohol levels
and to qualify for that place name the wine must be reviewed by a professional tasting panel

Santa Ynez Valley in Santa Barbara County, California is an AVA.

Label with Santa Ynez Valley

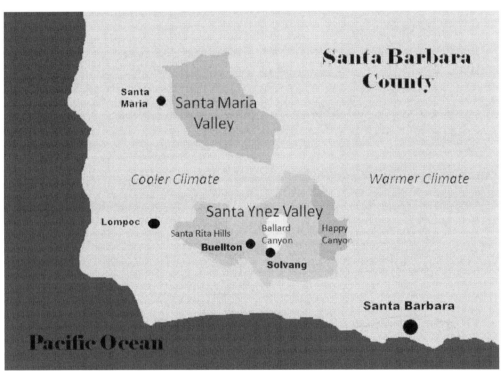

Map of Santa Barbara County

Santa Barbara County in the map above is a good study for the AVA concept. Note that the Santa Maria Valley AVA in the north is separate and self-contained, but the Santa Ynez Valley AVA itself contains three "nested" AVA's: Santa Rita Hills AVA, Ballard Canyon AVA, and Happy Canyon AVA. If the wine label reads "Santa Ynez Valley" the supposition is that the grapes were sourced from within the Santa Ynez Valley AVA but not within any of the nested AVAs, or from a combination of each. The winemaker, if in doubt, could always label the wine "Santa Barbara County" or even "California." The smaller the appellation, the higher the perception of quality (and the higher the price). Note we say "perception of" quality.

Dundee Hills in Oregon is an AVA. In fact, it is a sub-AVA of the much larger Willamette Valley AVA

Dundee Hills Wine Label

Oregon Wine Regions

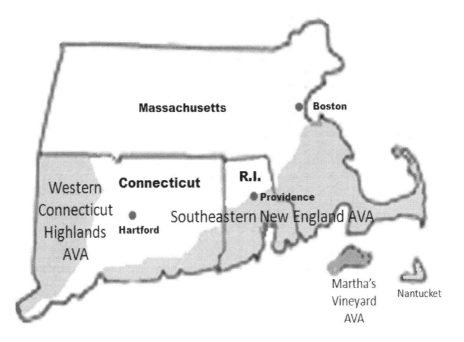

AVA Map of Oregon

Southern New England AVAs

Above is a map of the southern New England states. Notice that the Western Connecticut Highlands AVA is completely within the state of Connecticut, but that the Southeastern New England AVA straddles three states, and includes the Massachusetts island of Nantucket, but not the island of Martha's Vineyard, which is a separate AVA. It stands to reason that Martha's Vineyard would get its own AVA. After all, it is named after a vineyard. The only troubling part of this is that the island produces neither grapes nor wine. It does have a great number of well-connected summer residents.

The three wine labels from Rhode Island's Sakonnet Vineyard shown above illustrate a winemaker's choice to use different appellations for three different wines. On the left, the winemaker chose to release her Rhode Island Red under the Rhode Island appellation (remember that every US state is automatically an appellation). She could have probably used the Southeastern New England appellation for this but the state name was more in keeping with the wine name. On the right, she labeled the wine as Southeastern New England. Notice that she labeled the wine in the center "American Table Wine." This would tend to indicate that the percentage of the grapes used to make this wine was not high enough to qualify it for the Southeastern New England AVA or Rhode Island state appellation. Most probably, some or all of these grapes were shipped in from elsewhere, probably from New York State or even California.

Now here comes the confusing information (on the wine label, not here). According to TTB rules, if the winemaker uses an **AVA name** on the label, at least 85% of the wine must derive from that AVA. There is no requirement to divulge where the remaining 15% comes from. In the case of an **American state or county**, at least 75% of the wine must derive from that state or county to earn the right to a place on the label. State rules can tighten (but not loosen) these limitations—California requires wines labeled "California" to be 100%.

If a grape variety is mentioned on the label, the rule is 75%. This means that a wine labeled "California Pinot Noir" could be up to 25% Syrah, or Merlot, or something never meant to be blended with Pinot Noir, *with no way for the consumer to tell*. The tax people are regulating the labeling, not the food protection people.

Do you want to know how much sugar is in a wine? Too bad. The label tells you nothing. How much acidity? Ditto. How much alcohol? Well, that the label does reveal.

Meaningless American Wine Terms

>Reserve – no legal significance
>Old Vines – no legal definition (in any country)
>Sustainable – no legal definition
>Organic – meaningless unless certified organic
>Natural – as with foods, meaningless
>Special selection, limited release, private stock – no legal significance

Single Varietal Wines

>It is disturbing to us that wine labels only guarantee that a mentioned grape comprises 75% of the wine, since we Americans are heavily skewed toward single varietal wines: Chardonnay, Merlot, Sauvignon Blanc, Syrah – etc., and not blends
>And while we use place names, they are not as important as they are in Europe
>Why are single varietal wines, that is, grape names, so important in the American system?

It goes back to…no prizes awarded for guessing…Prohibition.

Many vineyards were forced to shut down entirely. Some stayed alive by producing grapes for the country's new hobby: home winemaking. Grapes were shipped with a warning: "Do not add yeast otherwise the grapes might ferment." Of course, these were actually instructions for do-it-yourself wine. Those vineyards that did not shut down entirely converted from fine wine grapes to varieties like Alicante Bouschet and Thompson Seedless, which could survive shipment to home winemakers around the country. These grapes at best produce mediocre wine.

In 1933, Prohibition was repealed, but it did its damage: far fewer vineyards, and inappropriate grapes for fine wine. You cannot just "plant" grapes and reap a crop a few months later. Vineyards take years to yield quality wine grapes. The breweries and distillers were able to go into immediate production of beer and spirits—all they needed was grain. The Great Depression was on, and the public wanted cheap beer, cheap spirits, and cheap wine.

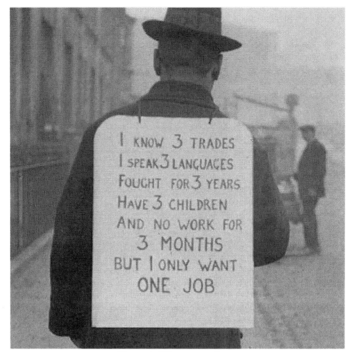

Great Depression

Producers churned out inexpensive sweet wines made from poor quality grapes largely produced in California's hot climate Central Valley. They used European place names to describe their wines, despite the fact that these wines and the grapes that made them had nothing to do with the European appellations they appropriated: Burgundy, Chablis, Chianti, Sherry, Port, Sauternes, Champagne, and many more.

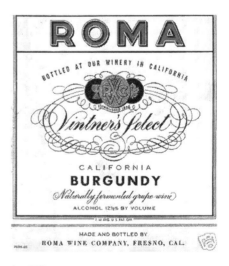

Old California Wines

World War Two in the 1940s did nothing in itself to turn the American wine industry toward fine wine production, but it exposed American soldiers to better quality European wines.

It took decades for fine wine to recover in the US. For most Americans, until at least the 1960s, good wine was something imported from Europe that you splurged for on special occasions. American wine was something you poured out of a jug. Winemakers who strove to change this perception fought an uphill battle. The land and the vines bided their time. Eventually, two influential champions of American fine wine arose.

- **Frank Schoonmaker** (1905-1976) was an influential wine writer. Writing in the 1940s and 1950s, it was largely Schoonmaker s idea to label American wines by their grape varieties as a means to indicate quality, to distance them from the mass-produced American wines that continued to use stolen European place names (without mention of the grape content). California place names like Napa and Sonoma did not yet have the association with quality they have today, so calling a wine Cabernet Sauvignon, Pinot Noir, or Chardonnay seemed the way to go. Progress here was slow.

- **Robert Mondavi** (1913-2008) founded his winery in Napa in 1966. A convert to Schoonmaker s single varietal concept, Mondavi put the full force of his magnetic personality behind it with crusade-like zeal. The quality wine industry took his lead, and varietal labeling became the norm.

In American wine, for better or for worse, grape type comes first, place second. Of course, American winemakers experiment with blends, and continue to promote the brand value of their counties and AVAs, but the American public looks at wines as being of specific grapes, and only a short list of international grapes at that.

American Wine Regions

California

Even through wineries exist in every American state, California continues to produce approximately ninety percent of all American wines (of all types, styles, and price ranges). This statistic is somewhat misleading, however, because California is big, and comprises a number of diverse wine producing regions, counties and AVAs. California effectively operates as if it were four different wine states

- the hot climate agricultural powerhouse Central Valley
- the Central Coast: the coastal areas between Santa Barbara and San Francisco Bay
- the Northern Coast: Napa, Sonoma, Mendocino, Lake counties and adjacent areas
- the cooler inland Sacramento-San Joaquin River Delta and the Sierra Foothills

Most of California is ideal wine country. It has a dependable growing season with ample sunshine. It seldom rains at harvest time. Pacific Ocean influence supports significant cool-climate regions. It has a wide variety of soils, climates, hills and valleys for vineyard placement.

California has two major problems as a wine producing region: labor availability and drought.

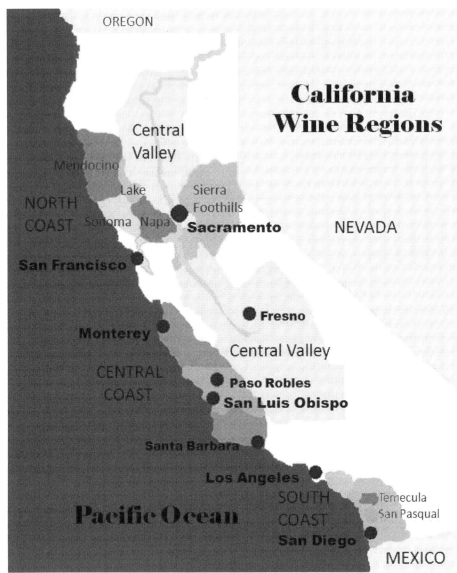

California Wine Map

In southern California, the **South Coast AVA** includes the counties of Los Angeles, San Diego, Riverside, Orange and San Bernardino. Tucked away among sprawling cities are some 3,000 acres of vineyards, much of it in the ocean-influenced Temecula Valley and San Pasqual Valley AVAs. For many years, production centered around Chardonnay, but Pierce's disease had driven growers to diversify into hardier grapes like Syrah, Tempranillo and Sangiovese.

The **Central Coast AVA** is immense, stretching the 250 miles from Santa Barbara in the south to San Francisco in the north in a six-county swath about 25 miles wide, and encompassing over 90,000 acres of wine grapes. Wines may, of course, be labeled "Central Coast." Because the area is so extensive, the label term "Central Coast" means little, except perhaps the supposition that the wine was produced under cool climate conditions. It is more meaningful to cover the Central Coast on a county- by-county basis. The three southernmost counties are most important. The northern counties, which include many urban area and Silicon Valley (and hence have very expensive land), make less of a vinous imprint.

We will start in **Santa Barbara County** on the Central Coast and work our way north.

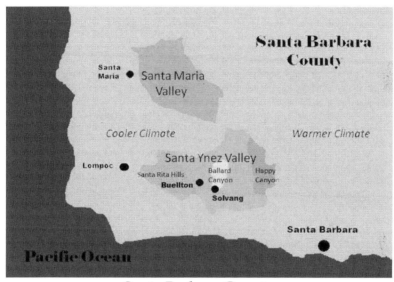
Santa Barbara County

Santa Barbara County and its **Santa Ynez Valley** have an unusual west-to-east topographical configuration. Cooling Pacific breezes extend a full twenty miles inland. The average temperature rises one degree per mile as you travel eastward and inland. As a result, the **Santa Rita Hills** AVA specializes in cool climate Pinot Noir and Chardonnay. Further inland, **Ballard Canyon** produces warmer climate Syrah, and further inland still, **Happy Canyon** brings us excellent Cabernet Sauvignon. The **Santa Maria Valley** in the cool-climate north is best known for Pinot Noir, Pinot Blanc, Chardonnay and some Syrah.

In Santa Barbara County you can take a side trip to the Lompoc Wine Ghetto, a grouping of drab industrial buildings that house over two dozen wineries and tasting rooms.

A Diagram of the Lompoc Wine Ghetto

San Luis Obispo County is directly north up the coast. In the original Spanish, San Luis Obispo stands for "St. Louis, the Bishop".

San Luis Obispo County

San Luis Obispo County has four primary wine regions. The **Arroyo Grande Valley**, **Edna Valley** and **York Mountain** AVAs are all within a few miles of the Pacific Ocean. Climate here is cool but remarkably steady, favoring Pinot Noir and Chardonnay, as well as aromatic white varietals like Pinot Gris, Riesling and Gewürztraminer. Soils are complex, often revealing fossils of ancient sea creatures, a quality that allows growers to plant varieties and clones that get the most from the county's diversity.

The fourth region is **Paso Robles**, which until a few years ago, at least politically, was one huge AVA stretching across the northeastern expanse of the county. Growers here lobbied the TTB to divide Paso Robles into no fewer than ten individual AVAs. They proved the impressive vinous diversity of the area and got their AVAs. The area has seen increased plantings of the Rhône varieties Syrah and Viognier, with the warmer mountainous eastern stretch becoming known for some fine Zinfandel, as well as Bordeaux varieties like Cabernet Sauvignon and Merlot. (Locals pronounce Paso Robles in an anglicized way, as Paso ROE-bulls, rather than the more Spanish-sounding Paso Robe-Lace.)

Next county up (but still considered Central Coast) is **Monterey County**.

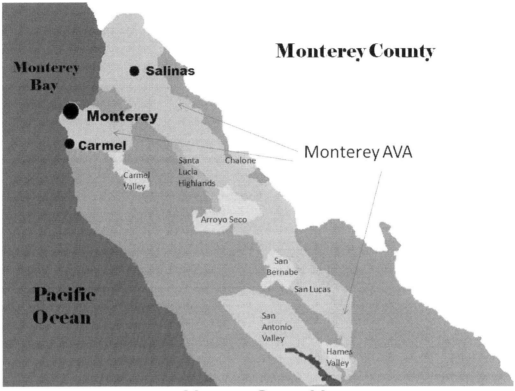

Monterey County Map

The Salinas River flows about a hundred miles southeast to northwest, flanked by the Gabilan Range to the east and the Santa Lucia Range on the west, emptying into the Pacific at Monterey Bay. The valley floor, characterized by sandy loam and gravel, is a fertile agricultural area, renowned for all kinds of crops (well described in John Steinbeck's novel, *East of Eden*), as well as a good deal of wine production. The limestone, granite and shale soil of the hills flanking the valley have seen increasing colonization by the vine. The **Monterey** AVA covers most but not all of the wine area, which includes eight smaller AVAs.

Underneath the Pacific Ocean facing into Monterey Bay and the Salinas Valley is an immense underwater canyon, larger than the Grand Canyon. The canyon generates cooling fog that funnels down the valley. The result, for the northernmost AVAs of the county, is a cool climate, but one with a long growing season, with long warm days to ripen the grapes, and cool nights to let them rest. The AVAs further south are hotter, but not beyond ocean influence.

Although fruit-forward Chardonnay and Pinot Noir account for much of Monterey wine production, growers are actively producing another forty varieties.

Central Coast—Further North

Between Monterey and San Francisco, the Central Coast AVA includes Alameda, Contra Costa and San Francisco counties, and parts of San Mateo, Santa Clara and Santa Cruz counties. This is excellent wine growing country, with well-drained gravel soils, warm days and cool nights because of the effect of the ocean and San Francisco Bay. The area has about six thousand acres of vines and one hundred wineries, but these must coexist with Silicon Valley and urban sprawl.

Well-known grapes like Chardonnay, Cabernet Sauvignon and Merlot account for a good half of production. This area includes the **Santa Clara Valley**, one of the state's oldest wine regions, a narrow strip just south of the big city of San Jose. The growing human population of the region may menace the environment and hyper-inflate land values, but it brings a steady stream of day-tripping customers to the area's wineries, allowing many of them to sell their wine at full retail.

Livermore Valley AVA

Livermore is situated in Alameda County, east of San Francisco Bay. Here, large operations Wente and Concannon coexist with many smaller producers. The valley has an east-west orientation and well-draining gravelly soil. Although breezes off San Francisco Bay assure good diurnal temperature differentials, Livermore is warmer than much of the ocean-influenced, Central Coast, with a climate suitable for Bordeaux varieties like Cabernet Sauvignon and Merlot as well as Rhône varieties like Syrah and Viognier, with some Chardonnay and Sauvignon Blanc. Human population pressure is the greatest threat to Livermore's vines.

Santa Cruz Mountains AVA

This AVA is not legally part of the broad Central Coast AVA, which it borders. It is south of San Francisco and west of Silicon Valley. On the eastern side of the region's high ridges (up to 2600 feet), the warm climate produces Cabernet Sauvignon, Merlot, Zinfandel and Syrah. On the ocean side of the ridges, Pinot Noir is the leader. The AVA has about 60 wineries.

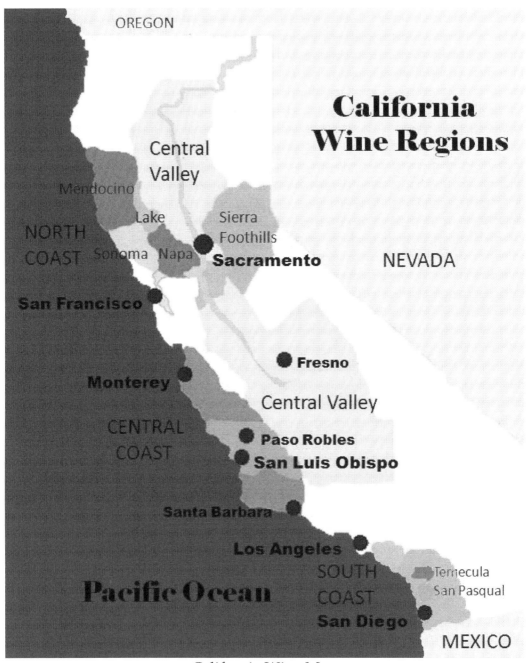

California Wine Map

Shown in yellow on our California wine map, the flat Central Valley stretches more than 450 miles southeast to northwest through the center of the state. The flat, largely irrigated valley is about 40 to 60 miles wide. It features some of the most productive agricultural land on the planet, producing more than half of the fruits, vegetables and nuts grown in the United States. This includes table grapes, raisins and bulk wine grapes, but the climate is too warm for fine wine production. Because of the hot climate, wine grapes with high natural acidity do best, including Chenin Blanc and Colombard. The Central Valley is not an AVA, meaning its wines can only be labeled under the broader "California" appellation.

The center of the valley is a climatic exception, however. Here the north-flowing San Joaquin River meets the south-flowing Sacramento River to form the Sacramento-San Joaquin River Delta, an extensive system of rivers, canal and marshes. This in turn drains into San Francisco Bay. The delta and the bay system tend to cool the middle of the valley, allowing quality wine grapes to grow in appellations such as Clarksburg (with 9000 acres of vines) and Lodi (with ten times as much). As the map of Lodi's seven AVAs clearly indicates, **Lodi** is well influenced by water systems. It also benefits from sandy clay soils that drain well. Lodi's reputation leads with its fine Zinfandel (nearly half of Lodi production). It also produces Syrah, Cabernet Sauvignon, Merlot and white wines like Viognier, Sauvignon Blanc and Chardonnay.

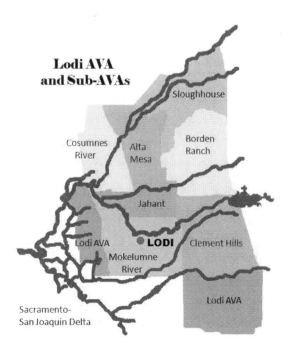

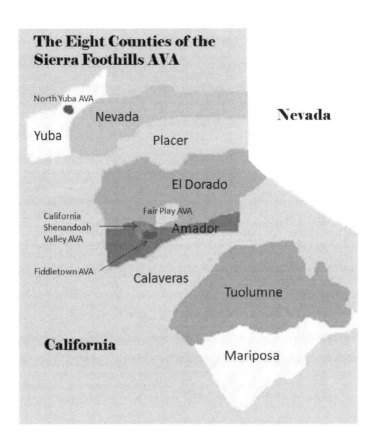

The Eight Counties of the Sierra Foothills AVA

North Yuba AVA

Nevada

Yuba

Nevada

Placer

El Dorado

California Shenandoah Valley AVA

Fair Play AVA

Amador

Fiddletown AVA

Calaveras

Tuolumne

California

Mariposa

Sierra Foothills

West of Lodi are the eight counties of the Sierra Foothills AVA. Although well inland, the climate is moderated by the area's elevation and also by the cooling influence of the Sacramento-San Joaquin River Delta system. This is Gold Rush country. The miners of the mid-19th century were a thirsty bunch. By the 1860s, the foothills had a thriving wine industry, particularly associated with Zinfandel. The gold mania subsided, but the vines continued to grow, in many cases under the loving and expert care of Italian immigrant winemakers. This wine culture, and the toughness of the vine itself, got Zinfandel to the other side of Prohibition. The worst threat to Zinfandel came in the late twentieth century when a new mania—this time for Cabernet Sauvignon, saw Zin vines pulled up and vineyards repurposed. In the nick of time, the thirst for white Zinfandel (which is made from the red Zinfandel grape), allowed Zin to take its place as "California's native grape." The AVA's hundred or so wineries produce Zin, often from old vines (which have no legal definition but are often many generations old), with lesser amounts of Cabernet Sauvignon, Syrah, and even smaller amounts of Chardonnay, Merlot, and Barbera.

Sierra Foothills has five sub-AVAs. The **California Shenandoah Valley** AVA, **El Dorado** AVA, **Fair Play** AVA, and **Fiddletown** AVA are bunched in the center of the region, in Amador and El Dorado Counties, and focus on Zinfandel. The **North Yuba** AVA in the northernmost county of Yuba is more removed form the cooling influence of the Delta and has a warmer climate suitable for Cabernet Sauvignon and the Rhône grapes Syrah, Grenache, Viognier and Roussanne.

North Coast AVA.

Six counties make up the North Coast AVA: Marin, Solano, Lake, Mendocino, Napa, and Sonoma. Wines sold under the "North Coast" label are usually blends of grapes from more than one of the counties.

Although **Marin County** just north of the City of San Francisco is highly affected by urban sprawl, the northern reaches of Marin have extensive agricultural lands that are legally protected from property development. While the entire north coast is known for cool climate viticulture, Marin, sandwiched between the ocean and the bay, may be downright cold. The saving grace is a long growing season. Marin has about 200 acres of grapevines, divided among a handful of family growers, producing Pinot Noir, Chardonnay, Gewürztraminer, and Riesling.

Solano County lies between the eastern reaches of the bay/delta system and the state capital of Sacramento. Two of Solano's AVAs are part of the North Coast AVA. The **Solano County Green Valley** AVA, just north of San Pablo Bay, produces Cabernet Sauvignon, Merlot and Syrah on about 800 acres. The **Suisun Valley** AVA, further north, is one of the state's oldest wine producing regions, producing a wide range of grapes on over 3,000 vineyard acres.

Lake County directly north of Napa, surrounds Clear Lake, California's largest lake. Although the county is inland and removed from the influence of the bay and delta system, the lake itself combines with substantial vineyard elevations to prevent the climate from getting too hot. Lake County AVAs include the **Clear Lake** AVA, the **High Valley** AVA, and the **Red Hills Lake County** AVA. The county's proximity to Napa makes it a prime purchasing source for winemakers from elsewhere, but it also has more than a dozen wineries of its own. Cabernet Sauvignon leads, with Sauvignon Blanc second.

In **Mendocino County**, on the Pacific Coast directly north of Sonoma, wine grapes are by far the most prominent legal agricultural product, covering 16,862 acres as of 2015: 4500 planted to Chardonnay, 2600 each to Pinot Noir and Cabernet Sauvignon, 1900 to Zinfandel, and 1400 to Merlot. Organic wine grapes account for a total of 3900 acres (and the county has been GMO free since 2004). Mendocino has ten AVAs.

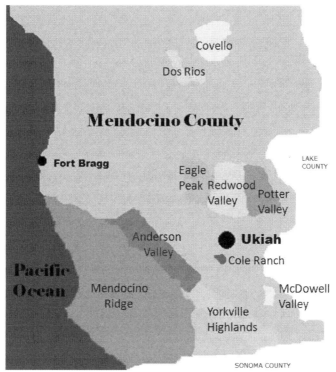
Mendocino County Wine Map

The **Anderson Valley AVA** is making a reputation for itself in sparkling wines, led by French Champagne house Roederer. The northern end of the valley (one of California's coolest regions) is closer to the Pacific Ocean than the warmer southern end. Anderson and the nearby **Mendocino Ridge AVA** produce Pinot Noir and Chardonnay for still and sparkling wines as well as Riesling and Gewürztraminer. A little further north, the **Redwood Valley AVA** is known for peppery Zinfandels, **Potter Valley** for Chardonnay, Pinot Noir and Sauvignon Blanc, **Eagle Peak** for Pinot Noir (from its single winery).

Further north still, the **Covello and Dos Rios AVAs** total only a few acres of vines between them, producing Cabernet Sauvignon, Cabernet Franc, Chardonnay, Merlot and Zinfandel in warmer inland climates than those appellations further south.

The **Yorkville Highlands AVA** is a continuation of the southeastward reaching Anderson Valley that at its southern end nudges the northern end of Sonoma's Alexander Valley. Yorkville Highlands has rocky soil with high gravel content and good drainage. The daytime climate is cooler than Alexander Valley but warmer than Anderson Valley. At night these highlands get chillier than either of their neighbors.

South of Mendocino's largest city Ukiah (which is not particularly large), the **Cole Ranch AVA** is the smallest appellation in the United States (only one winery producing Cabernet Sauvignon, Merlot, Pinot Noir and Riesling). In the county's southeastern corner, the **McDowell Valley AVA** makes Rhône wines from old-vine Syrah and Grenache. Some of these vines are more than 100 years old. McDowell is also known for dry rosés.

We have saved the two big players, **Napa** and **Sonoma**, for last. For starters, let us look at ways in which these neighbors are profoundly different form each other.

- Sonoma is twice the size of Napa
- Sonoma has four times the population of Napa
- Sonoma has a large city, Santa Rosa (population 175,000), while Napa has no large cities.
- Ocean-facing Sonoma has a cooler climate than inland Napa, although the southern reaches of both counties are also cooled by San Pablo Bay. Some of Sonoma s ocean fogs do reach eastward across the center of the county to affect Napa.
- Sonoma has a number of overlapping AVAs, while Napa s AVAs do not overlap.
- Sonoma produces agricultural products other than wine grapes (although grapes are number one), while Napa is all grape.
- The Mayacamas Mountains physically and climatologically separate Sonoma and Napa. Only two widely separated east-west roads connect the two counties.

Sonoma County

Sonoma County Wine Map

Sonoma is a patchwork quilt of wine appellations, several of which overlap. Visually, the lines formed by Sonoma's AVA boundaries push down from the northwest to the southeast. We need to draw another important line that challenges this up/down statement, penciling in the Petaluma Gap. The gap shoves cooling Pacific goodness laterally across Sonoma, in a band ranging from 20 to 30 miles wide. The western edge of the Gap is the coastal lowlands around Bodega Bay. The eastern edge is the mouth of the Petaluma River as it flows into San Pablo Bay, the northern reach of the San Francisco Bay system (which in turn connects to the Sacramento-San Joaquin River Delta). The gap cuts across the capacious **Sonoma Coast** AVA and is responsible for the cool climate of the **Russian River Valley** AVA and its nested sub-AVA, the **Green Valley of Russian River Valley** AVA, both known for Pinot Noir and Chardonnay. In 2015 the Petaluma Gap Winegrowers Association submitted a petition to the TTB to declare the gap an AVA. The jury is still out. Until the Petaluma people get their own AVA, the overarching Sonoma Coast AVA will have to do. Up the coast from Petaluma, the high elevation **Fort Ross-Seaview** AVA is completely surrounded by Sonoma Coast. Approved by the TTB in 2011, the AVA specializes in Pinot Noir and Chardonnay, but expects significant new planting of a wide variety of grapes. Fort Ross-Seaview is a good example of Sonoma's potential to develop new cool-climate growing regions.

Directly north of the Russian River Valley is the **Dry Creek Valley** AVA. Dry Creek is a tributary of the Russian River. Dry Creek is warmer and dryer than the Russian River Valley, but also benefits from ocean influence that leapfrogs the ridges between Dry Creek and the ocean. Before Prohibition, it was a Zinfandel specialist. Prohibition hit Dry Creek badly, and the region did not start to recover until the 1970s. Zinfandel once again reigns here, with much Cabernet Sauvignon (and Sauvignon Blanc for the white side of things). The **Rockpile** AVA juts into the northern edge of Dry Creek, producing Zinfandel, Cabernet Sauvignon and Petite Sirah.

Dry Creek's Michel-Schlumberger vineyard specializes in Cabernet Sauvignon with a French touch. Photo by Elliot Essman

To the east of Dry Creek lies the **Alexander Valley** AVA, a warm climate region known for its Cabernet Sauvignon. Alexander Valley is Sonoma's largest and most widely planted AVA. The Russian River, flanked by vineyards, flows down the Alexander Valley before it lurches west to form the Russian River Valley AVA and make its way to the Pacific. The Russian River provides early morning fogs that burn off as the day advances. During the day, the Alexander Valley is decidedly warm, but nights turn favorably cool, allowing grapes to ripen slowly for voluptuous Cabernet Sauvignon and Merlot and richly tropical Chardonnay. Grapes as diverse as Tempranillo, Barbera, Sangiovese, Syrah, Viognier, and Zinfandel inhabit this large region.

Southwest of Alexander Valley hard by the Napa County line is Sonoma's warmest region, the **Knights Valley** AVA, known for its Cabernet and Meritage (Bordeaux-style) blends. Directly south of Alexander is the **Chalk Hill** AVA, which overlaps a corner of the Russian River Valley (Sonoma *is* complicated). The name refers to the chalky soil of volcanic ash. Chalk Hill is warmer than the Russian River Valley but still benefits from some Petaluma Gap cooling. The cooling in fact continues its eastward path beyond Chalk Hill, relieving some of inland Napa's heat. Chalk Hill is known for white varietals like Chardonnay and Sauvignon Blanc. South of Chalk Hill is the new (2015) **Fountaingrove District** AVA, producing Cabernet Sauvignon, Chardonnay, Sauvignon Blanc, Merlot, Cabernet Franc, Zinfandel, Syrah, and Viognier. Fountaingrove is characterized by rolling hills with volcanic soils (Sonoma shows a great deal of past volcanic activity).

In the southeast corner of the county lies the **Sonoma Valley** AVA. It is important here to differentiate the Sonoma Valley AVA from the Napa Valley AVA. Sonoma Valley is only a small portion of Sonoma County, but the Napa Valley AVA, filled with sub-AVAs, is an overarching AVA that encompasses most of Napa County. **Sonoma Mountain** (a sub-AVA) in the west of Sonoma Valley blocks Petaluma Gap Pacific cooling influence, but the two appellations are close enough to San Pablo Bay to benefit from its air conditioner. The **Bennett Valley** AVA straddles areas of Sonoma Valley, Sonoma Mountain and Sonoma Coast, and *does* reflect cooling ocean influence. Barbera, Cabernet Sauvignon, Cabernet Franc, Chardonnay, Grenache, Merlot, Pinot Noir, Sauvignon Blanc and Syrah thrive here.

Another, fairly new, sub-AVA of Sonoma Valley is the **Moon Mountain District Sonoma County** AVA. As the name implies, this is high elevation land, ranging up to 2000 feet above sea level. Soil is once again volcanic. Up here, we find the legendary Monte Rosso vineyard. Or we could call it a zin-yard. The warm climate twins, Cabernet Sauvignon and Zinfandel, rule here, but further south the slopes feeding on San Pablo Bay produce some fine breezy Pinot Noir.

In the extreme south of Sonoma County hard by San Pablo Bay, Sonoma shares the **Los Carneros** AVA with southern Napa. The Sonoma portion of Los Carneros (often called just "Carneros,") can contribute grapes to Sonoma Valley labeled wines. The name Los Carneros means "the rams" in Spanish, a reference to its early function of these rolling hills as sheep grazing land. Because of the San Pablo Bay influence, Los Carneros is the coolest and most windy AVA in either Sonoma or Napa. The Pinot Noir and Chardonnay one would expect in such an environment have attracted a number of international Champagne producers, including Moët et Chandon (which runs Domaine Chandon California), and Taittinger (running Domaine Carneros).

Napa County

Raw numbers often speak louder than refined wine: Napa county accounts for a full twenty percent of the dollar value of California's wine grapes on just four percent of its volume.

Napa is so world renowned for its distinctive Cabernet Sauvignon that it is frequently considered Cab's second home base after Bordeaux.

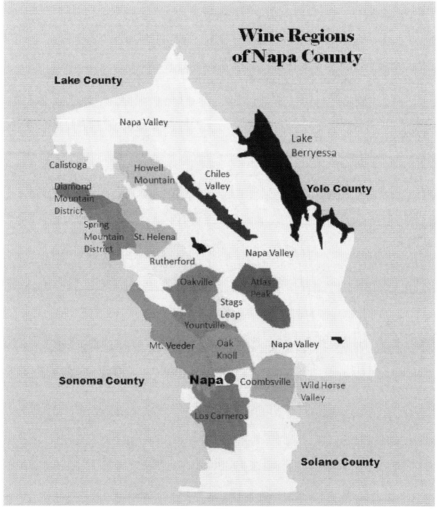

Napa County

These AVAs seem stacked one on top the other like a child's assemblage of blocks, with a handful of outliers. The Napa Valley AVA encompasses sixteen of these sub-AVAs which, while often snuggling in with each other, do not overlap (as one finds so often in neighboring Sonoma).

Napa wine did not attain its present world-class status overnight.

- Commercial production begins about 1860. By the turn of the twentieth century, Napa has over 140 wineries, some of which still operate: Chateau Montelena, Charles Krug, Schramsberg, Far Niente, Markham, Beaulieu, Beringer, and Mayacamas.

- Then Napa suffers a devastating three-pronged attack: phylloxera, Prohibition, the Great Depression.

- In 1938, Beaulieu hires legendary winemaker André Tchelistcheff, who brings in scientific techniques such as vineyard frost protection, oak barrel aging, malolactic fermentation, and cold fermentation.

- Beringer Vineyards starts a promotional campaign "All roads lead to Beringer" in 1939, inviting Hollywood royalty to visit, the first step in the wine country tourism that is so well developed in Napa today.

- Christian Brothers Winery expands its operations and disseminates its quality wine image under the leadership of winemaker Brother Timothy, whose smiling face on wine labels comes to be synonymous with wine in the eyes of the American public.

- World War Two ends, and wine consumption begins to pick up. Returning GIs, having had the experience of liberating fine European wines, ratchet up public demand for better wines.

- Robert Mondavi breaks from his family s Charles Krug winery in 1965 and sets up a large scale winery of his own in Oakville. Mondavi is indefatigable in his promotion of Napa wine, using varietal labeling to connote quality. Many other wine producers follow Mondavi s lead.

- In 1976, at a blind tasting in Paris, a Napa Cabernet and a Napa Chardonnay bested leading French comparables from Bordeaux and Burgundy. The French cried foul, but a repeat of the Judgment of Paris, thirty years later gets the same results.

- Massive investment from outside the world of wine streams into Napa. As just one of many examples, moviemaker Francis Ford Coppola and his wife Eleanor bought the legendary Inglenook winery in 1975, with profits from *The Godfather*. The couple have spent the last forty year restoring the property.

Today Napa has over 450 wineries, producing wines under the Napa Valley label and under its sixteen sub-AVAs. A number of Napa wineries have made serious reputations as architectural wonders (or, in some cases, curiosities). The region attracts over four million wine tourists each year.

Let us take a look at the array of Napa AVAs, many of them iconic in the world of wine. We will move south to north. In covering some of these wine names, it would seem germane to mention their cachet, their reputation, their tourist value, while keeping in mind that a lot of work, hard sweat, and risk capital goes into many of these wines. When reputation and actual quality come into alignment, you get a memorable experience. (Your wallet also ends up lighter.)

The **Napa Valley** AVA is virtually synonymous with Napa County itself, including all areas of the county that producer wine (in 16 sub-AVAs). Astonishingly, there are stretches of Napa County, mostly in the east and in the north, where no winegrapes grow. It is worth repeating here that, to the west, the Sonoma Valley AVA comprises only a portion of Sonoma County. According to the rules that allow a place name to be put on a wine label if 85% of the grapes come from that place, whether county or AVA, the phrase "Napa Valley" on a wine label means:

- at least 85% of the grapes come from the Napa Valley
- most probably none of the sixteen Napa sub-AVAs can individually account for 85% of the grapes
- winemakers often claim they are using the larger appellation to avail themselves of the best grapes they can find, regardless of their sub-AVA
- the reality might be that they are shopping around for the cheapest grapes they can find
- and remember the other side of the 85% rule   up to 15% of the grapes can come from anywhere in the state, with no requirement that the content be disclosed

We have already covered the **Los Carneros** AVA Napa shares with Sonoma. To recap: the rolling hills of Los Carneros abut San Pablo Bay at the southern end of both counties, making Los Carneros the coolest and most windy AVA in either Sonoma or Napa. Los Carneros specializes in Pinot Noir and Chardonnay, much of which goes into sparkling wine.

Napa shares the **Wild Horse Valley** AVA in its southeast with Solano County. San Pablo Bay exerts its cooling influence in the western half of the AVA, while the eastern half, shielded by hills, has a warmer climate. Soil is volcanic. Less than a hundred acres are planted, to Pinot Noir and Chardonnay.

The **Coombsville** AVA is Napa's newest (2011). Coombsville rises from near sea level at its western edge to 1,900 feet on the crest of the Vaca Mountain Range to the east. Lava and volcanic ash once flowed from these mountains, while river action wore down the hillsides yielding rocky, gravely soil that drains well. Cooling marine fog from San Pablo Bay is significant, even at elevation. Coombsville produces approachable Cabernet Sauvignon, Syrah, Chardonnay, and Pinot Noir with good structure and mouthfeel, earthy and mineral notes, layers of flavor and aromas, and soft tannins among the reds.

The **Oak Knoll District of Napa Valley** AVA is considered by many to be Napa Valley's "Sweet Spot." Close enough to San Pablo Bay to benefit from its cooling, Oak Knoll nevertheless has a long growing season. It is warm enough to ripen Merlot and Cabernet Sauvignon while at the same time cool enough to boast of delicate and restrained Chardonnay with crisp apple and mineral notes. The Sauvignon Blanc and Riesling are equally good.

The **Yountville** AVA produces Cabs more subtle, gentle and reserved than those from the warmer AVAs to its north (Napa gets warmer the further north you go from San Pablo Bay). Tannins are hard and acidity levels are good. Yountville also produces quality Merlot on Merlot-friendly clay alluvial soils.

It was a wine from what would become the **Stags Leap District** AVA that won the earth-shattering "Judgment of Paris" in 1976. Stags Leap is the only Napa AVA to justify its status on the basis of its soils, which vary from river sediments of loam with clay substructure, to volcanic mountain erosions. Its reputation is for powerful Cabs with firm tannins, elegance and grace. Stags Leap Merlot is unique, with velvety textures, perfumed cherry and red berry flavors, and soft tannins. The Sauvignon Blanc here is round and ripe, yet retains excellent citrus and apple flavors.

The **Mount Veeder** AVA features thin acidic volcanic soil on elevations from 500 to 2600 feet with steep angles that gives vines concentrated sunlight and fine drainage. Low yields give Cabernet Sauvignon, Merlot, and Zinfandel wines firm, tannic structure with strong earth-berry aromas and powerful flavors.

The **Atlas Peak** AVA in Napa's center is one of the higher elevation appellations, with little ocean or bay influence. Growers here produce Zinfandel, Cabernet Sauvignon, Cabernet Franc, Petit Verdot, Malbec, Merlo, Marsanne, Sangiovese, Chardonnay, and Sauvignon Blanc.

The **Oakville** AVA is where Robert Mondavi built his iconic winery in 1966. Oakville is moderately warm, with night and early morning fog acting to maintain grape acidity levels. Oakville has a large array of growers and wineries and is known for small boutique players who often limit production and availability. The Bordeaux trio of Cabernet Sauvignon, Merlot, and Cabernet Franc show ripe currant and mint flavors, rich texture, and full, firm structure tempered by rich fruit. Sauvignon Blanc and Chardonnay here are fruity and luscious.

The **Rutherford** AVA features well-drained soils composed of gravel, sand and loam with volcanic elements, resulting in legendary Cabernet known for its earthy mineral aspect (the Rutherford Dust). Reds like Merlot, Cabernet Franc, and Zinfandel are typically rich, medium to full bodied, elegant, with black-currant, cedar, cassis, black-licorice, spice box, cherry, and earth flavors. Production here in the dead center of Napa is relatively small. Rutherford is home to such well known wine names as Beaulieu, Rutherford Hill, and Francis Coppola's Inglenook.

One step further to the north, the **St. Helena** AVA is a major tourist stop. St. Helena (pronounced Saint Hel-EEN-a) covers 9,000 acres of flat narrow land between the Vaca and Mayacamas Mountains. In 1861, Charles Krug, the Napa Valley winemaking pioneer, opened his winery in St. Helena. The AVA is known for big Cabernet Sauvignon, Cabernet Franc, and Merlot wines with black jammy fruit. The Syrah is fleshy, supple and slightly earthy. St. Helena Zinfandel is well-structured with blackberry notes. The Sauvignon Blanc brings passion fruit and lemon, with a crisp and fresh quality, not "grassy".

Despite its distance from San Pablo Bay, the **Spring Mountain District** AVA gets the cool breezes from clear across neighboring Sonoma thanks to the energetic Petaluma Gap. Spring Mountain is the coolest and wettest AVA in the valley. Soils are a unique blend of volcanic and sedimentary rock. The five Bordeaux red blending varieties—Cabernet Sauvignon, Merlot, Cabernet Franc, Petit Verdot and Malbec—account for most of production, with some plantings of Zinfandel, Syrah, and Petite Sirah. Half the AVA's white grapes are Chardonnay, with Riesling and Sauvignon Blanc.

Another step to the north is the **Diamond Mountain District** AVA, which does not benefit from the cooling Petaluma Gap influence like Spring Mountain. Vineyards sit at on steep slopes at high elevations on porous volcanic soil. The name "Diamond Mountain" refers to small touches of volcanic glass the sparkle in the soil. Age-worthy Bordeaux varieties predominate.

Situated at the top of Napa's array of stacked blocks, the **Calistoga** AVA has very warm days moderated by the cooling influence of the Russian River at night, to generate exceptional diurnal temperature swings to ripen the Cabernet Sauvignon, Petite Sirah, Zinfandel and Syrah the appellation is known for.

The **Howell Mountain** AVA is primarily a Cabernet producer sited on a high ridge overlooking the town of St. Helena from the east. Howell is warm with little marine influence. Vineyards stand at from 1400 to 2600 feet on shallow infertile volcanic soils. Howell Cab is powerful and firm with blackberry-currant flavors, richly tannic, with excellent acidity for aging. The Chardonnay and Viognier show citrus and stone fruit flavors. Merlot and Zinfandel are also produced.

The **Chiles Valley** AVA in Napa's east sits high in the Vaca Mountains, high enough, in fact, to benefit from breezes coming in all the way from the Pacific Ocean. Some vineyards here were planted in Zinfandel in the 1870s. The valley's isolation served to spare the region from the scourge of phylloxera. The old-vine Zinfandel also managed to weather the storm of Prohibition. In addition to Zin, Chiles Valley is known for (no prizes awarded for guessing) Cabernet Sauvignon.

The Pacific Northwest – Oregon and Washington

We tend to think of Washington and Oregon together, but the wine climates for the two states could not be more different. Even though Washington is further north than Oregon, the climate in its main wine producing regions is hotter than Oregon.

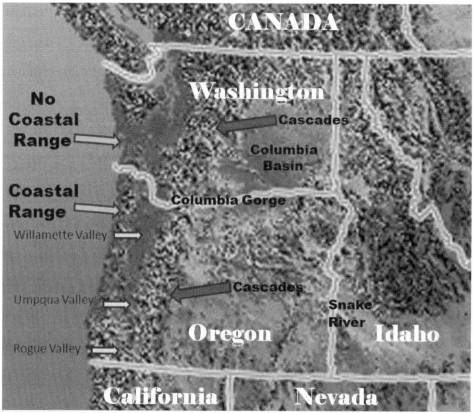

Topographic Map of the Pacific Northwest

As the topographical map of the two states indicates, the difference lies in the configuration of mountain ranges. In Oregon, a relatively low coastal range protects the interior from the worst of the Pacific chill. Some cool air does flow into the interior valley over the tops of the coastal range and through several gaps, supporting the cool climate wine region of the Willamette Valley. The Washington coast lacks a protecting coastal range, making western Washington too cold and wet for fine wine grapes (although there are wineries and tasting rooms in this populous region).

Further inland, the high Cascades act as a near total rain shadow in both states. The eastern side of the Cascades is arid, but irrigated, in both states, by water from the mighty Columbia River. Washington's main wine growing appellations are here. Several of them edge over onto the Oregon side of the Columbia.

Oregon Wine

Wine Map of Oregon

Oregon is the nation's third largest producer of vinifera wine after California and Washington. Major wine grapes include Pinot Noir (more than half the state's vineyard acreage), Pinot Gris (about 10% of acreage), Chardonnay (about 5%), Riesling, and Syrah.

Oregon has three major wine climate zones, none of them relating to the others.

- The Coastal Range supports the interior regions of the **Willamette Valley** AVA, the **Umpqua Valley** AVA, and the **Rogue Valley** AVA, running north to south down the entire length of the state. Umpqua and Rogue together constitute the **Southern Oregon** AVA.

- In the interior along the Columbia River, several AVAs which are primarily in Washington have Oregon components south of the Columbia River: the **Columbia Valley** AVA, the **Columbia Gorge** AVA, the **Walla Walla Valley** AVA. The **Rocks District of Milton-Freewater** AVA, although entirely in Oregon, is a sub-AVA of the Walla Walla Valley AVA, which is largely in Washington, creating some jurisdictional controversy.

- In far eastern Oregon, the state shares the **Snake River Valley** AVA with Idaho.

The **Willamette Valley AVA** south of the largest city Portland is Oregon's most prominent wine region. (Willamette is pronounced with a stress on the "am.") The state capital of Salem and the city of Eugene are both within the region. The largest AVA in the state, Willamette has over 200 wineries. The region is known for its mild climate year round. Summers are dry. Rain falls primarily in winter. Willamette has often been likened to cool-climate Burgundy in France, but its highest temperatures are slightly warmer, its coolest temperature somewhat cooler. Like Burgundy, the region gets a good deal of vintage variation. Heat waves or unexpected spells of chilling rain can seriously compromise a year's crop. Pinot Noir and to a lesser extent Pinot Gris are the two stars of the region, in both cases vinified in a less fruit-forward traditional French style that they are in California.

Willamette contains five nested AVAs: the **Dundee Hills** AVA, the **Eola-Amity Hills** AVA, the **McMinnville** AVA, the **Yamhill-Carlton District** AVA, and the **Chehalem Mountains** AVA . Chehalem in turn has its own nested AVA, the **Ribbon Ridge** AVA.

The **Southern Oregon** AVA is comprised of the **Umpqua Valley** AVA (immediately south of Willamette), and the **Rogue Valley** AVA (in the state's south just above the California line). Umpqua and Rogue have different characteristics and are separated by an expanse of mountains. The Southern Oregon AVA (a so-called "super-AVA") was created in 2004 to allow the two regions to market wine under a joint label.

German immigrants planted the first vines in the **Umpqua River Valley** in the 1880s. Umpqua is slightly warmer than Willamette, and, like Willamette, the region produces Pinot Noir, Tempranillo, and Syrah among the reds, Pinot Gris and Riesling among the whites. Umpqua has two sub-AVAs: **Red Hill-Douglas Country** and **Elkton**.

Further south, the **Rogue River Valley's** vineyards concentrate on the Rogue River's three major tributaries. The **Illinois River Valley**, cool climate high country, produces Pinot Noir and Chardonnay. The **Applegate Valley** AVA (Rogue's only sub-AVA) has a warmer climate more suited to Cabernet Sauvignon and Merlot, with Syrah, Chardonnay and Zinfandel. Thickly settled (it includes the cities of Ashland and Medford), **Bear Creek Valley** is warmer still, and produces Cabernet Sauvignon, Merlot, Chardonnay, Cabernet Franc, Malbec, Sauvignon Blanc, and Syrah.

In north central Oregon the two major regions, both shared with Washington, are the **Columbia Valley** AVA, and the **Columbia Gorge** AVA. Both AVAs are warmer and drier than the regions nearer the coast. The Oregon portion of Columbia Valley has 1200 acres of vineyards, growing a wide variety of grapes, leading with Syrah, Cabernet Sauvignon, Merlot, and Sangiovese. Wine here tends to be fruit forward, but keeping some of the balance and structure of European wines. The Columbia Gorge is marketed as "a world of wine in 40 miles" because of the variety of climates, terrains, and grape varieties in such a small space, covering two states. Grapes (the list is large) include Zinfandel, Syrah, Pinot Noir, Cabernet Sauvignon, Sangiovese, Riesling, and Pinot Gris.

The large **Snake River Valley** AVA (shared with Idaho) on the eastern edge of the state is both cool and dry, with a short growing season. In this climate, cold-hardy white grapes like Riesling, Gewürztraminer, and Chardonnay prosper. The region also has an ice wine industry. Some warmer pockets within Snake River produce Cabernet Sauvignon, Merlot, and Syrah.

Washington State

Washington State Wine Regions

Wine Map of Washington

Washington is the nation's second largest wine producer (but it accounts for only one tenth the volume of California). Only one percent of Washington's wine grapes grow west of the Cascades, although numerous wineries make their home in the Puget Sound area, maintaining their cellar doors at convenient day trip distance from the big population centers like Seattle and Tacoma. While the state has its share of estate wines, one of the key configurations in Washington wine is the separation of growers and winemakers. Many growers came to the grape from growing other fruits.

Washington's major wine regions to the east of the Cascades get very little rain, making irrigation a necessity. The Columbia, Walla Walla, Snake and Yakima rivers provide the water. Because of the high latitude, summer ripening days are often two hours longer than in California. The aridity causes distinct diurnal temperature swings, favoring retention of grape acidity. The grapes get through the summer all right, but every few winters extreme frosts may damage the vines. Washington wine growers have developed numerous methods for dealing with this winter frost, including the use of wind turbines, but one of the best methods is to plant grapes that handle the winters better (Merlot loses in this scenario; Riesling wins). Much of the topsoil is sandy loam studded with basalt rock specks. The phylloxera louse does not like these conditions. The aridity also helps keep major vine diseases and pests in check. As a result, Washington is one of the few areas in the world where vinifera vines can grow on their own roots. This is well and good, given that grafting wounds on vines make them particularly sensitive to winter damage.

Washington viticulture is highly mechanized. Here, wine grapes coexist with a rich array of other fruits, particularly apples. Washington's primary grapes include Cabernet Sauvignon, Riesling, Chardonnay, Merlot, and Syrah, but the growers experiment with many wines not seen elsewhere in America, examples being Lemberger (Blaufrankisch in Austria), and the Georgian white grape Rkatsiteli. Wines tend be fruit-forward with bright acidity and noticeable tannins.

The **Columbia Valley AVA** takes up nearly a quarter of the state (and also spills over into Oregon). With the exception of the **Columbia Gorge** AVA (shared with Oregon), the **Lake Chelan** AVA in the state's north, and the **Lewis-Clark Valley** AVA in the state's southeast (shared with Idaho), all the grape producing areas in eastern Washington fit within Columbia Valley. Sub-AVAs of Columbia Valley include the **Ancient Lakes** AVA**,** the **Horse Heaven Hills** AVA, the **Naches Heights** AVA, the **Wahluke Slope** AVA, the **Walla Walla Valley** AVA**,** and the **Yakima Valley** AVA**.** Yakima in turn has its own trio of nested AVAs: the **Rattlesnake Hills** AVA, the **Red Mountain** AVA, and the **Snipes Mountain** AVA.

Much of the Columbia Valley's geology and topography is the result of the Missoula Floods (also known as the Spokane Floods or the Bretz Floods) that occurred at the end of the last ice age. This flood (released from a glacial lake near Missoula, Montana) inundated a large area leaving silt and gravel beds. These sediments formed the soils of the region.

The **Columbia Gorge** is marketed as "a world of wine in 40 miles" because of the variety of climates, terrains, and grape varieties in such a small space, covering two states. Grapes (the list is large) include Zinfandel, Syrah, Pinot Noir, Cabernet Sauvignon, Sangiovese, Riesling, and Pinot Gris.

The **Lake Chelan** AVA encompasses the southern and eastern shores of Lake Chelan. The lake was formed by the scraping action of ice age glaciers. The soils the glaciers left are sandy and coarse, with notable amounts of quartz and mica. The lake modifies the climate, resulting in a longer growing season and a reduced risk of frost. Italian immigrants settled in the area and began to grow wine grapes before the turn of the 20th century, but instead of becoming a wine producer, the region made a name for itself with apples, pears, peaches and cherries. Around the turn of the 21st century, wine producers became attracted by the long growing season with sunny days and lake-cooled nights. The region now has 20 wineries producing Syrah, Malbec, Pinot Noir, Riesling, Viognier, Pinot Gris, Gewurztraminer, Sangiovese, Merlot, and Cabernet Franc.

The **Ancient Lakes** AVA gets its name from the remnants of the great Missoula flood. The flood scraped the top soils down to the basalt level and gouged out canyons called "coulees" among which many vineyards are planted today. The area sits in the eastern foothills of the Cascades, making the rain shadow of those mountains nearly complete the climate among the driest in the Columbia Valley. White grapes predominate: Chardonnay, Pinot Gris, and Riesling.

The **Horse Heaven Hills** AVA borders the Yakima Valley AVA on the north and the Columbia River on the south. Elevations range from 200 feet in the south to 1,800 feet at the northern boundary. The appellation gets very little rainfall. Grapes are planted in the south-facing slopes of hills that bear the brunt of strong winds that come in from the west through the Columbia Gorge, reducing the threat of rot and fungal diseases and creating desirable vine stress that improves the concentration of the wines. The warmth of the Columbia River moderates the temperature. Washington's largest winery, Columbia Crest, is located in the appellation. A fifth of all wine grapes in Washington are grown in Horse heaven Hills, including Cabernet Sauvignon, Syrah, Merlot and Chardonnay.

The **Naches Heights** AVA is a dry plateau, west of the city of Yakima, ranging in elevation from 1200 to 2400 feet. Seven vineyards here plant red Bordeaux varieties (Cabernet Franc, Cabernet Sauvignon, Malbec, Merlot and Petit Verdot), white Bordeaux varieties (Semillon and Sauvignon Blanc), Rhône varieties (Syrah, Mourvèdre and Viognier), Italians (Barbera, Gewürztraminer, Nebbiolo, Sangiovese, Sagrantino and Pinot Grigio) and even Portuguese varieties (Souzao, Tinta Cao, Touriga Nacional, and Tinta Roriz.)

The **Wahluke Slope** AVA with 8500 vineyard acres accounts for 15% of state production. The area is isolated, warm, and very dry. The deep topsoil is largely windblown sand. Vineyards are arrayed on a broad, south-facing slope, with little variation in soil or climate among them.
The wines here are characterized by full body and prominent varietal character. Top grape varieties include Merlot, Syrah, Cabernet Sauvignon, Riesling, Chardonnay, and Chenin Blanc.

The **Walla Walla Valley** AVA , which pokes into part of northern Oregon, is known for its iconic sweet onions, wheat production, and strawberries. Soils are good draining wind-deposited loess. During the growing season, dry Walla Walla enjoys hot days and dramatically cooler nights (because of the aridity). Wine growing began in the 19th century, declined with killing winter frosts and, of course, Prohibition, and saw a rebirth in the 1970s. Cabernet Sauvignon accounts for 41% of plantings, Merlot 26%, Syrah 16%, with Cabernet Franc, Sangiovese, Chardonnay, and Viognier among a score of other varieties.

The **Yakima Valley** AVA has the distinction of being the first AVA in Washington State (1983). With a thousand acres of vineyards, Yakima has the largest concentration of wineries and vineyards in the state, accounting for 40% of the state's wine. The most widely planted wine grapes are Chardonnay, Riesling, Merlot, Cabernet Sauvignon, Pinot Gris, and Syrah. Nearly 40% of Washington State's yearly wine production is made from Yakima Valley grapes. Yakima also produces prodigious quantities of apples, cherries, nectarines, peaches, pears and plums, as well as 80% of the hops grown in the United States. Yakima has three nested AVAs:

- At elevations ranging from 850 feet to 3,085 feet, the **Rattlesnake Hills** AVA, sits much higher than the remainder of the Yakima Valley. Vineyards are typically located on ridges and terraces with good air drainage that decreases the danger of frost damage, both in winter and in early spring.

Prominent grapes include Cabernet Sauvignon, Malbec, Merlot, Syrah, Chardonnay and Riesling.

- The **Red Mountain** AVA is acclaimed for its red wines from Cabernet Sauvignon, Merlot, Sangiovese, Cabernet Franc and Syrah.

- The **Snipes Mountain** AVA is a high elevation area of rocky soils that, unlike the rest of Yakima, was largely untouched by the Great Missoula Flood. It specializes in Cabernet Sauvignon, Malbec, Syrah, Grenache and Chardonnay.

Lewis-Clark Valley has high temperatures compared to the regions that surround it. The AVA is mostly in Idaho, near the city of Lewiston. When it approved the AVA, the TTB adjusted the border of the Columbia Valley AVA to avoid any overlap. This is appropriate, since unlike the flood-affected Columbia Valley, the Lewis-Clark Valley was created when tectonic forces pushed up mountains, and the Clearwater and Snake rivers cut into those mountains. Climate in the warmest pockets of the appellation can support late-ripening varieties like Cabernet Sauvignon and Grenache. The appellation also has cooler zones where Chardonnay, Pinot Noir, and Merlot do well.

The Challenge of the "Other 47" States

For reasons involving Pacific Ocean currents, the configuration of mountain chains, volcanic activity and even the Great Missoula Flood, the western edge of the North American continent, (including the American states of California, Oregon and Washington, the Canadian province of British Columbia, and the Mexican state of Baja California), is well suited to the growing and vinification of vinifera grapes. In the vast center of the continent, viticulture is challenged by great extremes of temperature in both summer and winter. In the southeastern quarter of the United States, tropical humidity is the great stumbling block to vinifera cultivation. The northeast (where this writer lives) suffers from a double whammy: miserable humidity coming up from the south and vine-killing winter chill sweeping down from the arctic. For many years, once California punched its way to the top of the American vinous world, growers in the "rest" of the country attempted to produce wines from the same international grapes the Californians were planting, Cabernet Sauvignon and Chardonnay above all. Viticulture might fail entirely because of climate induced disease, and when it did succeed, the resulting wines lacked the vivacity and vitality of their California models. Wise winemakers eventually faced the music and started to concentrate on grapes that were appropriate for their climates and environments. These grapes were either French-American hybrids or select vinifera varieties that better fit the climate.

Let us re-cap here the difference. North American fully non-vinifera grapes do not make the kinds of wines most of us like to drink. A species like Vitis labrusca, which includes the Concord grape so well enjoyed for eating out of hand, grape juice, and grape jelly, when made into wine, has a "foxy" taste reminiscent of wild strawberries that have been wrapped in wet fur. The Concord is well suited, however, to environments which are downright cold (and it also resists phylloxera). Attempts to beat phylloxera by crossing vinifera grapes with non-vinifera grapes failed (root grafting succeeded), but in the process a number of **French-American hybrid grapes** were created that did well in the cold harsh climates of the upper Midwest, New York State, Ontario, and even China and Japan. Baco Noir, Chambourcin, Vidal Blanc, Frontenac, Marechal Foch, and Seyval Blanc are just a few of these excellent grapes. The wines they produce can be absolutely delightful, without a trace of foxiness, they just have an image problem (like any grape that doesn't fit into the pantheon of "international" varieties).

- Only nine percent of the grapes produced in **New York State** are Vitis vinifera: Riesling, Chardonnay, Merlot, Cabernet Franc, Pinot Noir, Pinot Gris.

- Another eight percent are hybrids: Cayuga White, Chambourcin, Dechaunac, Vidal Blanc, Seyval Blanc and three specifically developed for the New York environment by the state s vine research center at Cornell University: Noriet, Corot Noir, and Valvin Muscat.

- The remaining 93% of New York s grapes are non-vinifera   Vitis labrusca, the Concord, Catawba, and Niagara varieties

All of these grapes, even the vinifera varieties, show some form of cold hardiness.

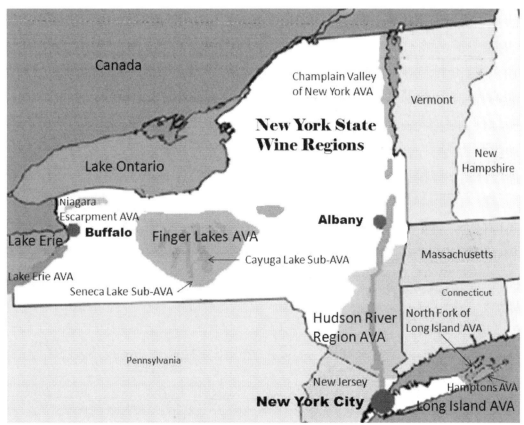

Wine Map of New York

New York is a geologically and topographically diverse state, stretching from the Atlantic Ocean through to the Great Lakes. The Allegheny River in western New York State is actually part of the Mississippi River Valley. New York has big cities (and one giant one), vast suburban areas, and yet significant wilderness and agricultural areas. The state's six wine regions, all designated AVAs, each have nothing in common with the other five except or the fact that each has a name that refers to a body of water (which in all cases, tends to modify the climate).

The **Lake Erie** AVA runs along the lake split among western New York, northern Pennsylvania, and northeastern Ohio. The Concord grape predominates here with most of production going into juice, jelly, eating grapes and low-quality sweetened wine. Some growers are starting to experiment with vinifera plantings.

The **Niagara Escarpment** AVA in western New York has a similar environment to the vineyard areas on the Ontario side of the international border. Twenty wineries make up the Niagara Wine Trail producing Merlot, Cabernet Franc, Cabernet Sauvignon, Chardonnay and Riesling as well as a variety of fruit wines. Viticulture in this cool climate would not be possible without the moderating effect of Lakes Erie and Ontario.

With 11,000 acres under vine, the **Finger Lakes** AVA is New York's largest. Even more so than around the Great Lakes, this interior region would be far too cold for vines without the heat-absorbing and radiating qualities of these eleven narrow glacial lakes. Most vineyards are clustered around the sloping shores of Canandaigua, Keuka, Seneca, and Cayuga lakes. Seneca and Cayuga each qualify as sub-AVAs. More than 120 wineries inhabit this well-developed resort area, many specializing in selling to tourists. Riesling is the leader, with Pinot Noir and some French-American hybrids.

The Finger Lakes has an important place in American wine history as a result of the experiments of Dr. Konstantin Frank, a Ukrainian immigrant, at the Cornell University Geneva Experiment station in the 1950s and 1960s. Dr. Frank proved that *appropriate* vinifera grapes could withstand the cold winter if they could be grafted onto the right native vine roots. In the case of the Finger Lakes, that grape is Riesling. Riesling handles winter frost well. That said, nothing could stop the vine-killing 2014 freeze, caused by a "polar vortex." Riesling vines died, and the federal government declared nineteen of New York's counties disaster areas.

New York's newest delimited wine region is the **Champlain Valley of New York** AVA, approved in September 2016, in the state's extreme northeast. In this cold but tourist-rich region, hardy hybrid grapes run the show: Marquette, Frontenac, and Leon Millot among reds; La Crescent, Seyval Blanc, Brianna, Chardonnel (a cross between Chardonnay and Seyval Blanc), and St. Pépin among whites.

The **Hudson River Region** AVA edges to within day commuting distance of New York City. Most vineyards are situated on the west side of the Hudson, often overlooking the river. The region has the distinction of having the oldest continuously operated winery in the United States: Brotherhood, founded in 1839. The French hybrid Seyval Blanc shares honors with Chardonnay and Riesling for the most popular grape. Millbrook Vineyards and Winery, well inland on the east side of the river, has long been an innovative maker of cool-climate vinifera wines, both red (Pinot Noir, Cabernet Franc, and Merlot) and white (Chardonnay, Riesling and Tocai Friulano). It is perhaps telling that Millbrook, which does a brisk tasting room business, rounds out its offerings with a Cabernet Sauvignon from San Benito County, California rather than trying to coax that demanding grape to ripen in Dutchess County, New York.

The growing season for the Finger Lakes and Lake Erie AVAs is about 200 days, the Hudson River Region's is only 190 days, but the vineyards at the eastern extreme of Long Island enjoy about 230 days a year of growing time. The important wine regions are the outstretched twin forks of Long Island constituting the **North Fork of Long Island** AVA and the **Hamptons, Long Island** AVA. A larger Long Island AVA, covering Nassau and Suffolk Counties, was created later to protect the Long Island brand. In this case, the sub-AVAs existed *before* the regional AVA. Vineyards here benefit from the warming influence of three bodies of water: the Atlantic Ocean to the south, Long Island Sound to the north, and Peconic Bay between the north and south forks. The Hamptons tends to be cooler and wetter than the North Fork. Long Island winemakers are doing well with Cabernet Franc and Merlot (which benefit from those extra weeks of growing season). Chardonnay and Riesling also do well, but the energetic growers of this tourist-friendly region are trying their hands at dozens of other vinifera grape varieties.

Ranking the American states as wine producers leads the researcher to contradictory sets of data (except that all data criteria put California as number one). You are forced to choose a list that *seems* most useful. The danger is that you might chose a ranking list skewed toward those states that have the best public relations departments. With that disclaimer, this writer chooses to rely on data from the National Association of American Wineries and their ranking of the states based on number of wineries (rather than vineyard acreage or volume of wine sold). The top five by this criterion are: California, Washington, Oregon, New York, and Virginia. (California has more wineries than the other 49 states combined.) These are also the states covered in detail in the World Atlas of Wine. Texas is nearly tied with Virginia on the NAAW list, and exceeds it on some other lists, so we will also cover that state.

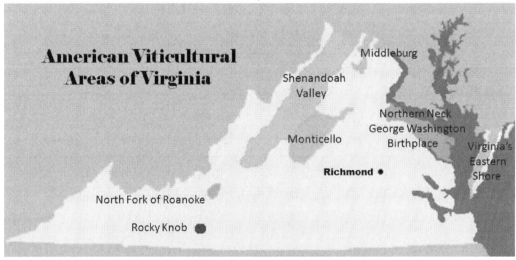

Wine Map of Virginia

We have already discussed **Virginia** in this course in our discussion of Founding Father Thomas Jefferson's failed efforts to grow vinifera grapes on his estate at Monticello. Tom's problem, though he did not know it at the time, was the phylloxera louse. Even without phylloxera, the region's endemic humidity would have promoted fungal issues that would have worn Jefferson out. To be precise, these issues would have worn Jefferson's *slaves* out, but that is material for another course. The same Monticello vineyards are producing vinifera grapes now thanks to rootstock grafting and judicious grape selection. The **Monticello** AVA is one of seven in Virginia. The Commonwealth's top five varietals are Chardonnay, Cabernet Franc, Merlot, Vidal Blanc (a French-American hybrid), and Viognier. Viognier has open clusters that allow air to circulate among and between the grapes, helping to avoid fungal infection caused by the humidity. Chardonnay still leads in production, but Viognier is now promoted as Virginia's signature grape.

It is worth remarking here that Virginia's official state motto is *sic semper tyrannus*, Latin for "Tyrants always get the ignominy they so richly deserve." In 1969, Virginia decided that "Virginia is for Lovers" made better PR. The phrase (which pre-dated "I – heart – New York") is still in use. So if Viognier is now the state's signature grape, so be it. The word Viognier even *looks like* Virginia. Cabernet Franc is touted as Virginia's signature red.

The **Middleburg** AVA is Virginia's newest, in the Piedmont region of the north, abutting the Potomac River, 50 miles west of Washington, DC. Soil is granite-based clay. Boxwood, one of the leading producers, produces red wine only from the Bordeaux grapes of Cabernet Franc, Cabernet Sauvignon, Merlot, Petit Verdot and Malbec. Other Middleburg wineries produce Viognier, Chardonnay, Riesling, and some are experimenting with Nebbiolo, which is extraordinarily difficult to propagate outside of its home in Italy's Piemonte.

The vineyards of the **North Fork of Roanoke** AVA sit between 1,200 feet and 2,200 feet in elevation on the eastern slopes of the Allegheny Mountains. The elevation makes this a cool-clime region despite its latitude. Cabernet Franc, Cabernet Sauvignon, Merlot, Sangiovese, Viognier, Petit Verdot, Syrah, Chardonnay, and Malbec are among the grapes produced.

The **Rocky Knob** AVA in the Blue Ridge Mountains of southwest Virginia is small, with elevations reaching from 1600 feet to 3600 feet. Soils are a mixture of gravel and silt loam. Strong winds in this mountainous area protect the vines from fungus and excess humidity. No wine is being produced under this appellation at present.

The **Shenandoah Valley** AVA is large, and spills over into the West Virginia panhandle at its northern end. The valley is flanked by the Blue Ridge Mountains to the east and the Allegheny Mountains on the west. Growing season is warm, and the ridges act as a rain shadow, keeping the appellation dry. Wineries here produce a combination of vinifera varietals, French-American hybrids and a some wines from the Norton grape, a native American variety that is free of that "foxy" quality.

The **Northern Neck George Washington Birthplace** AVA comprises a peninsula between the Potomac and Rappahannock rivers in the Tidewater region of Virginia. The tip of the AVA juts into Chesapeake Bay. Production is split between vinifera grapes (Cabernet Franc, Cabernet Sauvignon, Chardonnay), and French-American hybrids (Chambourcin, Seyval Blanc, Vidal Blanc).

The **Virginia's Eastern Shore** AVA lies near sea-level on the southern end of the Delmarva Peninsula. The soil is sandy and deep, the weather mild because of ocean and bay influence. Here, Chatham Vineyards on Church Creek grows Chardonnay, Merlot, Cabernet Franc, Cabernet Sauvignon and Petit Verdot.

Texas Wine Regions

Wine Map of Texas

Texas is a mighty big state, so keep in mind that the regions on the AVA map above are bigger than they look.

The **Texas Hill Country** AVA in central Texas is the nation's second largest AVA. (The Upper Mississippi River Valley AVA, which covers parts of Illinois, Iowa, Wisconsin and Minnesota, is the largest, but doesn't produce much in the way of wine.) Only a small portion of the region, about a thousand acres, is planted to quite a wide variety of vines, including the Cabernets, Sangiovese, Tempranillo, Tannat, Barbera, Sauvignon Blanc, Viognier, and Chardonnay. Texas Hill Country has two small sub-AVAs. The **Fredericksburg in the Texas Hill Country** AVA is known for its Cabernet Sauvignon and Chardonnay. The **Bell Mountain** AVA produces Cabernet Franc, Cabernet Sauvignon, Chardonnay, Chenin Blanc, and Colombard.

The vineyards of the **Texas High Plains** AVA stand on flat terrain at elevations between 3,000 and 4,000 feet above sea level between the city of Lubbock and the New Mexico line. The elevation and aridity result in lower temperatures at night. The *tierra roja* soil is composed of sandy loam over limestone. This is a dry region, but it sits atop the Ogallala Aquifer, which stretches into eight states. High winds virtually strip the vines of pests and disease. This desolate region is more of a growing area than a winemaking one, although it contains at least six wineries. All the conditions here are right for this region to become a top quality source for fine wine grapes. Growers already ship their grapes far and wide. Cabernet ripens nicely in these conditions, but you will also find Italians like Aglianico, Barbera, Montepulciano, and Sangiovese and the Rhône grapes like Syrah, Grenache, Roussanne and Viognier, plus Sauvignon Blanc and Tempranillo.

The **Texoma** AVA is north central Texas, south of Lake Texoma, the Red River and the Oklahoma border. This is where 19th century viticulturist Thomas Volney Munson developed the technique of grafting vinifera grapevines onto native-American roots to successfully combat phylloxera and save wine from obliteration.

The **Texas Davis Mountains** AVA is in the western part of the state surrounded by the Chihuahua Desert. With elevations ranging from 4500 to 8300 feet above sea level, the AVA is decidedly cool. Given its remoteness, it only has 50 acres planted to Cabernet Sauvignon and Sauvignon Blanc. By contrast the AVA covers 270,000 acres.

The west Texas **Escondido Valley** AVA produces Cabernet Franc, Cabernet Sauvignon, Chardonnay, Chenin Blanc, and Colombard but has no wineries. Soil is silt and loam.

The **Mesilla Valley** AVA is mostly in New Mexico. The Texas portion is located north and west of El Paso at relatively high elevations. Soils are mostly sand, loam, and clay loam. Mesilla (meaning "little table" in Spanish) is very hot and dry but these conditions are ameliorated by cooling winds that funnel through the valley. The long growing season assures optional ripeness for Cabernet Sauvignon, Dolcetto, Zinfandel, Mourvèdre, Sangiovese and other grapes that take well to warmth.

Canada features two distinctive wine producing regions several thousand miles apart, in southern British Columbia and southern Ontario.

Wine Map of Ontario

The **Niagara Peninsula** of Ontario benefits from the moderating effects of Lake Erie and Lake Ontario and has more than 13,000 acres of vineyards. White hybrids include Seyval Blanc and Vidal, red hybrids Baco Noir, Chambourcin and Maréchal Foch. Niagara also grows Gewürztraminer, Riesling, Chardonnay, Pinot Gris, Pinot Blanc, Pinot Noir, Cabernet Franc and Merlot. Niagara also makes a specialty of producing ice wine. Here the grower lets the grapes freeze while still on the vine, resulting in a sweet concentrated wine.

The **Lake Erie North Shore** region of southwestern Ontario benefits from Lake Erie's status as the shallowest and warmest of the Great Lakes. Grapes include Syrah, Baco Noir, Cabernet Franc, Pinot Noir, Vidal Blanc, and Cabernet Franc. Here, too, ice wine is produced.

Prince Edward County on the north shore of Lake Ontario is a designated wine area producing Pinot Noir, Chardonnay, Pinot Gris, Cabernet Franc, Riesling, and Syrah on shallow limestone soils. The vines ripen well over the lake-enhanced summer, but killing winter freezes are a real problem. Around the country's largest city, the **Toronto and York** area, dozens of wineries cater to day-trippers with an array of cool climate vinifera and hybrid varieties. Winter freezing is a major problem, however.

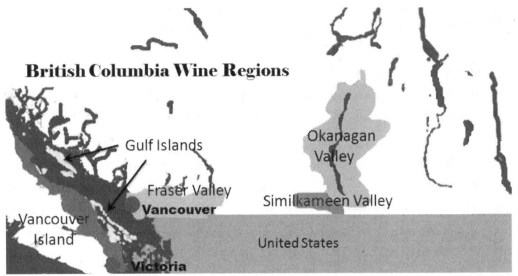

Wine Map of British Columbia

The **Okanagan Valley** is British Columbia's most prominent fine wine region. Okanagan is Canada's only desert. Okanagan's continental climate is moderated by Lake Okanagan and the series of watercourses that connect to it. The Cascade Mountains create a rain shadow effect as in adjoining areas of Eastern Washington. Even more so than Washington, Okanagan's northerly grape ripening days are extra long. Okanagan had a stop-and-go history for a hundred years, until the modern wine industry began here in the 1970s. Growers now plant more than 60 vine varieties destined for nearly every style of wine: still, sparkling, fortified and dessert, including ice wine. Varieties include standard grapes like Cabernet Sauvignon, Merlot, Pinot Noir, Pinot Gris, and Cabernet Franc. German influence brings Riesling and Gewürztraminer. With global warming, plantings of warm climate varieties are on the rise, including Sangiovese, Syrah, Tempranillo, Trebbiano, Pinotage, Malbec, Barbera and Zinfandel. The nearby **Similkameen Valley** hard by the international border, specializes in Merlot, Cabernet Franc, Cabernet Sauvignon, and Chardonnay.

Further west in British Columbia, the **Fraser Valley** near Vancouver accounts for a full half of the province's agriculture including 30 vineyards and 15 wineries. In this flat region of rolling hills, climate is dry and irrigation is often necessary. Top grapes include Pinot Noir, a number of white and red hybrids developed by Swiss grape geneticist Valentin Blattner, and the Bacchus grape, a German vinifera crossing. With the mildest climate in all Canada, southern **Vancouver Island** and the nearby **Gulf Islands** produce wines from Pinot Noir, the red hybrid Maréchal Foch, Pinot Gris, and Ortega (a German white vinifera crossing named after the Spanish poet José Ortega y Gasset).

Mexico

Wine Map of Mexico

The making of wine in **Mexico** dates back nearly five centuries to Hernando Cortés, the first conquistador. If Spain's mission in the New World was to Christianize the natives and spread the faith, it needed sacramental wine. The wine, of course, was useful for other forms of emotional solace. Unfortunately, in 1699 Charles II, King of Spain, banned new vineyard plantings in Mexico (except for sacramental purposes) to protect the wine industry in Spain, leaving the Mexican wine industry to wither on the vine. Promising Mexican vinifera wine had to wait until the 21st century, but it has come back with some force.

Mexico has three wine producing regions among its 31 states. The northern region includes Baja California and Sonora. The La Laguna region straddles Coahuila and Durango, and includes the Parras Valley. The center region includes the states of Zacatecas, Aquascalientes, and Queretaro.

In the **Parras Valley** between Coahuila and Durango, Casa Madero, built in 1597, can claim to be the oldest winery in the Western Hemisphere. In the 18th century, Basque immigrants settled in the Parras Valley. They brought Garnacha (Grenache), Mazuelo (Carignan) and other red grapes to the region. The arid valley compensates for its low latitude with formidable altitude (a mile high in some places). Springs provide the water. Today, the valley produces Cabernet Sauvignon, Syrah, Tempranillo, Chardonnay and Chenin Blanc, as well as brandies.

Since we mentioned brandies, be it known that most of the wine produced in Mexico is designated for brandy, the most widely consumed spirit in the country. Agave-based spirits like Tequila and Mezcal come in a distant second.

As if they had a mind of their own dedicated to searching out better wine climates, the vines of the Parras Valley filtered up to the northern part of Baja California, a region that benefits from both altitude and Pacific Ocean influence. The Santo Tomas winery was founded in 1888. Italian immigrants founded the L.A. Cetto winery in 1926, which today runs a huge spread of 2500 acres in the **Guadeloupe Valley**, just north of Ensenada and within striking distance of Tijuana and the U.S. border. The Guadeloupe Valley and its neighbors the San Vicente Valley and the Santo Tomás Valley today produce 90% of Mexico's wines. Guadeloupe is an area of a few large producer like Cetto who coexist with a number of boutique wineries. The valley enjoys sunny days and cool Pacific nights. Soil is deep granite. Vineyard elevations range from 650 to 1650 feet. The region is widely publicized as "La Ruta del Vino." This beehive of vinous activity lacks a signature grape, instead growing fifty varieties, both red and white. The area has a wine school that helps draw tourists, and some makers are producing organic grapes and promoting sustainable viticulture. The proximity to the United States is a major plus.

Down in the Mexico's center region, in Zacatecas, Aquascalientes, and Queretaro, vineyards sit at 6000 feet and can be downright cold, despite the low latitude. Spanish cava producer Freixenet has invested money in the region to produce dry sparkling wines called *vinos espumsos*. Cabernet Sauvignon, Sauvignon Blanc, Zinfandel and Pinot Noir find their way into still wine here.

Chapter Thirteen

World Wine Regions
South America

Brazil

Brazil has a large population with a considerable thirst for wine, but much of the country has a tropical climate, not really suited for fine wine production. Grapevines need a winter in which to go dormant, and they do not like excess heat and humidity. Despite this, the country grows wine grapes on 170,000 acres. Less than ten percent of the grapes are vinifera grapes. Most plantings in Brazil are of indigenous grapes or hybrids that can better stand the heat and humidity.

The Brazilian state of Rio Grande do Sul sits in the extreme south, bordering wine producing countries Uruguay and Argentina. In addition to almost reaching the 30th parallel, the usual minimum latitude for fine wine production, the region enjoys considerable elevation, up to 4500 feet above sea level. It has the added advantage of a population that reflects considerable immigration from Italy. The major international grape varieties as well as Portuguese varieties make up the wine menu here. While we might someday see some of these wines on the American market, the Brazilians drink rather than export most of their wine.

Bolivia makes up for its low latitude by extremely high altitude. Most Bolivian wine traditionally went for brandy, especially the clear grape brandy called Pisco, but some growers are starting to plant international varieties at altitudes ranging from 5500 to nearly 8000 feet. A similar situation exists in **Peru**, the taste leader in the Pisco world.

The people of **Uruguay** are very fond of wine. Basque immigrants brought the Tannat grape from southwest France to the country in the 1870s, and, like the French grapes Malbec and Carmenere that became the signature red grapes of Argentina and Chile, respectively, Tannat became Uruguay's own. French investment in the country's wine industry is significant, supporting a range of international grape varieties in addition to Tannat. Most vineyards are clustered in the south of the country across the Rio de la Plata from Argentina.

Argentina and Chile may share a long north-south Andean border and the Spanish language, but they differ widely with respect to climate. Chile has cooling Pacific influence. The Atlantic gives no corresponding benefit to Argentina. Chile exploits the Pacific benefit up and down a wide stretch of latitude. Argentina fine-tunes its available altitude for its vineyards.

Wine Map of Argentina

Argentina produces full-flavored deeply-colored red wines at significant altitudes, and aromatic whites at even higher altitudes. The **Mendoza** region looks up to the high Andes to the west. Elevations here push 4,000 feet, the air is dry, and day/night variation makes for flavor and acidity in the region's characteristic Malbec (the grape came over from France in the 1860s). Unfortunately, spring frosts can endanger vines, as can summer rains, and hail is a consistent menace.

Mendoza is a huge producer, making two-thirds of Argentina's wine. Average vineyard elevation is 2,000–3,600 feet above sea level.

The departments of **Maipú** and **Luján** are the principal producing regions of Mendoza, but the **Valle de Uco** with its **Tupungato** Department is an up and comer. Malbec is the most important grape, with Cabernet Sauvignon, Tempranillo, Chardonnay and the pink-skinned Criolla Grande and Cereza grapes. The soil of Mendoza is mostly loose alluvial sand over clay. Water descends from the Andes in several river systems, which in turn flow into a network of irrigation channels, canals, and reservoirs that in many cases date back centuries.

North of Mendoza, closer to the equator and lower in altitude, the province of **San Juan** is Argentina's second largest producer. San Juan is considerably hotter than Mendoza and produces red varietals from Syrah and Bonarda, as well as brandy, vermouth and fortified wines along the line of Sherry. The next door province of **La Rioja** traces winemaking back to the earliest Spanish missionaries. Heat and lack of water are issues in La Rioja. It specializes in the white grapes Muscat of Alexandria and Torrontés.

Still further north, and hence at lower latitudes, the provinces of **Catamarca, Jujuy and Salta** include some of the highest vineyards in the world: up to 8000 feet. Catamarca is the most widely planted. The **Cafayate region of Salta**, with its mile high vineyards, is making an international reputation for its environment: temperatures reaching 100 degrees Fahrenheit during the days (on vineyards closer to the sun), with nighttime temperatures dropping into the fifties, one of the widest day-to-night temperature swings in the wine world. The Torrontés from here is richly acidic and pure. Cafayate is attracting significant foreign investment.

In **Patagonia** to the south, the province of **Río Negro**, with its chalky soils, has a consistently cool climate (thanks to Antarctic influence). Rio Negro has traditionally served as Argentina's principal fruit growing region. Dry weather and winds here keep vine diseases down, and growing season is patiently long. Bordeaux varieties like Cabernet Sauvignon were brought here in the early 20th century. French and Italian wine houses are investing in this region, reaping a return expressed in Torrontés, Sémillon, Riesling, Merlot, Cabernet Franc, Pinot Noir, and a lighter version of Malbec. To the west bordering Chile is the province of **Neuquén**, more a matter of 21t century wine expansion, producing Sauvignon Blanc, Chardonnay, Pinot Noir and Malbec. In the far south, in the province of **Chubut** (off our map), Mendoza's Bernardo Weinert is planting early ripeners like Pinot Noir, Chardonnay, Gewürztraminer and Riesling to produce high acid, low alcohol German-style whites.

Wine Map of Chile

Even though the Spanish introduced the grapevine to Chile, French influence, now in its third century, has been consistently strong. French wine consultants are active in Chile, seeing that French financial infusions bear fruit. French vines varieties rule Chile. Of course, they predominate elsewhere, but in Chile, the French influence extends to winemaking. That means Bordeaux blends, usually led by Cabernet Sauvignon, Chile's most produced grape, accounting for a third of all Chilean vines. Where Cabernet goes, also goes Merlot. For decades, Merlot had an identity crisis—literally, as Merlot and the Bordeaux blending component Carménère were often comingled and confused. Vine scientists—ampelographers—had to come in and untwine these two vines. Carménère is nearly extinct in Bordeaux, but it has found a new identity in Chile where it was introduced in the 1850s. It is hence parallel in function to Malbec in Argentina, Tannat in Uruguay, Cabernet Sauvignon in Napa, Shiraz in Australia, Chenin Blanc in South Africa, and Sauvignon Blanc in New Zealand—all French emigrants that have become the signature grapes of countries in the New World.

If the French presence were not enough, Chile is in many ways the ideal country in which to produce wine. Most of its regions are dry, but it has ample irrigation water from the Andes. Its ultra-long pacific coast interacts with the Humboldt Current coming up from Antarctica, creating unparalleled cool-climate viticultural possibilities. In Chile you can fine-tune both latitude and altitude. The country has ample supplies of inexpensive labor. What's more, phylloxera never reached Chile, so most vines are propagated on their own roots.

This last attribute, un-grafted vines, has a down side. Once grafting to defeat phylloxera became the norm, rootstocks were developed to respond to a wide range of environmental challenges such as resistance to other diseases and pests, soil salinity, calcium content, soil acidity and alkalinity, too much water, too little water, cold resistance, heat stress, and so forth. Chile's un-grafted vines cannot avail themselves of any of these benefits. For years, many Chilean growers could not pay attention to these kinds of "modern" details. Chile had a reputation for inexpensive, quaffable wines. That is changing rapidly in the 21st century, as highly trained European winemakers come to fine tune and micromanage their Chilean wineries and vineyards.

We will look at Chile's wine regions starting in the north and working our way south. The **Elqui Valley**, just off our map, was for many years primarily a producer of grapes for Pisco but has more recently become a Syrah specialist—on granite hillside vineyards at elevations of over 6500 feet. **Limari** is a much more open wine valley, directly cooled by the Pacific because of the absence of a coastal range (coastal ranges buffer most of Chile's regions). The result is Sauvignon Blanc, Chardonnay and Pinot Noir.

The **Aconcagua** region takes its name from the highest mountain in the Andes, which looms over the appellation at 23,000 feet. The warm **Aconcagua Valley** has 2500 acres of Cabernet Sauvignon, Carménère and Syrah. The **Casablanca Valley**, closer to the ocean, makes Sauvignon Blanc, Chardonnay and Pinot Noir. South of Casablanca, the **San Antonio Valley**, closer still to the Pacific, produces Sauvignon Blanc, Chardonnay and Pinot Noir and Syrah.

Are we starting to get a theme here? We are: French grapes.

A hop over the national capital of Santiago brings us to the **Central Valley**: Maipo (pronounced MY-po), Rapel (made up of Cachapoal and Colchagua), Curicó and Maule. **Maipo** is the warmest of the Central Valley appellations, dotted with wineries and vineyards within smog distance of the capital, and basically one word describes it: Cabernet, some of it world class.

Rapel's constituents Cachapoal and Colchagua are the regions usually found on wine labels. **Cachapoal**, particularly its sub-region of Apalta, is known for Cabernet and Syrah. The clay soils of **Colchagua** naturally favor Merlot, which likes that kind of environment.

Curicó, the next region down, is warmer, since the Coastal Range veers farther east and blocks Pacific influence. Curicó is the source of everyday drinking wines from Cabernet Sauvignon and Sauvignon Blanc.

Maule is the oldest wine region in Chile. Here some old vine Cabernet and Merlot produce age-worthy Bordeaux-style blends. Parts of Maule have the clay soil Merlot adores.

The Central Valley has width as well as length. East-west orientation can affect vines as much as the north-south direction. Nights are colder nearer to the Andes, favoring retention of color and acidity. The land in the west gets afternoon cooling from the Pacific. The best wines tend to come from the mountain side, raised at significant elevation. Since 2011 Chile has allowed winemakers to use a trio of east-west label descriptors: *Costa* (coast), *Entre Cordilleras* (between the mountains, i.e., between the Coastal Range and the Andes), and *Andes*.

The three regions of **Chile del Sur** (southern Chile), **Itata**, **Bio Bio**, and **Malleco**, are not only closer to the South Pole but they lack protection from a coastal range. Think cold and wet. These regions are big producers of the Pais and Moscatel vines that for centuries have supported jug wine production in the country. As with any such area (anywhere), pockets of quality stand out, producing Pinot Noir, Chardonnay, Riesling and Gewurztraminer (the last two are **not** French!) Wine colonizers are trekking even further south of the Malleco Valley, catching and barbecuing penguins as they search for the holy grail of cool-climate Burgundian and German growing conditions.

Chapter 14

World Wine Regions
Australia

Australian school children in their distinctive Aussie hats.

These Aussie schoolchildren in the photo above, including the author's granddaughter balancing on the rail in front, know to protect themselves from the unrelenting Australian sun. The country's grapevines go out there without the benefit of hats. Australia bears the brunt of the El Nino and La Niña climate systems. Drought is a constant menace, as are state-gutting bushfires, which will incinerate vineyards as they will anything else in their path. The tough Aussies always find ways to cope.

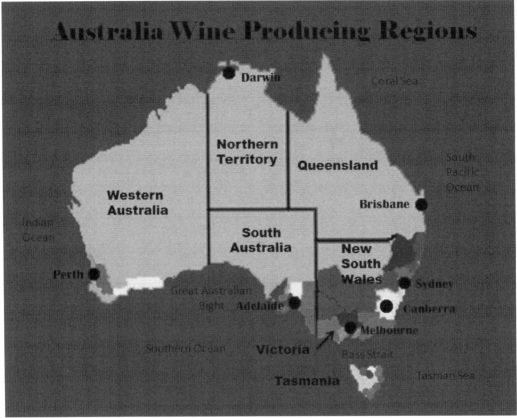

Australia Wine Map

A quick blink at the Australia wine map tells us that most of the continent is too close to the equator for vine growing. Australians claw out good vineyard sites by hugging the south of the continent, taking advantage of the proximity of bodies of water, planting vineyards at elevation—or all three. Actually, a fourth factor is critically important: willingness to experiment with what they call "alternative" grape varieties. Zinfandel, Tempranillo, Sangiovese, Viognier, Pinot Gris, Barbera, Nebbiolo, Dolcetto, Aglianico, Negroamaro, and many others have little trouble qualifying for Australian test runs. Even the Greek Assyrtiko, which maintains acidity nicely in hot climates, had established an Australian bridgehead.

Shiraz (Syrah in Aussie-speak) is still the leader, produced in nearly every appellation and sub-appellation in many different styles, Chardonnay is number two, Cabernet Sauvignon three.

Australia uses a system of Geographical Indications (GIs) that is largely similar to the American appellation system. A GI may appear on a wine label if the wine contains a minimum of 85% of fruit from that region. The largest appellations are states and zones. These divide into regions (the official term) and in some cases sub-regions. For example, in the state of South Australia, Barossa is a zone. Within it are two regions: Barossa Valley and Eden Valley. Eden Valley in turn has a sub-region called High Eden.

For convenience, we are going to call all these appellations "regions."

More than half of Australia's wine is produced in bulk for export in the largest zone, South Eastern Australia. Do not confuse this with South Australia, which is one of Australia's states. The South Eastern Australia appellation legally refers to wine made from grapes grown anywhere in Australia except Western Australia. In reality, most wine with this labeling is produced from grapes grown in three interior regions: Riverina in New South Wales, Murray Darling, which straddles the border between New South Wales and Victoria, and Riverland in South Australia. Extensive river systems in this warm interior climate support irrigation for grapes and many other crops, but water availability and quality is a constant issue. Wines from this region are altogether average, and account for more than half of all Australian wine imported into the United States. Australia is a lot more than Kangaroos hopping out of a wine label, of course.

South Australia Wine Map

The state of **South Australia** produces half of Australia's wine and has the nation's premier district for quality wine, the **Barossa Valley**. German immigrants blazed the wine trail in Barossa in the 19th century. The name is Spanish, a reference to the 1811 battle of Barrosa between the English and French in the Peninsula War (the name is misspelled, but no one suggests changing it now). Barossa's climate is hot and dry, with cool nights. Its gem is concentrated, fruit-forward, soft tannin, jammy Shiraz with notes of anise, licorice, and leather. Barossa also has old-vine Grenache and Mourvèdre (which they call Mataro). These two grapes partner with Shiraz to produce the GSM wines that are popular in Australia. Of course, the region produces Cabernet Sauvignon and Chardonnay.

Just east of the Barossa Valley is the **Eden Valley**, higher country. Eden's primary grape is also Shiraz, but it has made a reputation as a producer of dry Riesling, with notes of rich lime, floral and mineral. **Clare Valley** to the north of Barossa has an even better reputation for Riesling, also producing concentrated Shiraz and Cabernet.

Just south of the state capital of Adelaide, the growers of **McLaren Vale** grow everything: Shiraz, of course, but also Grenache, Mataro, Sangiovese, Vermentino, Roussanne, Tempranillo, Nebbiolo, Zinfandel, Sagrantino, the Georgian grape Saperavi, to name just a few. **Adelaide Hills** just to the east of the capital has made a name for its citrusy Sauvignon Blanc, which has less of a grassy character than New Zealand Sauvignon Blanc. **Langhorne Creek** further south and nearby **Currency Creek** produce Sauvignon Blanc, Cabernet Sauvignon, Merlot, Shiraz and Chardonnay.

Two hundred miles to the south of Adelaide, the **Limestone Coast** zone enjoys wine-friendly limestone soils and warm, dry Mediterranean climate. The most prominent region here is **Coonawarra**, which had become the epicenter for Australian Cabernet Sauvignon. Coonawarra has a distinctive soil called "terra rossa," or red earth. **Padthaway** and **Wrattonbully** have similar soils to Coonawarra and are known for Cabernet Sauvignon, Merlot, Shiraz and Chardonnay. Cooler **Mount Gambier** shows potential for Pinot Noir. Right on the coast, **Mount Benson** and **Robe** produce a number of varieties with Cabernet Sauvignon holding number one in each.

The Red Earth of Coonawarra.

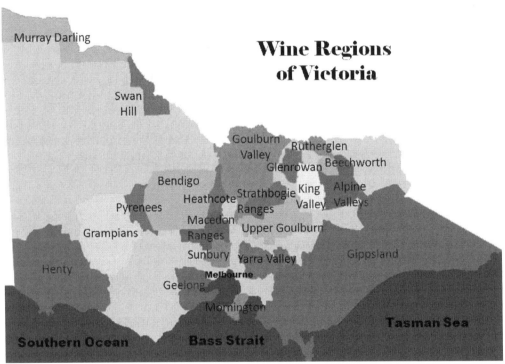

Wine Regions
of Victoria

Murray Darling

Swan
Hill

Goulburn
Valley
Glenrowan
Rutherglen
Beechworth

Bendigo
Heathcote Strathbogie King Alpine
Valley Valleys
Pyrenees Ranges
Macedon
Grampians Ranges Upper Goulburn

Sunbury Yarra Valley Gippsland

Henty
Melbourne
Geelong

Mornington

Tasman Sea

Southern Ocean Bass Strait

Victoria Wine Map

The state of **Victoria** is mainland Australia's smallest state, and also the coolest. Victoria boasts over 600 wineries, most of them small family operations. As a cursory look at the wine map shows, the state seems a veritable patchwork of regions. The state has six zones.

The **Northwest Victoria** zone includes the irrigated regions of **Murray Darling** and **Swan Hill**, both of which Victoria shares with New South Wales. This is Victoria's hottest wine region. Murray Darling is known for bulk wines, Swan Hill for fruit-driven Chardonnay, Shiraz and Cabernet Sauvignon.

The **Gippsland** zone is also a region. This large area is the scene of much new development, but it is initially carving out a reputation for Pinot Noir.

In the **Central Victoria** zone, **Bendigo** is large region with a variety of land formations: volcanic plains, alluvial flood plains, rolling granite hills and sedimentary rises. Soils are sandy gravel, volcanic basalt or clay loams. Bendigo has a Mediterranean climate with warm, dry summers and mild, wet winters. Shiraz leads the reds that dominate, with Cabernet Sauvignon, Pinot Noir, Merlot, Cabernet Franc, Malbec, Mataro, Sangiovese and the Portuguese grape Touriga Nacional. The red Cambrian soils of **Heathcote** produce Shiraz above all, with outstanding examples of Sangiovese, Tempranillo, Petit Verdot, Cabernet Sauvignon, Merlot and excellent Rieslings and Viognier. The **Goulburn Valley** has a typical inland valley floor warm climate and substantial diurnal temperature ranges. The meandering Goulburn River has a cooling effect, however. Loose textured sandy, gravelly soils translate into Riesling, Cabernet Sauvignon, Marsanne, and Shiraz. The **Strathbogie Ranges** have vineyards at up to 2000 feet. Domaine Chandon uses the high acid Pinot Noir and Chardonnay produced here for sparkling wine. **Upper Goulburn** sits between the Great Dividing Range and Strathbogie Ranges at a high altitude that favors crisp aromatic white wines, fine sparkling wines and elegant, textural red wines.

The **Northeast Victoria** zone is inland and quite hot. The region specializes in fortified dessert wines that are uniquely Australian in style. **Rutherglen**'s "stickies" are made from late harvest Muscat and a grape called Topaque. These wines age years in cask. Rutherglen also makes still red wine from the Durif grape, an obscure variety that just might be related to California Petite Sirah. **Glenrowan** is renowned for its full-bodied red wines from Shiraz, Durif and Merlot, fortified Muscat wines and crisp whites from Chardonnay, Trebbiano, Sauvignon Blanc and Fiano. **Alpine Valleys** is cooler because of its elevation. Growing season is quite long for wines characterized by forward fruit and bracing acidity. Chardonnay, Shiraz and Cabernet Sauvignon lead the pack, but a range of varieties, some "alternate," are finding adherents in the region: Sangiovese, Barbera, Nebbiolo, Vermentino, Savagnin, Teroldego and Marzemino. **Beechworth** is an old gold mining town producing fruit-forward Chardonnay, as well as Pinot Gris, Shiraz, Tempranillo, and a number of Italian reds.

The **Port Philip** zone centers on the great city of Melbourne. South of the city, **Geelong** has a maritime climate that proves ideal for Pinot Noir. Ditto for the **Mornington Peninsula** across Port Phillip Bay. To the northwest, inland **Sunbury** has Shiraz, Cabernet Sauvignon, Cabernet Franc, Merlot, Chardonnay, and some Riesling. To the northeast, the **Yarra Valley** has a great deal of topographical variety, warm in the valleys and much cooler up in the hills. Soils are sandy loam in some regions, red volcanic earth in others. Pinot Noir and Chardonnay are the stars in both still and sparkling wine. The elevation of the high **Macedon Ranges** keeps the region cool for Pinot Noir and Chardonnay.

The **Western Victoria** zone adds a final level of complexity to the Victorian labyrinth. **Grampians** is a craggy area in the western extreme of the Great Dividing Range, known for Shiraz and Cabernet Sauvignon, despite its moderately cool climate. The rolling hills of the **Pyrenees** have soil that can range from grey-brown and brown loam to red sandstone and red clay quartz. Shiraz and Cabernet Sauvignon are the leaders, with Sauvignon Blanc, Chardonnay, Viognier, Merlot, Cabernet Franc, Grenache, Sangiovese, Nebbiolo and Tempranillo. Cool climate **Henty** by the Southern Ocean makes Riesling and good cool-climate Shiraz.

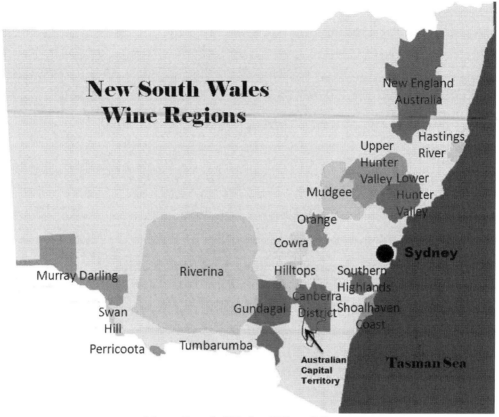

New South Wales Wine Map

New South Wales

New South Wales saw the first plantings of wine grapes 200 years ago. It is now better known to the world as the site of that opera house. I will never forget a balmy evening in April on my first of (now) ten trips to Australia at one of the outdoor bars that cascade down from the opera house on Sydney Harbor. The music was pumping, as it was at the bar after that, and the one down the way from that. I am writing this as some effort to explain that the Aussies do not like to accept limitations. In Australia, it is perfectly acceptable to vaunt that opera house and yet not be able to pronounce La Boheme, much less attest that you have sat through it. Aussies are a "can do" people. And so, if you tell them you cannot produce good wine in the subtropical reaches a hundred miles north of Sydney, they will open a bottle of **Hunter Valley** wine and wait for you to be impressed. And you will be.

Hunter has hot summers and wet autumns. Rain tends to fall at harvest time, as it rarely does in the wine paradise of South Australia. You get vintage variation in Hunter, a factor that rarely applies to the country's wines. What you also get is phalanxes of city people coming northward with money. Hunter is known for its superb restaurants, golf resorts, recreational opportunities, and its organized array of tasting rooms. The ability to sell at full retail at the cellar door is a powerful benefit to keep the wine flowing.

The soils of the Lower Hunter make up for the challenging climate. The grapes in the southern foothills vines grow off eroded volcanic basalt, resulting in low vine vigor and great concentration of mineral aromas and flavors. At higher elevations the soil, still volcanic, turns red, and supports some earthy Shiraz that is as soft as the rolling hills (which to my mind was a second England). Hunter produces Semillon (which they spell without the accent and pronounce as it is spelled) on sandy alluvial creek beds. There is plenty of sprightly Chardonnay available, but the Hunter Semillon has become a specialty. (Single varietal Semillons are rare elsewhere.) The Semillon grapes leave the vine at low sugar levels and ferment to about 11%, alcohol, with no malolactic fermentation (avoiding that buttery quality). The new wine is grassy and citrusy, but it will age in bottle if you are patient to bring out many layers of toast, dried fruit, and spice. The Upper Hunter keeps primarily to the traditional Chardonnay. Lower and Upper Hunter together qualify as a zone.

The **Central Ranges Zone** includes Mudgee, Orange, and Cowra. **Mudgee** abuts Upper Hunter directly to the west. Winemaking here dates back to German immigration in 1858. The name is Aboriginal meaning "nest in the hills." Mudgee is located on the western slopes of the Great Dividing Range (Hunter is on the east). Spring comes cold to Mudgee, often delaying bud break, but summers are long and warm, with harvest occurring a month before Hunter. Soils are sandy loam over clay. Three quarters of production is red here: Shiraz, Cabernet Sauvignon, and Merlot. **Orange** is dominated by Mount Canobolas. As a result, Orange is characterized by relatively steep vineyards on volcanic basalt soil. A range of meso-climates apply, the greater in elevation, the cooler. Grapes are the same as Mudgee. Even though **Cowra** is the southernmost region in the Central Ranges, it is the warmest, being lower in elevation. It is hot and dry here. In descending order of production, Cowra's grapes are Chardonnay, Shiraz, Semillon, Cabernet Sauvignon, Verdelho, Merlot, and Sauvignon Blanc.

The **Southern New South Wales** zone includes **Hilltops**, which has a distinctly continental climate and dry summers that necessitate irrigation. Soils are dark granitic clay. Production, mostly for blending elsewhere, leads with Shiraz, also Cabernet, Chardonnay, Merlot and Semillon. **Canberra District** around the national capital is a largely irrigated region, soils of brownish clay, producing Shiraz, Cabernet, and Merlot. **Gundagai** is a land of diverse climates, and red earth soils, producing Chardonnay, Shiraz, and Cabernet. **Tumbarumba** has a short growing season, granitic basalt soils, specializing in Pinot Noir, Chardonnay, and Sauvignon Blanc, with some sparkling wine.

In the western part of the state, the Big Rivers zone includes the regions of **Murray Darling**, **Perricoota**, **Riverina** and **Swan Hill**, all hot climate, highly irrigated producers of largely bulk wine (although these types of regions always have pockets of quality).

The **South Coast** zone includes two regions. **Shoalhaven Coast** is a high humidity area that owes much of its retail success to cellar door sales of Chardonnay, Cabernet, Shiraz and the French-American hybrid Chambourcin (which does well in humid climates like the American northeast). The **Southern Highlands** is a temperate region with basalt and shale soils producing Chardonnay, Pinot Noir, Riesling and Merlot.

In the subtropical north of the state, the rolling hills of **Hastings River** account for Semillon, Chambourcin, Shiraz, and Chardonnay. **New England Australia** has a remarkably mild climate for its low latitude. Chardonnay, Riesling, and Sauvignon Blanc lead among whites, Shiraz, Cabernet Sauvignon, and Pinot Noir among the reds.

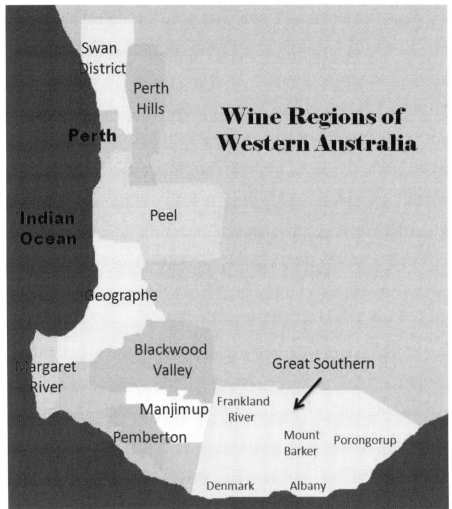

Western Australia Wine Map

Western Australia is the country's largest state and yet its wine production is relatively small: about five percent of the national total. Western Australia wines get quality accolades and awards far out of proportion to their volume, however.

Great Southern is Australia's largest wine region, and it is one of the country's coolest. It divides into five sub-regions. **Albany** has a maritime climate, moderated by the Southern Ocean, with moist, cool winters and warm, dry summers, giving us Pinot Noir and Shiraz. **Denmark** is quite similar in configuration to Albany, a little cooler and wetter. **Porongurup** is the easternmost Great Southern sub-region, stretching out along the slopes of the Porongorups, an isolated mountain range The sub-region has cool to mild winters and warm, sunny summers. Soils are ancient, deep karri loams from weathered granite. Delicate Riesling leads the pack here, with Chardonnay, Pinot Noir, and Pinot Meunier (one of the Champagne blending grapes). **Mount Barker** has also a reputation for floral, delicate Riesling. **Frankland River** is in the northwestern corner of the region, warmer than the others because of its inland location, suitable for Bordeaux type red wines and Shiraz.

Margaret River gets consistent accolades from the wine press. This is a region of numerous small producers—more than two hundred. Spring can be cool and windy here but summers are warm and dry. Cabernet Sauvignon flourishes throughout the region, along with its Bordeaux partners Merlot, Malbec and Petite Verdot. Shiraz sneaks its way in as well. The southern chunk of the region has more Antarctic than Indian Ocean influence and yields some Sauvignon Blanc, Semillon, Chardonnay and Riesling.

Geographe, on the Indian Ocean north of Margaret River has a variety of soils: the coastal plains are sandy and the interior uplands granite, with alluvial soils in between. The result of this configuration is a range of wine grapes: Bordeaux reds, Chardonnay, Tempranillo, Sauvignon Blanc and Semillon.

Blackwood Valley enjoys summers that are cool and dry. Soils are commonly gravelly loam. The most prominent grape varieties of the region include Cabernet Sauvignon, Shiraz, Merlot, Chardonnay, Sauvignon Blanc and Semillon, with smaller plantings of Riesling, Viognier and Pinot Noir.

Manjimup is a high elevation forested area, planted largely to Pinot Noir but diversifying into Cabernet Sauvignon, Merlot, Chardonnay, Sauvignon Blanc and Verdelho. The region is also known for its rare black truffles.

Pemberton has carved out a reputation for Sauvignon Blanc, Chardonnay and Pinot Noir as well as Rhône varieties. Soils in the cool region are either gravely loam over medium clay or karri loams, formed from gneissic rock.

Peel is a coastal region with dry summers that do not get too hot because of coastal breezes. Sections closer to the coast have limestone soils, further inland granatic gravely soils predominate. White wines lead: Chenin Blanc, Chardonnay and Verdelho.

Perth Hills has both altitude and sea breezes. Summer evenings are warm, leading to continuous ripening. Red wines (Shiraz, Cabernet Sauvignon, Merlot, Pinot Noir) have a slight edge over white (Chardonnay).

The **Swan District** is the hottest, driest wine-producing region in Australia. Most soils are alluvial. White wine styles lead the region's significant production: Verdelho. Chenin Blanc, and Chardonnay. Some fortified wines are produced.

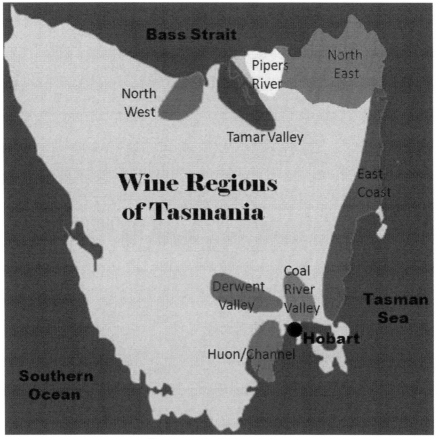

Tasmania Wine Map

Tasmania's wine regions are unofficial. The island is all a single zone, although that may change as vine plantings increase and investment by large wine firms floods into the island. The west coast of the island is too wet for viticulture, while the dry east coast faces irrigation and water issues. Nevertheless, Tasmania is burgeoning, with its decidedly cool climate, made all the more appealing as global warming pushes the arc of Australian wine production to the south. Some quick climate math tells us that in both hemispheres, the optimal cool climate band is moving to higher latitudes. This is no problem in the northern hemisphere, but the southern hemisphere risks running out of land. Tasmania benefits from the math. Pinot Noir leads in Tasmania with 44% of vines, its Burgundian partner Chardonnay has 23%. These two form the basis for a significant sparkling wine industry. Sauvignon Blanc, Pinot Gris and Riesling round out the largely white wine focus of the island.

The **Tamar Valley** (which produces 40% of Tasmania's wine) and neighboring **Pipers River** on the island's northeast see their temperatures moderated by the Tamar River. They have a climate equivalent to that of France's northernmost wine region, Champagne. White grapes thrive here. Chardonnay with high natural acidity generally undergoes malolactic fermentation to soften the acids. It is made more complex with barrel fermentation. The Riesling is steely and fragrant, with the natural acidity characteristic of the grape that allows it to age in bottle a dozen years. The Gewürztraminer is a more delicate affair, showing spices and rose petal. Sauvignon Blanc and Pinot Gris are also produced, as are sparkling wines. High quality Pinot Noir is served on its own or becomes a sparkling wine component.

The **East Coast** produces approximately twenty percent of Tasmania's wine. The area has an optimal combination of cool climate and dry weather, promoting slow ripening for intense flavors of light-bodied Pinot Noir and citrus-rich Chardonnay.

Derwent Valley and **Coal River** in the south are dry regions, affected by the rain shadow of Mount Wellington. They produce Pinot Noir, Chardonnay and Riesling.

The **Huon Valley** is Australia's southernmost region, producing Pinot Noir and Chardonnay, Riesling and Sauvignon Blanc, as well as the hardy German varieties Sylvaner and Müller Thurgau.

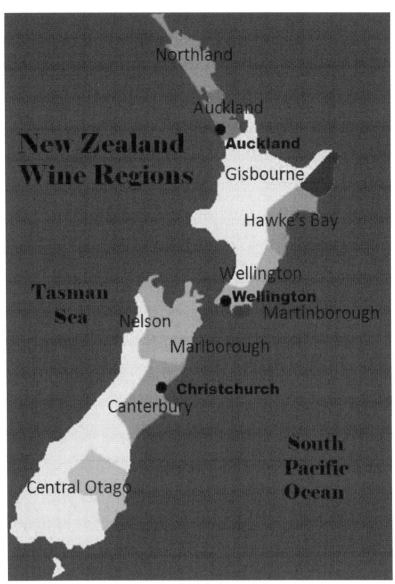

New Zealand Wine Map

Although **New Zealand** winemaking goes back to the 19th century, it was not until the 1970s that the first stirrings of the island country's modern wine industry began. The vector for this was Sauvignon Blanc, the region was **Marlborough** on the northeastern corner of South Island. In 1970, Marlborough (named after John Churchill Duke of Marlborough an ancestor of a prominent wine devotee), produced hardy any grapevines. After two decades of attempting to make Sauvignon Blanc in the oaked Fumé Blanc style pioneered by Californian Robert Mondavi, Marlborough developed its own style of stainless-steel fermented un-oaked Sauvignon Blanc. This wine combines the grassiness and tropical fruit typical of New World Sauvignon Blanc with the citrusy acidity of Old World offerings, with a particular Kiwi synergy that leads some wine critics to call this wine the world's best Sauvignon Blanc. Marlborough Sauvignon Blanc has an exciting quality to it that for some reason the Californians and Chileans cannot match. Marlborough has a cool maritime climate with a long steady sun-filled growing season that helps bring out the natural balance of acids, sugars, and flavor intensity in the grapes.

Further south (in fact, the southernmost wine region in the world) is **Central Otago**, renowned for its Pinot Noir. High mountains up to 12,000 feet protect the region from destroying winds from the west. The region has the country's only continental climate, with hot temperatures during the summer and winters cold enough for ice and snow. During the growing season, the area sees wide day/night temperature swings. Vineyards tend to inhabit hillsides to maximize sun exposure and reduce the risk of frost. Soils consist of rough-edged mica and other metamorphic schists in silt loams. The Pinot Noir (70% of production) has intense fruit, assertive structure and silky texture. Among whites, Riesling is the most well regarded, Pinot Gris the most produced. These two, with Gewürztraminer, are vinified in the full range of styles from bone try to sticky sweet.

The **Canterbury/Waipara Valley** region on east coast of the South Island around the city of Christchurch is cool and dry with light not very fertile soils. Sauvignon Blanc and Pinot Noir lead, with some Pinot Gris. **Nelson** encompasses the northwest corner of South Island, separated from Marlborough by mountain ranges. Nearly forty varieties flourish in these rolling hills, but Sauvignon Blanc reigns triumphant, responding to worldwide demand. Pinot Noir and Pinot Gris production is substantial, but the prior leader, Chardonnay, now lags behind,

We cross the often-tempestuous Cook Straight to North Island. There, **Hawke's Bay** on the eastern side is New Zealand's second biggest wine producer after Marlborough. It is the oldest wine area. This large region has an array of soils and terrains, but is perhaps the sunniest region in the country. Winemakers, from small artisanal producers to large wine conglomerates, produce red Bordeaux blends, Syrah, some Chardonnay and, in a new trend, Syrah's white Rhône companion Viognier. **Gisbourne** sits on the east coast directly north of Hawke's Bay, producing soft fragrant Chardonnay with peach, pineapple, and melon accents as well as Gewürztraminer.

In the southwestern stretch of North Island, the **Wellington/Wairarapa** region includes the distinctive production area of **Martinborough**. Close to the national capital of Wellington, the region is characterized by small-scale producers who specialize in Pinot Noir. Many of these wines are getting excellent marks from international wine critics.

Auckland, the most populous city in the country, is the hub of the wine region by the same name. This warmest of New Zealand's wine regions produces red wines from grapes that thrive on heavy clay soil, including Bordeaux blends, in addition to much variety including Gewürztraminer grown in the shadow of Auckland's airport. Many of the winemakers here, as is true elsewhere in the country, are of Lebanese and Croatian descent. The **Waiheke Island** sub-region is achieving renown with high quality Bordeaux blends, Montepulciano, Petit Verdot, Chardonnay and Viognier. The **Matakana** sub-region, despite its humidity, is doing well with Pinot Gris, Syrah and Bordeaux reds.

Northland, which also has a Croatian heritage, has a nearly subtropical climate, producing Chardonnay with tropical fruit notes, Pinot Gris, and Viognier, and among reds some spicy Syrah, Bordeaux blends, Pinotage, and deep-colored aromatic Chambourcin.

Since we have just mentioned Pinotage, South Africa's signature red grape, it is time to look at this final southern hemisphere wine producer.

Chapter Fifteen

World Wine Regions
South Africa

South Africa Wine Map

South Africa was lost to the world of fine wine for many years. For most of the twentieth century, grape production centered around the country's brandy industry. By the time this system was ready to change, South Africa's path to the world wine market was clapped shut as a result of sanctions having to do with the country's long standing apartheid system of racial separation. When apartheid ended in 1994, South African winemakers were able to set their sights on international markets and make wines that appealed to those markets. They are still at it.

South Africa's vineyards hug the Cape of Good Hope in the country's southwest. Even here, the climate ought to be too hot for quality viticulture, if it were not for the cold Benguela current that streams up from Antarctica. Summers are warm, ripening seasons long and slow. Soil types run the gamut as does the configuration of the land, making for a great deal of vineyard diversity. The Cape in fact has some of the oldest geological formations in the world of wine, and tremendous biodiversity. Ninety percent of South Africa's fine wine qualifies for official sustainability status.

Among white grapes, Chenin Blanc (called Steen) has long been the leader, follow by Sauvignon Blanc and Chardonnay, and then Colombard, Muscat of Alexandria, Sémillon and Viognier.

Cabernet Sauvignon is the most red planted grape, comprising 12% of vineyard area with Shiraz (Syrah) just behind at 10%. Merlot comes next and then Pinotage, South Africa's own grape. Bred in 1925, Pinotage is a South African crossing of Pinot Noir and Cinsault. A good Pinotage will have flavors and aromas of bananas and tropical fruit, but some tasters get an acetone effect, a taste of paint. Pinotage is not for everyone. It may well be blended with Syrah or Cabernet.

Legally South Africa's wine areas divide into **Geographical Units**, the largest and most meaningful of which is the Western Cape. Western Cape is divided into five **Regions**: Breede River Valley, Cape South Coast, Coastal Region, Klein Karoo, and Olifants River. The Regions are in turn divided into **Districts** which in turn divide into **Wards**. As one example, the famous wine of Constantia fits into this system like this:

- Geographical Unit: Western Cape
- Region: Coastal Region
- District: Cape Peninsula
- Ward: Constantia

If an appellation is mentioned here, assume it is a **District** unless otherwise indicated.

Constantia, just south of Cape Town (in fact one of the city's wealthier suburbs), produced a world famous dessert wine from Muscat grapes during the 18th and 19th centuries The wind called the Cape Doctor comes in from the ocean to cool the area. Soils are clayish reddish brown in some areas, with sandy soils in others. Constantia now produces grassy Sauvignon Blanc with smaller plantings of Semillon, Cabernet Sauvignon, Merlot and Chardonnay, as well as some late harvest Muscat dessert wines. Just north of Cape Town, the gently rolling terrain of cool climate **Durbanville** also produce grassy Sauvignon Blanc, Chardonnay, Shiraz, Pinotage and Merlot.

East of Cape Town, lovely **Stellenbosch** sits nestled in mountains. It is the Cape's most famous District and has been producing since the 17th century. Soils vary from alluvial loam in low-lying areas to decomposed granite in the hills. Breezes off False Bay to the south act as air conditioning. So long a Chenin Blanc producer, Stellenbosch now produces Cabernet above all, seconded by Sauvignon Blanc, and then Shiraz and Merlot. **Paarl** to the immediate north is further away from False Bay and hence warmer. Much of its wine is blended with wines from Stellenbosch and other nearby areas and labeled as "Coastal Region."

Then name **Franschhoek** means, literally, "French Corner." Just east of Stellenbosch, it was settled in the 17th century by French Huguenots and is the locale of a number of historic cellars. Like Stellenbosch it is a major tourist destination. The climate is mild in summer. Sauvignon Blanc, Merlot, Chardonnay and Sémillon thrive on potassium rich soils of loam and granite shale.

The **Cape South Coast** is not one of the traditional growing areas, springing up as a wine region only in the final quarter of the 20th century as wine pioneers moved into Benguela Current influenced areas once considered too cool for viticulture. **Walker Bay** is one of these new areas, known for its insistent Sauvignon Blanc and its Burgundian styled Chardonnay and Pinot Noir. **Elgin** in the 21st century has populated vineyards on high slopes (up to 1300 feet) for maximum exposure to sea breezes. Once again, Sauvignon Blanc, Chardonnay and Pinot Noir lead.

The **Elim/Cape Agulhas** area at the southern tip of **Overberg** is also the extreme southern tip of the continent. Climate is harsh, with winds battering the area from three sides—year-round. Vines respond by growing low, producing smaller than usual berries that ripen only slowly, bringing intense fruit and formidable acidity. The soil varies from shale and sandstone to '*Koffieklip*' ('coffee stone'), which is used to build local houses. It all combines to create herbaceous and mineral Sauvignon Blanc and Shiraz. A wine frontier indeed.

North of Cape Town, Durbanville, and Paarl, the large district of **Swartland**, long a producer of bulk wine, has seen a great deal of quality wine trailblazing since 2000. The land here is rolling plains. Hot and dry conditions reduce the risk of fungal diseases, and result in low yields of very concentrated fruit. Tough bush vines predominate in Swartland's hottest corners. Soils of shale alternate with granite. These soils can often hold enough water to allow dry farming. The tough bush vines dig very deep to attain this hydration, resulting in further concentration of flavors. Chenin Blanc, Shiraz and Pinotage are the traditional varieties planted here, but pioneers, attracted by the low cost of land, are not averse to planting alterative varieties. Reds doing the colonizing include Carignan, Cinsault, Grenache, Mourvèdre, and the Portuguese Tinta Barocca. Whites include Chenin Blanc, Clairette Blanc, Grenache Blanc, Marsanne, Roussanne, and Viognier. **Darling**, a cool-climate enclave, benefits from Atlantic breezes and is known for Sauvignon Blanc. **Tulbagh**, east and inland from Swartland, sits in a u-shaped valley that brings in breezes from the south to cool off the evenings and prolong ripening. Shiraz, Grenache, Mourvèdre and Viognier often go into Rhône blends. Chardonnay, Chenin Blanc and Sauvignon Blanc are also produced.

Piketberg is a warm climate region north of Swartland. Most wines are made by cooperative cellars from irrigated vineyards. **Olifants River Valley** pushes further north to 31 degrees south latitude, stretching toward the limits of the traditional 30 to 50 degree temperate viticulture zone. Cool Atlantic breezes allow this. The coastal areas produce herbaceous Sauvignon Blanc and Chenin Blanc while the interior gives us Pinotage, Shiraz and Cabernet Sauvignon.

Four hundred miles north of Cape Town, at 28 degrees south latitude, two hundred and fifty miles inland, the **Orange River** region, just south of the Kalahari Desert, is South Africa's northern viticultural extreme. It is hot and dry here, but the Orange River helps regulate the temperature. The region is known for bulk production of Colombard, Chenin Blanc and Muscat of Alexandria, all white grapes. Further inland is **Douglas**, a green oasis where the Orange and Vaal rivers meet.

.

The **Breede River Valley** is a large wine region, sheltered on three sides by mountain ranges. This is warm, dry, irrigated country producing mainstream wines from Shiraz, Pinotage, Cabernet Sauvignon and Chardonnay, much of it vinified by cooperatives. Prominent districts include **Worcester, Robertson**, **Breedekloof**, and **Swellendam**.

To the east of Breede River is the hot climate Region of **Klein Karoo**, a semi-desert that produces a number of wine types, including fortified wines from Muscat and still wines from Cabernet, Chardonnay, and Portuguese red varieties. High altitudes (up to 2300 feet) and some southerly breezes moderate the heat. **Calitzdorp** is an enclave within Klein Karoo known for its Port-like fortified wines, made from Portuguese grapes like Touriga Nacional and Tinta Barocca. **Langeberg-Garcia** sits at the southern edge of Klein Karoo and has chalky mountain soils that support Sauvignon Blanc with good structure and minerality. Verdelho, Semillon, Grenache, Cabernet Sauvignon, and Shiraz round out the selection.

Chapter Sixteen

World Wine Regions
France

France produces more fine wine than any other country. France also produces a great deal of mediocre wine, but that does nothing to diminish the country's place as a fine wine role model. See the History of Wine section for some reasons why. The culmination of two thousand years of French wine history is the country's system of geographical wine appellations, the highest level of which is the standard-setting Appellation d'Origine Contrôlée (AOC) system.

In the United States and most of the rest of the New World (Canada, Mexico, Argentina, Chile, Australia, New Zealand, and South Africa) wines are primarily named after the **type of grapes** from which they are made. Place names are used (Napa Valley, Mendoza, Barossa Valley, Marlborough), but the only requirement for those wanting to use place names on their labels is that the wine come from that place. The winemaker using a place name on the label can use any grape or combination of grapes, any vine growing practice, any winemaking technique, whatever yeast he or she wishes, and so forth. Further, in the U.S., only 85% of the wine has to be from that place (the rest can be from anywhere).

Not so in France. The INAO (Institut National de l'Origine et de la Qualité), founded in 1935, sets French standards. To qualify for AOC status, the INAO specifies:

> the wine's geographical area
> allowed grape variety or combination of varieties
> pruning and vineyard management rules
> whether irrigation is permitted
> harvesting rules and maximum vineyard yields
> type of yeast allowed in the winery
> minimum and maximum alcohol levels
> and anything else they can think of

But the wine is not home free even here. It must be reviewed and approved by a professional tasting panel.

Let us look for starters as to how these rules affect the grapes that are used to make French AOC wines. Here are some examples:

- Hermitage, the great wine from the Rhône: at least 85% Syrah with up to 15% of white Marsanne or Roussanne grapes (most hermitage is in fact 100% Syrah).

- Cahors, from Southwest France: minimum of 70% Malbec with up to 30% Merlot or Tannat.

- Anjou: At least 80% Chenin Blanc, the remainder a blend of Chardonnay and Sauvignon Blanc.

- Châteauneuf-du-Pape: Red varieties allowed are Cinsault, Counoise, Grenache Noir, Mourvèdre, Muscardin, Piquepoul Noir, Syrah, Terret Noir, and Vaccarèse (Brun Argenté). White and pink varieties are Bourboulenc, Clairette Blanche, Clairette Rose, Grenache Blanc, Grenache Gris, Picardan, Piquepoul Blanc, Piquepoul Gris, and Roussanne. These grapes are not restricted as to proportion. Despite these rules, most Châteauneuf-du-Papes lead with Grenache and round it out with Syrah and Mourvèdre, the classic GSM blend.

- Chablis: 100% Chardonnay

Every French AOC wine has similar strictures. Except in Alsace (which is known for its single varietal Riesling, Gewürztraminer and Pinot Gris), French law traditionally forbad the grapes or grapes to appear on the label. New EU regulations now allow this, as means of better reaching New World markets.

A French winemaker who labeled his or her wine with its grape variety or varieties would not be popular with most other winemakers, because he or she would be diluting the all-important French concept of *terroir*, the unique quality of a physical place that expresses itself in the wine.

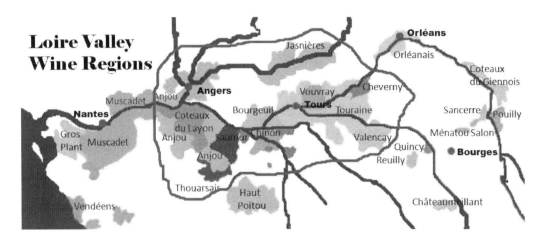

Map of Central Loire Valley

In the circled area of the Loire Valley in the map above, all the appellations (except the Cabernet Franc regions of Bourgeuil and Chinon in the center) produce wine primarily from the Chenin Blanc grape. Despite this fact, winemakers, marketers and devotees would never call the wine of Vouvray "Chenin Blanc" any more than they would call the wine of Coteaux du Layon "Chenin Blanc." To do so would contravene the concept of terroir. The grape type is, in the French view, incidental.

Burgundy
Wine Regions

 Chablis

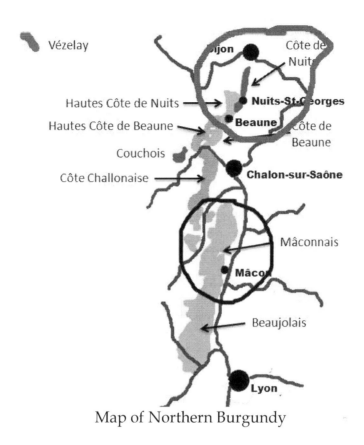

Map of Northern Burgundy

Similarly, in the Côte de Nuits section of northern Burgundy (circled in red), these exquisite vineyards produce nothing but Pinot Noir, and yet they all have distinct terroirs: Gevrey-Chambertin (or its nine grand cru vineyards-Le Chambertin, Chambertin-Clos de Beze, Mazis-Chambertin, Chapelle-Chambertin, Charmes-Chambertin, Mazoyeres-Chambertin, Griotte-Chambertin, Latricieres-Chambertin and Ruchottes-Chambertin), Morey-St-Denis (with five grand cru vineyards-Clos de la Roche, Clos St. Denis, Clos des Lambrays, Clos de Tart and Bonnes Mares which it shares with the village of Chambolle-Musigny), Chambolle-Musigny (grand cru vineyards of Bonnes Mares and Musigny), Vougeot (Clos de Vougeot), Vosne-Romanee (six grand cru vineyards-Romanée-Conti, La Tâche, Richebourg, La Romanée, Romanée-St. Vivant and La Grand Rue), and so forth. To call any of these wines
"Pinot Noir" would be at best meaningless, at worst sacrilege.

Further south, in the Mâconnais (circled in black) Pouilly-Fuissé, Pouilly-Loché Pouilly-Vinzelles, and Saint-Véran are all 100% Chardonnay, but to call the wine "Chardonnay" would dilute the concept of individual terroirs.

AOC wines are the country's top wines, and the ones we are likely to see on wine shop shelves. The next level down relates to the regional wines. The old designation *Vin de Pays* (wine of the country) is gradually being replaced by the new European Union Term *Indication Géographique Protégée* (IGP) (Protected geographical origin PGI). The lowest level is Vin (simply, wine) or Vin de France, replacing the old Vin de Table.

The Wine Regions of France

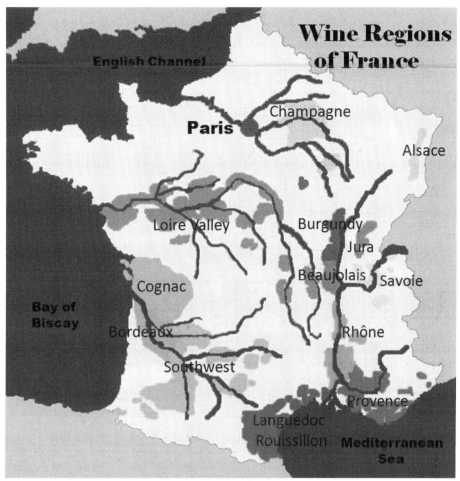

Wine Map of France

The map above shows the major wine producing regions of France. Note all the blank spots, where wine is not produced. We will be explaining the significance of some of these areas later on.

Bordeaux

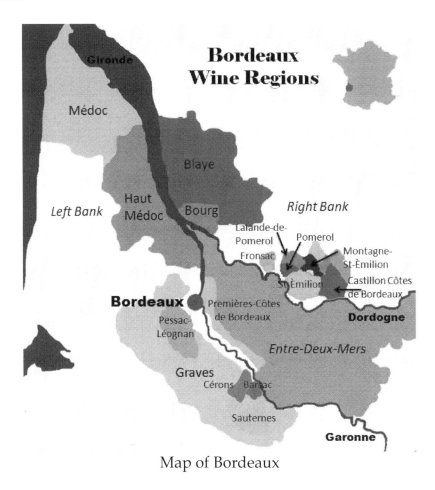

Map of Bordeaux

The region of Bordeaux has nearly 300,000 acres of vines covering 54 different appellations. In an average year, the region produces seven hundred million bottles of wine at every quality level. Much of the wine of Bordeaux, red and white, is completely ordinary. Some of the wines of Bordeaux are among the most prized and expensive in the world.

Bordeaux sits on layers of limestone and has soils generally high in calcium. In Bordeaux, two rivers, the Garonne and the Dordogne, merge to form the estuary called the Gironde, which flows out to the Atlantic. These bodies of water divide Bordeaux into several areas that produce different types of wine. The "Left Bank" refers to the land to the west of the Garonne and the Gironde. Major sections of the Left Bank include the Médoc and Graves. The "Right Bank" refers to the land east of the Dordogne and the Gironde. The term "Entre Deux Mers," literally "between two seas," refers to the area between the two rivers.

Bordeaux has what is known as an oceanic climate, with warm summers and not-so-cold winters. Because it is nearer to the ocean, the Left Bank is somewhat warmer than the right Bank.

Most Bordeaux wines, either red or white, are blends. The red "Bordeaux varieties," a term used internationally to refer to these grapes, are Cabernet Sauvignon, Merlot, Cabernet Franc, Malbec, Petit Verdot and, infrequently, Carménère The white Bordeaux varieties are Sauvignon Blanc, Sémillon and Muscadelle.

Left bank Bordeaux red wines will typically lead with Cabernet Sauvignon and smooth out the blend primarily with Merlot and Cabernet Franc. Right bank Bordeaux red wines will typically lead with Merlot and add tannins and oomph with Cabernet Sauvignon and Cabernet Franc. In either case, a 70:15:15 ratio is about average, though individual winemakers differ.

Why are Cabernet Sauvignon and Merlot blended with each other?

> Cabernet Sauvignon provides structure, tannins and acids, dark-fruit flavors of blackcurrant and bell pepper.
> Merlot is juicer, a "fatter" variety; has less structure, but good palate weight and fruit flavors.
> Cabernet's robust structure is fattened out with Merlot's juicy fruit – a marriage with excellent long-term potential when assembled with care.

Note here that in warm-climate regions like Napa in California, Cabernet Sauvignon ripens longer than in Bordeaux, leading to riper tannins, decreasing the need to blend Merlot in with the Cabernet Sauvignon as a means to tame Cabernet's tannins.

In the United States we are used to consuming Cabernet Sauvignon and Merlot as single varietal wines, but American "Meritage" wines seek to blend the two to create what is commonly called a "Bordeaux Blend."

Wines labeled "Entre Deux Mers" are usually dry white wines from Sauvignon Blanc, Sémillon, Muscadelle or Ugni Blanc. Most wine produced in the Entre Deux Mers region is sold as generic Bordeaux. Red wine production is on the rise in Entre Deux Mers.

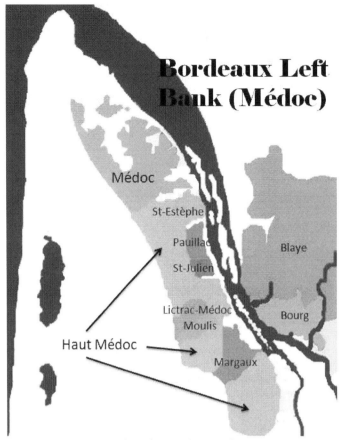

Map of Left Bank Bordeaux

Red wine labeled Médoc or Haut Médoc can be quite ordinary, wine labeled with one of the villages of the Haut Médoc (St. Estèphe, Pauillac, St. Julien, Margaux) might be of a better quality (and hence more expensive), but a select grouping of vineyards in the region produce some of the finest wines in the world. In 1855 wine brokers ranked the left bank wines and created a system of *grands crus*, or great growths. The lowest level of distinction is "Fifth Growth," the highest "First Growth." The system continues in place. There are eighteen fifth growths, ten fourth growths, fifteen third growths, and fourteen second growths. The five first growths are all famous names:

> Château Lafite Rothschild
> Château Latour
> Château Mouton Rothschild
> Château Margaux
> Château Haut-Brion

All of these first growths are in the Médoc except Château Haut-Brion, which is in Graves.

Samuel Pepys

On Friday 10 April 1663 Samuel Pepys writes in his famous diary "…to the Royall Oak Tavern, in Lumbard Street…and here drank a sort of French wine, called Ho Bryan, that hath a good and most particular taste that I never met with." This is considered the first wine review, and Château Haut-Brion is still going strong.

Wine producers in Bordeaux refer to their establishments as Châteaux. This is true even if the winery is in modest building, or even a garage, although some of the great Bordeaux wine houses are indeed architecturally significant.

For perspective, a 2016 web search of representatives of the five different classed growths of the same vintage comes up with the following prices, in US dollars:

Fifth Growth: Château Lynch-Bages, Pauillac, 2010, $169
Fourth Growth: Château Duhart-Milon, Pauillac, 2010, $190
Third Growth: Château Palmer, Margaux, 2010, $260
Second Growth: Château Léoville-Las Cases, St.-Julien, 2010, $305
First Growth: Château Haut-Brion, Pessac, Graves, 2010, $975

Many of these famous Châteaux produce **second wines** from grapes not selected for the main wine (first label). These wines usually refer to the name of the Château on the label, with some variation. For example, Fifth Growth Château Lynch-Bages produces Echo de Lynch-Bages. You can get the 2010 vintage for $49.

Graves

South of the Médoc and the city of Bordeaux, on the same side of the river, **Graves** includes the sub-regions of Pessac-Léognan, Sauternes and Barsac. True to its name, Graves is known for its gravely soil. **Pessac-Léognan** is home to Château Haut-Brion. Further to the south, Sauternes and its sub-region Barsac are known for intensely sweet dessert wine that have been made from grapes infected with "noble rot," the favorable branch of the fungus *botrytis cinerea* which shrivels the grapes on the vine and so concentrates their flavors, adding its own botrytis elements. Sauternes has a system of first and second growths. One Château stands out among all the rest and is classified Superior First Growth (Premier Cru Supérieur), Château d'Yquem. You can get the 2010 for about $700. A 1959 will run you about $2300—for a half bottle.

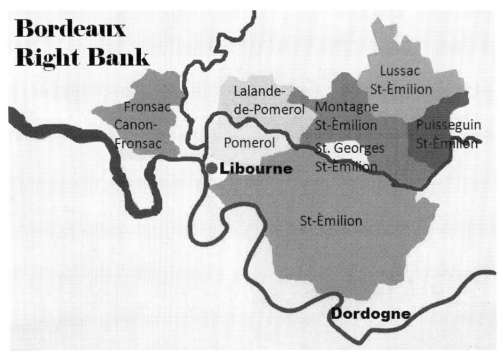

Map of Right Bank Bordeaux

The Right Bank is also called the Libournais, after its main town Libourne. Two renowned appellations are **Pomerol** and **St. Émilion**. Each has less expensive satellite appellations. Wines here in this cooler climate center around Merlot, which likes the clay soil, and Cabernet Franc. Red wines here are softer and plumier than Cabernet Sauvignon-led left bank wines. Pomerol has no systems of class growths, and yet its flagship wine, Château Pétrus, is just as highly regarded (and expensive). The 2010 Château Pétrus is offered on one website for $4100, discounted from $5400. St. Émilion has its own system of grands crus, with a special upper notch for two producers, Château Ausone ($1245 for the 2010) and Château Cheval Blanc (a steal at $985). In the north of the Right Bank sits **Bourg and Blaye**, large producers of Merlot, Sauvignon Blanc for sparkling wines, and Ugni Blanc for brandy.

Wine Map of Burgundy

Burgundy and Bordeaux are often spoken of in conjunction because of their equivalent renown, and the fact that they both begin with the letter "B," but, in actuality, they have little in common. **Burgundy** is much further north and inland from Bordeaux, and has a cooler climate with much greater vintage variation. Burgundy's wine, red and white, are single varietals as contrasted with Bordeaux's blends. It is all wine, but a radically different kind of wine.

The calcareous soil of **Chablis** is closer to the Aube region of Champagne than it is to the main region of Burgundy, 85 miles away. AOC regulations insist on 100% Chardonnay. The wine ferments in steel tanks, and does not see oak, resulting in great purity of aroma and taste, high acidity, and a quality called "flintiness" or "steeliness." Seven Grand Cru Chablis vineyards inhabit a single hill overlooking the town of Chablis. Premier cru is the next level down, AOC Chablis a further step down (and the biggest production) and Petit Chablis a lesser quality designation from outlying regions. Chablis producers have fought a long battle to prevent their place name from being used for generic white wines in other countries, often a losing battle.

Burgundy has a higher number of AOCs than any other region of France. The Burgundians are extremely terroir-conscious, a perspective that goes back to the days when monks fine-tuned the wine, paying attention to every minor different in aspect to the sun, moisture retention, soil quality. Starting just south of Dijon, the **Côte d'Or** encompasses the **Côte de Nuits** and the **Côte de Beaune**. The legendary Grand Cru wines flourish on the middle and upper part of the limestone slopes with their chalky soils, where (monks figured out that) they have the best exposure to the sun and the best drainage. Premier Crus sit on the less favorable sections of the slopes. The flats account for the less prestigious village wines. Lowest rung are wines labeled **Bourgogne AOC.** The **Côte de Nuits** can boast of all but one of Burgundy's red Grand Cru appellations, while the **Côte de Beaune** immediately to its south has all but one white grand Cru appellation. Remember, in Burgundy red is Pinot Noir and white is Chardonnay.

The great red burgundies have an earthy quality and may improve with age, both in cask and in bottle. They are full-bodied, redolent of black currant, cherry, fresh red fruits, earthy mushroom and a shelf full of spices. They taste of the land on which they are lovingly coaxed to ripeness. The great white Burgundies have a rich mouthfeel, tremendous intensity, minerality, sometimes nuttiness, sometimes a hint of honey, with restrained elements of oak. In either case, the terroir these wines express is not reproducible. It is not even reproducible in Burgundy itself every year, since in this uncertain climate you get vintage variation, a few good years, a few not so good years.

To the south of the **Côte d'Or** is the **Côte Chalonnaise**, which has Premier Cru but no Grand Cru vineyards. **Rully** has 23 premier cru vineyards producing still white wine and *Crémant* sparkling wine. **Mercurey** has 30 Premier Cru vineyards and is the largest volume producer of mostly red wine. **Givry** is mostly red wine and has 17 Premier Crus. **Montagny** has 49 Premier Crus and produces only white wines. **Bouzeron** is the only AOC for Burgundy's second white grape, Aligoté.

The **Mâconnais** district is the southernmost, if you do not count Beaujolais which is administratively a part of Burgundy. Wines labeled **Mâcon** may be white, red or rosé. The label **Mâcon-Villages** only applies to white wines. **Mâcon-Villages** with a village designation is used for whites or reds depending on the village designated. In the southern part of Mâcon are several Chardonnay-only AOCs: **Pouilly-Fuissé**, **Pouilly-Loché**, **Pouilly-Vinzelles**, **Saint-Véran**, and **Viré-Clessé**. Remember, to the French, the wine from each place is distinct and unique, notwithstanding the fact that they are all vinified with 100% Chardonnay.

The Wine Regions of France

The Loire Valley

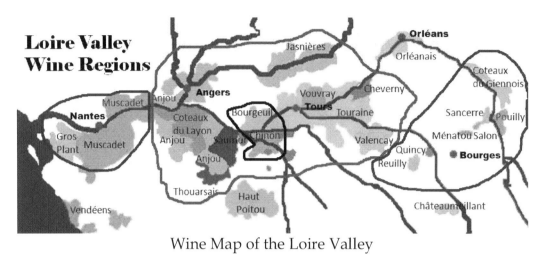

Wine Map of the Loire Valley

The Loire is the longest river in France. It originates in the Massif Central in the Cévennes range, flows south to north and makes an abrupt turn to the west at Orléans, flowing then toward the Atlantic Ocean. The northern region, considered one of the most pleasant climates in France (with few extremes of temperature), has a well-developed wine culture.

The map above looks complicated, but we can make it more accessible by dividing it up into primary wine grape regions. (Note these are the major grapes. In many cases the primarily white wine appellations also produce smaller amounts of red and rosé wines from Gamay, Pinot Noir, and Cabernet Franc. The primarily Chenin Blanc regions may also produce other whites from Sauvignon Blanc and Chardonnay.

- The **Upper Loire**, circled at right, is the traditional home of Sauvignon Blanc, led by the appellations of **Sancerre** and **Pouilly Fumé**. The wine is light, dry, acidic, with mineral, gunflint, steely and citrus notes.

- The large **Middle Loire** section, circled in red, is the traditional home of Chenin Blanc. This middle section divides into two major parts:

   o the **Touraine** region in the east of the section, named after the city of Tours, producing every possible gradation of Chenin Blanc, dry, sweet and sparkling, with the greatest variety going to the town of Vouvray.

- o the **Anjou** region in the west of the section is named after the city of Angers. Anjou is known for Chenin Blanc in many manifestations: sweet at all levels (especially in the **Coteaux du Layon)** and dry (in the case of its appellation of **Savennières**, an extremely dry, age-worthy white wine). The **Saumur** appellation is famous for its sparkling Crémant de Loire.

- The appellations of **Bourgeuil** and **Chinon**, circled in black in the center of the map, are known for single varietal Cabernet Franc (which has its origins in Bordeaux).

- The **Lower Loire**, circled at left around the city of Nantes, produces white wines called **Muscadet** from the Melon de Bourgogne grape. The grape is neutral, and the best examples of Muscadet-Sèvre et Maine are often bottled without racking or filtering, so they age in bottle on their lees. Muscadet is often enjoyed with the area's seafood. The region's other grape, the Gros Plant Nantais, makes a highly acidic white wine with little international appeal.

The Loire town of Vouvray produces Chenin Blanc wines in all levels of sweetness, still and sparkling. Photo by Elliot Essman

Houses built into the limestone tuffeau soil of Vouvray. Note the vines at the top, which grow in tuffeau soil. Photo by Elliot Essman

A winemaker in his Cabernet Franc cellar at Chinon. Photo by Elliot Essman

Cabernet Franc vines seen from the castle at Chinon. Photo by Elliot Essman

The Wine Regions of France

Alsace

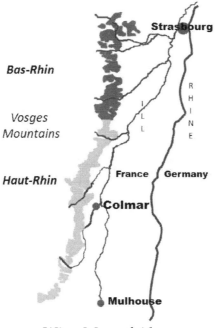

Wine Map of Alsace

The vineyards of **Alsace**, are situated on a narrow strip of land between the Vosges mountains and the Rhine River (the border with Germany). The Vosges form a rain shadow, so the region is among the driest in France. The northern section of Alsace is called the Bas-Rhin (lower Rhine), the southern section the Haut-Rhin (upper Rhine)

Alsace produces world-class dry Riesling, highly aromatic Gewürztraminer, and spicy, full-bodied Pinot Gris. Alsatian wines were traditionally dry, but recently there has been a trend to produce sweeter late harvest wines.

Alsace is the one part of France where wines are traditionally labeled as single varietals. Alsatian wines are bottled in the traditional tall narrow Alsace *flute*.

Fifty-one vineyard sites merit the ranking of AOC Alsace Grand Cru.

The Crémant d'Alsace AOC applies to sparkling wines.

The Wine Regions of France

Champagne

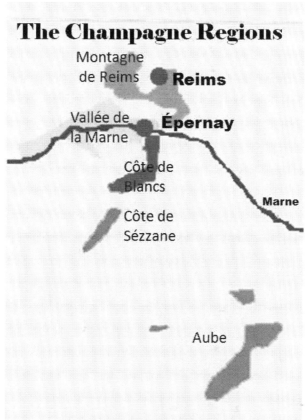

Wine Map of Champagne

Champagne is the northernmost wine region of France. To produce the sparkling wine called Champagne, the maker must first create a still wine out of the juice of grapes grown in the delimited Champagne region. This region is relatively large and spread out, with different sections specializing in the three grapes most commonly used for Champagne. The white grape Chardonnay brings acidity and, after various production processes, a biscuit flavor. The red grapes Pinot Noir and Pinot Meunier give the ultimate wine structure and finish. They usually do not add color, since their juice is extracted from the grapes with minimal skin contact.

Arbanne, Petit Meslier, Pinot Blanc and Pinot Gris may legally be used to make Champagne, but these grapes are used today by only a small number of traditional producers.

The soil of Champagne is characterized by chalk, since the region is part of a basin that extends all the way to eastern England. The white cliffs of Dover show the same chalk. The chalky soil drains well and reflects every precious ray of summer sunlight in this northerly region.

Champagne has five grape growing regions.

On a plateau south of Reims, the **Montagne de Reims** produces quality Pinot Noir, even though this is the northernmost of the sections.

The **Vallée de la Marne** straddles the Marne river west of Épernay. These low-lying, south-facing vineyards produce full, round, ripe wines. Pinot Noir and Pinot Meunier predominate, with increased plantings of Chardonnay.

The **Côte des Blancs** is a hook-shaped ridge extending south from Épernay. The best vineyards sit on the eastern side of the ridge. This section produces mainly Chardonnay.

The **Côte de Sézanne** benefits from a longer ripening season because it is further south. It is almost entirely Chardonnay.

The **Aube** sits far to the south, some 65 miles south of Épernay, much closer in fact to Chablis in Burgundy than it is to the main regions of Champagne. It specializes in Pinot Noir. Although it is considered by many a lower quality area good for little more than sourcing grapes for non-vintage Champagne, it is also the home to maverick growers who are producing their own distinctive Champagnes instead of selling their grapes to the large Champagne houses.

The **Montagne de Reims** and the **Côte des Blancs** contain the greatest concentration of Grand Cru and Premier Cru villages. The Comité Interprofessional du Vin de Champagne (C.I.V.C.). grades villages on the prospective quality of their grapes. The Grand Cru villages get a 100% grade, the Premier Cru villages grades from 90 to 99%. The villages that qualify for neither designation get grades between 80 and 89%. The prices growers get for their grapes depends on these percentage grades.

The Champagne Business

More than one hundred Champagne houses produce the beverage from grapes they purchase from literally thousands of growers, many of whom are very small. Many thousands of smaller producers grow most or all their grapes themselves. Champagnes have a system of two letter label abbreviations that indicate the type of producer.

- **NM**: *Négociant manipulant*. These buy grapes and make the wine. The category includes most internationally known houses.
- **RM**: *Récoltant manipulant*. Growers who make their own wines, called in English "grower Champagnes."

The big wine houses go to great lengths, using professional tasters, to make their product consistent form year to year. The smaller grower-producers show greater variation year to year, and often have idiosyncratic styles. Many devotees consider grower Champagnes more interesting.

Other codes include:

- **ND**: *Négociant distributeur*. A wine merchant selling wine made by others under its own label
- **CM**: *Coopérative de manipulation*. Cooperatives that make wines from the growers who pool their grapes.
- **SR**: *Société de récoltants*. Another form of cooperative
- **RC**: *Récoltant coopérateur*. A cooperative member who sells the cooperative's wine under its label
- **MA**: *Marque auxiliaire* or *Marque d'acheteur*. A brand name Champagne that is unrelated to either a producer or a grower, as in a warehouse club or supermarket brand

See the section on sparkling wine making for a discussion of how Champagne is made.

The Wine Regions of France

Beaujolais

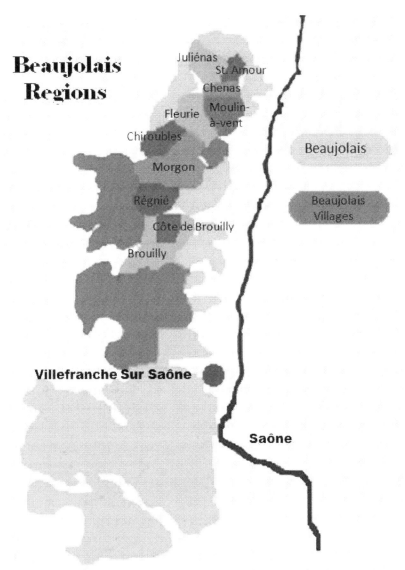

Wine Map of the Beaujolais Region

Beaujolais is administratively part of Burgundy, but its primarily red wine is made from a different type of grape: Gamay instead of Pinot Noir. There is history to this.

In 1395, Philip the Bold, powerful Duke of Burgundy, decided that the Gamay grape, which he called "a very bad and disloyal plant," was inferior (to Pinot Noir) and banished Gamay from his realm. Sixty years later, Philip the Good also came down hard on the grape. The two Phils might have been on to something: Gamay does not do particularly well on the limestone soils of Burgundy proper. It did thrive further south on the sandstone, granite and schist soils of Beaujolais. It ripens two weeks earlier than Pinot Noir and is easier to grow (of course, *most* grapes are easier to grow than Pinot Noir).

Philip the Bold

Beaujolais produces more wine that all of the rest of Burgundy, including Chablis. The wine is light and fruity, very easy to drink. Most of it is plain **Beaujolais**, produced in great qualities on the sandstone soils of the southern part of the region.

Some of this Beaujolais is the famous (or infamous) **Beaujolais Nouveau**. Under the aegis of wine promoter Georges Dubouef , who coined the term Beaujolais Nouveau, the light fruity virtually tannin-free wine became all the rage on the international market. Beaujolais Nouveau is released the third Thursday of November each year, and it is wise to consume it by the fourth Thursday, Thanksgiving Day, because it is not designed to keep.

It is made using a process called "carbonic maceration" rather than the standard alcoholic fermentation common in other wines. During carbonic maceration, the winemaker pumps carbon dioxide into a sealed fermentation vessel filled with whole clusters of uncrushed grapes. The CO_2 seeps into the individual grapes and starts a fermentation process on a grape-by-grape basis, producing alcohol as well as the esters ethyl cinnamate which adds strawberry and raspberry aromas and benzaldehyde, responsible for cherry and kirsch aromas. Eventually the weight of the grapes and the pressure of the CO_2 caused the skins to break, juice trickles down to the bottom of the vessel, and ambient yeasts accomplish a standard fermentation.

Wine from ninety-six villages may be labeled Beaujolais, but thirty-nine of these villages qualify for the appellation **Beaujolais Villages**. These villages are more likely to rest on schist and granite soil and produce better quality wine meant to last a year or two. Ten appellations in the northern reach of Beaujolais comprise the **Cru Beaujolais**, the highest quality tier. These wines are labeled with their village or location names and do not need to indicate "Beaujolais" on the label (although sometimes they do, for our benefit). The ten are:

Brouilly: The largest Beaujolais Cru, around Mont Brouilly, noted for aromas of blueberries, cherries, raspberries and currants.

Côte de Brouilly. A hilly sub-region within Brouilly

Régnié: Makes fuller body wines with red currant and raspberry flavors. Thought to the site of the first vineyards planted in Beaujolais by the Romans

Morgon: Earthy, deeply colored wines which take on a silky texture when aged. Aromas of apricots and peaches

Chiroubles: With some of the highest altitudes in Beaujolais, known for delicate perfume that often includes aromas of violets.

Fleurie: Velvety, delicate wines that can age up to four years.

Moulin-à-Vent: Literally "windmill." Formidable full-bodied wine often aged in oak

Chénas: Aroma of wild roses.

Juliénas: Rich, spicy and floral

Saint-Amour: Spicy flavors and aromas of peaches.

The Wine Regions of France

The Rhône Region

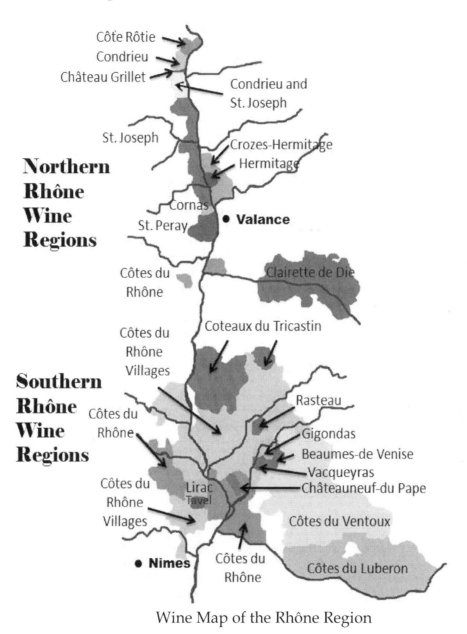

Côte Rôtie
Condrieu
Château Grillet

Condrieu and
St. Joseph

St. Joseph

Crozes-Hermitage
Hermitage

**Northern
Rhône
Wine
Regions**

Cornas
St. Peray

● **Valance**

Côtes du
Rhône

Clairette de Die

Coteaux du Tricastin

Côtes du
Rhône
Villages

**Southern
Rhône
Wine
Regions**

Côtes du
Rhône

Rasteau

Gigondas
Beaumes-de Venise
Vacqueyras
Châteauneuf-du Pape

Côtes du
Rhône
Villages

Lirac
Tavel

Côtes du Ventoux

● **Nimes**

Côtes du
Rhône

Côtes du Luberon

Wine Map of the Rhône Region

They say that Burgundy and Beaujolais lie between the mustard and the onions. What this means is that the regions are situated between the cities of Dijon, world famous for its mustard, and Lyon, whose cooking is associated with onions. You will eat well whichever city you visit.

The river Saône accompanies you through the mustard to onions region, but once it reaches the gastronomic capital of Lyon, the **Rhône**, coming in from Lake Geneva, swallows it up and takes over the southward march. In wine terms, the northern and southern Rhône regions are two separate personalities. The south, the more extensive of the two, accounts for 90% of Rhône valley production.

The **northern Rhône** is far greener than the south, and several degrees cooler on average. Climate is continental, and the mistral winds howl through the canyons in winter and even spring. The valley here is narrow, leaving thin echelons of vines balanced on granite cliffs, with little room for expansion. The northern Rhône is home base for four formidable grapes that are in the process of challenging Bordeaux and Burgundy for world dominance: the red Syrah and the whites Viognier, Marsanne and Roussanne.

Côte-Rôtie hangs onto the west edge of the valley as if for dear life. The name means "roasted slope," which is true to life, given the concentration of the sun on the cliff. The appellation divides into two sections depending on soil. The Côte Brune ("brown slope") in the north has dark, iron-rich schist and the Côte Blonde ("blond slope") further south has pale granite and schist soil. The schist keeps the heat in during the day and protects the vines when those cold mistrals blow. To combat erosion on these steep slopes, growers terrace their vineyards and enclose them with stone walls, but the system is not foolproof. It is not uncommon to see growers hauling buckets of soil and rocks up the hill to reunite them with the vineyards. Some of the vines are over a century old, and most vines an average of forty. Côte-Rôtie, at best, is tiny, if not minuscule.

Côte-Rôtie marries the two great grapes of the northern Rhône, though they are of different colors. Syrah forms the base, with up to 20% Viognier (although in most cases the Viognier will weigh in at less that 10%). The grapes must be co-vinified, crushed and fermented together rather than being blended as separately fermented wines. These wines can last decades. Aroma is unique: green olive, bacon, violet, raspberry with flavors of black pepper, white pepper, blueberry, blackberry, plum, and leather.

Directly to the south of Côte-Rôtie is the equally small appellation of **Condrieu**, and the even smaller one-vineyard appellation of **Château Grillet**, both producing Viognier only. This is this up and coming world grape's home base. Soils here differ from Côte-Rôtie, sanded granite rather than schist. This Viognier expresses peach, white flowers, dried fruit, spices like anise, melon. This is a full-bodied and rich wine that, although dry, expresses a rich ripe sweetness. Vinopinion is split as to whether Condrieu should be consumed young or allowed to age some years. Expensive.

Below Château Grillet is **Condrieu and Saint-Joseph**, a bridge between the two appellations. The larger appellation of **Saint-Joseph** allows red wines of Syrah with up to 10% Marsanne and Roussanne, as well as white wine from Marsanne and/or Roussanne. Continuing south on the west side of the river, **Cornas** produces all-Syrah reds, and **Saint-Péray** still and sparkling wines of Marsanne and/or Roussanne. On the east side of the river, across from the southern stretch of Saint-Joseph, **Crozes-Hermitage** produces reds of Syrah and up to 15% Marsanne and Roussanne; whites of only Marsanne and Roussanne.

Surrounded on three sides by Crozes-Hermitage, on a hill overlooking the river, **Hermitage** gives us reds of Syrah and up to 15% Viognier; whites of only Marsanne and Roussanne. The red Hermitage, usually 100% Syrah, is one of the great wines of the world.

Some history first. If you know anything about history—and you should, since it brought you here—you would be aware of the Albigensian heresy, which presaged Protestantism by several centuries. You can look that up. In any case, when the French knight Gaspard de Stérimberg returned in 1224 from trying to wipe out the Albigensians, he was wounded. The queen of France gave him permission to build a chapel on the hill and live there as a hermit, hence the name Hermitage. The chapel is now part of a wine estate. In 1642, French King Louis XIII made Hermitage an official court wine, gave some as a gift to England's Charles II, and once the English fell for it, the tiny dot on the hill (345 acres of vines) earned its permanent place on the world wine map.

Hermitage starts out an undisciplined youth, with aromas of black fruit, herbs, olives, cassis, iron and earth and tannins that can only be called rude. The maturing wine comes together in a delightful softness as the black fruit changes to red. The nose gets deeper earth, more mature olive, tobacco, a cabinet of spices. On the palate, the fully-grown wine is exquisitely soft. The finish is so smooth and long that once it abandons your mouth it takes up permanent residence in a special "Hermitage niche" in your brain that you never before knew you had. Hermitage will make you wait a decade or longer, but of course you have the option to exchange money for a wine that is already grown up. A few months ago this writer found four bottles of 17-year-old Hermitage for $80 each, and was foolish enough to only buy the one. Thank goodness for that brain niche.

The Southern Rhône has the name of the river in common with the northern Rhône, but little else. Between the two is a significant stretch without viticulture, and then the valley spreads out, fanning out appellations on both side of the river, the east somewhat more than the west. Climate here is solidly Mediterranean, meaning summers are warm and dry, with irrigation permitted in some appellations. Among red wines of the southern Rhône, Grenache, Syrah, Mourvèdre, Cinsault and Carignan are leading grapes, the first three forming the model for various "GSM" wines produced all over the world. Whites include Ugni Blanc, Roussanne, Bourboulenc, Picpoul, Clairette, and sometimes Viognier.

Côtes du Rhône is produced in areas that do not qualify for more limited appellations. **Côtes du Rhône Villages** applies to wine produced in a number of favored villages. Côtes du Rhône reds usually lead with Grenache. The individual AOC appellations, called *crus*, many of which at one time could at best claim Côtes du Rhône status, are the next step up in quality.

The most prestigious individual appellation is **Châteauneuf-du-Pape** which, as we have already discussed, allows a blend of up to ten red varieties and nine whites, for its red wine, with no restriction as to proportion. As in Côtes du Rhône, Grenache usually leads, and the GSM combination is quite common. History again: the name means "new castle of the Pope." In 1308 Pope Clement V, who was originally French, moved the Papacy from Rome to the French city of Avignon, not far the southern Rhône region, where it remained for 67 years. Clement and his successors came to like and support the local wine. Clement's successor John XXII built the castle that still stands as the symbol of the appellation. CDP is often sold in thick bottles which sport an embossed replicate of a papal seal.

Châteauneuf-du-Pape is a high production area, producing more wine, mostly red (white is allowed but not rosé), than the entire northern Rhone region. In certain areas round rocks called *galets roulés* sit on top of the clay soil. The rocks collect the heat from the sun, releasing the heat at night to keep up the ripening process. Many vineyards do not use the *galets* because they seek to delay the ripening process in order to preserve acidity.

It is tough to generalize what Châteauneuf-du-Pape wine is like because it has so many permutations. In a recent web search, we found examples selling from $20 to nearly $2000 with numerous prices points in between. The red wine could be earthy and meaty with notes of leather and tar, but rich and spicy with some age. A common aromatic note is "garrigue," an amalgamation of dried hillside herbs typical of southern France. White Châteauneuf-du-Pape (only 5% of production) is extremely varied in character. It can be made from any or every one of those allowed white grapes.

Gigondas, northeast of Châteauneuf-du-Pape, is considered Châteauneuf-du-Pape's "little brother." Red and rosé wines are permitted, but no whites. Red Gigondas must be made from a maximum 80% Grenache, a minimum 15% Syrah and/or Mourvedre, and a maximum 10% from the other Rhône varietals, excluding Carignan. Once again, we are probably looking at the popular GSM blend.

Vacqueyras, next door to Gigondas, is much like it. Whites are allowed, yet 97% of production is red.

Beaumes de Venise, which borders both Gigondas and Vacqueyras, includes two different AOCs that produce radically different types of wine. Here vines grow on the lower slopes of the Dentelles de Montmirail, a collection of jutting spires of Jurassic limestone.

The **Muscat de Beumes de Venise AOC** got its cru status in 1943 for its fortified wine from the Muscat grape, but its renown predates that date by two millennia. Pliny the Elder (23-79 AD) praised the Muscat wine of Beaumes. In 1248, Louis IX took the wine with him on his seventh crusade. The next century the Popes in Avignon took a shine to the wine. The golden Muscat vines are planted on narrow terraces, known as "restanques" or "faysses", and supported by walls. The sun's warmth radiates down off the limestone slabs of the Dentelles de Montmirail. The white wine is golden in color, with a nose of flowers and tropical fruits, and a long finish. Fermentation is arrested at between five and ten percent alcohol level by adding pure alcohol of at least 96%, when the musts contain 5% to 10% alcohol. The finished wine must contain at least 100g/L of sugar (10% sugar level) and have an alcohol content of at least at least 15%. The plain vanilla **Beumes de Venise AOC** got cru status only in 2005 for red wines. Considering that Grenache must be at least 50% of the blend, Syrah 25%, with the remainder divided between Mourvèdre and a few others (up to 5% white), this wine is looking awfully like a close cousin to Gigondas, Vacqueyras, Châteauneuf-du-Pape and the GSM blend.

Vinsobres is another AOC that largely follows a GSM configuration.

In the **Côtes du Vivarais** in the northwest of the region, red wines (80% of production) are made from Grenache, Syrah, Cinsault, and a few other grapes. Rosé (15%) uses the same mix. White wines (5%) are made from Clairette Blanche, Grenache Blanc, and Marsanne.

Grignan-Les Adhemar appears as the **Côteaux du Tricastin** on our map. An accident at the Tricastin Nuclear Power Center in 2008 released uranium into the environment and negatively impacted sales of the wine, so the name of the AOC was changed. The appellation sits at the border between the continental climate of the northern Rhône and the Mediterranean climate of the southern Rhône. Winemaking here goes back two millennia Wines are nearly all red, led by Grenache and Syrah, with Cinsault, Mourvèdre and Carignan.

Rasteau specializes in the fortified Vin Doux Naturel (VDN) in red, rosé or white, and a small proportion of dry red wines. Grenache Noir, Grenache Gris and Grenache Blanc are allowed in the VDN. These can also include up to a 10% contribution from any of the eighteen varieties allowed in red, rosé or white Côtes du Rhône. The alcohol level of the finished wine must be at least 15 per cent, a maximum of 21.5 per cent by volume, with sugar at a minimum of 45 grams per liter (4.5%.). The dry red Rasteau is commonly made from 100% Grenache Noir.

Lirac produces red wines from Grenache (40% min.), Syrah and Mourvèdre (min 25% together), Cinsault and Carignan (max. 10%) Rosé uses the same varieties, with up to 10% of the allowed varieties for whites. White Lirac uses Clairette, Grenache Blanc and Bourboulenc, with no variety allowed to be more than 60%.

Tavel wines are all rosé. Tavel has been highly regarded over the centuries. It was the favorite of Louis XIV, the Avignon popes, novelist Honoré de Balzac, and the 20th-century writer, Ernest Hemingway. Grenache, Cinsault, Syrah and Mourvèdre are the main grapes used. The wine is very dry and has greater body and structure than many rosés. It may improve with age.

In the **Côtes du Ventoux**, red and rosé wines are made from Grenache, Syrah, Cinsault, Mourvèdre, and Carignan (maximum 30%). White wines are produced from Clairette Blanche, Bourboulenc, Grenache Blanc, and Roussanne (maximum 30%). The reds (80% of production) are light and fruity.

In the **Côtes du Luberon**, red wines are made from Grenache and Syrah (minimum 60%, of which Syrah is a minimum of 10%), Cinsault (maximum 20%), Carignan (maximum 20%) , with Counoise, Gamay Noir, Mourvèdre, and Pinot Noir. For rosé the same varieties are used as for the red, with up to 20% of the allowed varieties for the white wine. Whites are made from Ugni Blanc (max. 50%) Roussanne & Marsanne (combined max of 20%), Clairette Blanche, Grenache Blanc, Vermentino, and Bourboulenc.

In the **Die region** between the northern and southern sections of the Rhône, **Clairette de Die** is a sparkling white wine made from Muscat Blanc à Petits Grains (75% minimum) and Clairette (25% maximum).The wine has peach and apricot flavors and rose and honeysuckle aromas, is usually drunk young, and is served chilled.

Crémant de Die is a dry, sparkling wine of apple and green fruit flavors and fragrance made by the traditional Champagne method of a first fermentation in the vat followed by a second fermentation in the bottle. Clairette, Aligoté and Muscat are the allowed grapes.

Coteaux de Die is a still dry white wine produced from 100% Clairette.

Châtillon-en-Diois is a still wine produced in three colors. The red and rosé are produced from Gamay, Pinot Noir and Syrah.

The Wine Regions of France

Provence

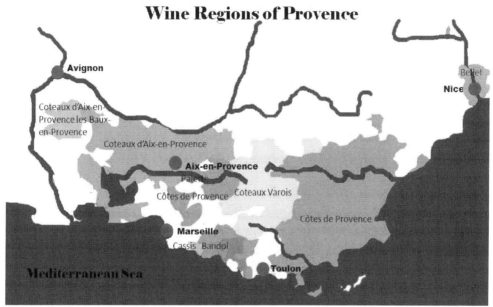

Wine Map of Provence

Provence subsisted for years on often ordinary rosé, purchased as a thirst quencher by many a tourist in this paradise under the sun. Rosé still accounts for 50% of production, but quality red and whites are now holding their own. The region has been making wine for over 2500 years. The Greeks founded Marseille in 600 BC as Massalia. The Romans followed, calling the area "our province" (*provincia nostra*), hence the name Provence. This was the first Roman province outside of Italy.

The climate of Provence is decidedly Mediterranean, with very warm summers. The mistral wind that comes in from the north is an issue. It blows away potential vine diseases but can also damage the vines. Vineyards are planted on hillsides away from direct wind contact to protect the vines, and secure vine training systems are in place. Soils show great variety.

The **Côtes de Provence** AOC is a large noncontiguous region covering over 85 *communes* in the eastern part of Provence. Côtes de Provence accounts for nearly 75% of Provence wine production—rosé is at least 80% the production of the appellation. Red wine is on the ascendency with 15%. The remaining 5% is white. Red grapes used include Carignan, Cinsault, Grenache, Mourvèdre and Tibouren with some Cabernet Sauvignon and Syrah. For rosé wines, at least 20% must be blended from wine produced by the soignée method of maceration.

The **Coteaux d'Aix-en-Provence** is the region's second largest appellation, north and west of the Côtes de Provence. Red wine accounts for 65% of production, 35% rosé and 10% white. Grapes include Grenache, Cinsault, Mourvèdre, and some Cabernet Sauvignon. The major white grapes are Bourboulenc, Clairette, Grenache Blanc, Chardonnay, Sauvignon Blanc and Sémillon. Within the Coteaux d'Aix-en-Provence is the smaller **Les Baux-de-Provence**. The climate of the region is very hot with the surrounding valley known as the Val d'Enfer (Valley of Hell). Red grape varieties account for around 80% of the wine led by the familiar trio of Grenache, Mourvèdre and Syrah. This was the first AOC to require that all vines be produced biodynamically, many producers having already converted to organic viticulture.

Bandol is produced around the village of that name in eight communes with silicon and limestone soils which, along with the warm coastal climate, are ideal for the major variety Mourvèdre, which is late ripening. For both the red and rosé wines, Mourvèdre must account for at least 50% of the blend, with Grenache and Cinsault. Syrah and Carignan are restricted in Bandol to a maximum of 15% of the blend or 10% individually. Nearly 70% of the production is red wine. Red Bandol wine is dark in color with rich flavors of black fruit, vanilla, cinnamon and leather and usually requires at least 10 years of aging before it fully develops. The white wines of Bandol are composed primarily of Clairette Blanche, Bourboulenc and Ugni Blanc.

Cassis is primarily a white wine appellation, producing Clairette, Marsanne, Ugni Blanc and Sauvignon Blanc on limestone soil. The dry white wines are full-bodied, low in acidity and have herbal aromas that pair well with the local seafood.

The **Coteaux Varois** is in the central region of Provence. Over 60% of production is rosé with around 33% red wine and small amount of white wine. The major grape varieties are Grenache, Cabernet Sauvignon, Cinsault, Mourvèdre, Syrah and Carignan.

Palette is a small AOC near Aix-en-Provence. Reds and rosés must be composed of a minimum 80% Grenache, Mourvedre and/or Cinsault with the remaining 20% a possible blend of Syrah, Carignan, Castet, Manosquin, Muscat Noir and Cabernet Sauvignon. Whites are composed of at least 80% Clairette with Bourboulenc, Trebbiano, Grenache Blanc and several white varieties. Muscat is permitted to round out the remaining 20%.

Bellet north of Nice produces an even mix of the three colors. Its proximity to the Piemonte region of Italy reflects in its grapes: The key white grape is Vermentino, with support from four classic white grapes of southern France—Blanqueiron, Bourboulenc, Roussanne and Clairette. Muscat Blanc and Chardonnay can be used, but only in the white wines. The key red grapes are Braquet and Fuella Nera (*Folle Noire* or *Jurancon Noir*), with backup from Cinsault and Grenache. Locals and hordes of tourists drink the entire production of Bellet, so it is rarely exported.

The Wine Regions of France

Languedoc-Roussillon

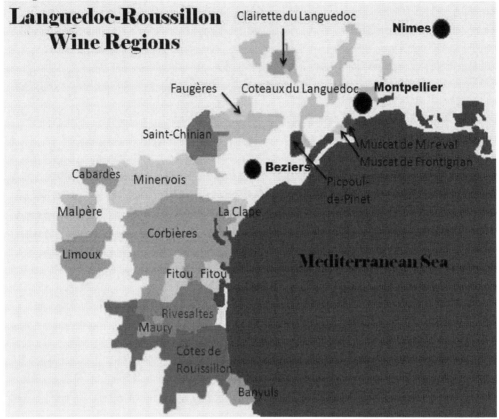

Wine Map of Languedoc-Roussillon

The regions called Languedoc-Roussillon in the south of France along the Mediterranean coast runs from the Spanish border east to Provence. Languedoc is the eastern/northern part of the region, Roussillon the western/southern stretch. The total region contains more than 700,000 acres of vines and is the largest wine producing region on the planet, accounting for more than a third of all French wine. This was the area largely responsible for the "wine lake" of the late 20th century and subsequent European Union efforts to decrease wine production with the aim of increasing both wine quality and wine industry viability. Over the past several decades, the area has attracted outside investment aimed at quality, as well as maverick winemakers seeking to blaze new trails. The majority of Languedoc wine is still produced by the region's more than 500 cooperatives.

Like Provence and the southern Rhône, the region enjoys a Mediterranean climate with warm dry summers. Vineyards in the Languedoc stretch along the coastal plains of the Mediterranean while in Roussillon they cling to the narrow valleys around the Pyrenees. The *tramontane* wind comes in from the northwest, keeping the climate dry. Water is an issue, especially with global warming. Some areas are being allowed to irrigate, and others irrigate on the sly in contravention of French and EU regulations.

A range of grapes are prominent in this large region. Among reds, the dynamic duo of Cabernet Sauvignon and Merlot have made their inroads. The Rhône grapes of Grenache, Syrah and Mourvèdre are widely grown, as are Cinsault and Carignan. Among whites, Chardonnay is widely grown for regional wines and in the sparkling Crémant de Limoux. Other whites include Viognier, Roussanne, Marsanne, Vermentino (Rolle), Bourboulenc, Clairette Blanche, Grenache Blanc, Grenache Gris, Picpoul, and Maccabéo, and a range of Muscat varieties used for fortified wines.

AOC Languedoc was launched in 2007 as an all-encompassing quality wine appellation covering the entire region, from Nîmes — just west of the Rhône — down to the eastern Pyrenees. This subsumes the **Coteaux du Languedoc** appellation that previously covered only the high country in the northeast of the region. Coteaux du Languedoc still appears on wine labels. AOC Languedoc wines can be made from: Grenache, Syrah, Mourvèdre, Cinsault and Carignan for the reds and rosés; Grenache Blanc, Clairette, Bourboulenc, Viognier, Picpoul, Marsanne, Roussanne, Vermentino and Ugni Blanc for the whites. As is the case with any broad regional appellation, winemakers within the various *crus* can label their wine with those crus if they qualify for them. Let us take a look at some of these crus, moving from right to left on our map, starting with the region's numerous sweet fortified wines and then moving on to still dry wines.

Most of the fortified wines are vins doux naturels (VDNs), literally "naturally sweet wines." The "natural" sweetness comes from grape juice that is not allowed to ferment. The *mutage* method is used: adding a distilled grape spirit to stop fermentation before all the grape sugar ferments to alcohol.

Just to the southwest of the university city of Montpelier, the neighboring appellations of **Muscat de Mireval** and **Muscat de Frontignan** produce VDNs from Muscat Blanc à Petits Grains grapes. In the northeast corner of the **Minervois** appellation (which largely produces still wines), **Muscat de Saint-Jean-de-Minervois** is also based on Muscat Blanc à Petits Grains. Further south, **Muscat de Rivesaltes** is made from Muscat of Alexandria and Muscat Blanc à Petits Grains grapes. **Rivesaltes** (with no "Muscat") refers to the same region's VDNs produced from Grenache Noir, Grenache Gris, and Grenache Blanc (and varying in color accordingly). **Maury**, just southwest of Rivesaltes, makes similar Grenache-based VDNs. In the extreme south, approaching the border with Spain, **Banyuls** produces VDNs in a number of colors, also based on Grenache Noir, Grenache Gris, and Grenache Blanc. Small amounts of Muscat grapes are allowed in these wines.

Among the still wines of the region, the **Clairette du Languedoc** appellation produces wines only from the white Clairette grape, but in a wide range of styles. Some are light and crisp, while others are full-bodied, sweet (but not fortified) and reddish brown, labeled sometimes as "rancio" (intentionally oxidized) if they have been aged at least three years.

The coastal appellation of **Picpoul de Pinet** is a full-bodied white wine with citrus aromas and flavors, made exclusively from the local Picpoul grape.

Sited on an ancient seabed giving it schist soils, **Faugères** is renowned for full-bodied red wines made primarily from Syrah, Grenache and Mourvèdre, with some Cinsault and Lladoner Pelut. It produces some white wines from Grenache Blanc, Marsanne, Roussanne and Rolle (Vermentino).

Saint-Chinian gives us blended red, white, and rosé wines. Most wines are robust reds traditionally led by Carignan. The fruity rosés are commonly based on Cinsault. Grenache, Lladoner Pelut, Mourvèdre and Syrah go into the mix. White wine grapes include Grenache Blanc, Marsanne and Roussanne. AOC regulations mandate that all wines be blends.

Minervois is named after the village of Minerve, referring to the Roman Goddess Minerva, a testament to the long history of winemaking in the region. Minervois is an area whose reputation is on the rise. In red Minervois wines, Grenache, Syrah and Mourvedre (our old friend GSM) must together constitute 60% of the blend, possibly complemented by Carignan and Cinsault. White wines are made from Vermentino, Roussanne, Marsanne and Grenache Blanc.

Corbieres is an important, productive region producing red, rosé and white wines. Both red and rosé wines are based on Grenache, Syrah, Mourvèdre and Carignan, with the rosés also enjoying contributions from Picpoul and Grenache Gris. White are blends of Bourboulenc, Grenache Blanc, Maccabeu, Marsanne and Roussanne. To the south of Corbieres, **Fitou** produces similar wines. Located on the coast hard by the northeast corner of Corbieres, **La Clape** produces highly regarded red wines from Grenache, Syrah and Mourvèdre as well as whites from Grenache Blanc, Clairette, Bourboulenc, Marsanne, Roussanne and Piquepoul.

Cabardés produces red and rosé wines in the hills just north of Carcassonne. The area, which has made wine since the Roman era, is on the border between Languedoc-Roussillon and France's Southwest region. The grapes reflect this split personality: Syrah and Grenache from the south of France, Cabernet Franc, Cabernet Sauvignon and Merlot from the southwest and Bordeaux. Think of it as the best of both for rich red wines and intensely flavored dry rosés. The wines of **Malpère** directly to the south have a similar configuration

Limoux is known for both still and sparkling wines. It is yet another appellation (or pair of appellations) that has one foot in Languedoc-Roussillon and the other in the Southwest region. Here, grapes grow at higher elevations than in the rest of Languedoc-Roussillon, in a cooler climate. Still red Limoux must be at least 50% Merlot, with Cabernet Sauvignon, Cabernet Franc, Malbec, Grenache, Syrah and Carignan. White Limoux Blanc is made from Mauzac, Chenin Blanc and Chardonnay. The Mauzac, a white grape of the Southwest called "Blanquette" locally, is the major grape of **Blanquette de Limoux**, the sparkling wine the area is best known for. Chenin Blanc and Chardonnay go into the mix. To appeal to present day international tastes, **Crémant de Limoux** is made from a higher percentage of Chardonnay and Chenin Blanc.

Roussillon's specialty is sweet VDNs like **Riversaltes, Maury, and Banyuls**. The catch-all **Côtes du Roussillon** appellation covers the various still wines of this part of France. Red Côtes du Roussillon is typically Grenache, Syrah and Mourvedre, with possible help from Carignan and Cinsault. Rosés can use these plus Grenache Gris and Macabeu. Whites are predominantly Grenache Blanc and Macabeu, with Marsanne, Roussanne and Rolle. **Côtes du Roussillon Villages** labeling applies to four better quality villages and is commonly made from Carignan, Grenache and Syrah.

The Wine Regions of France

Southwest France

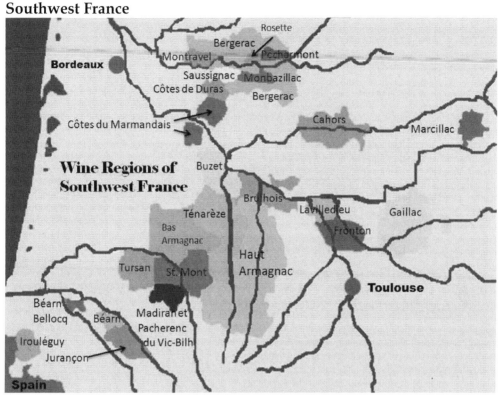

Wine Map of Southwest France

First: Even though the Bordeaux region is in the southwest of France, when we refer to "southwestern France" we mean the southwestern part of the country *excluding* Bordeaux, to the east and south of that famous region. The southwest has a number of extremely diverse regions. Some mirror the grape configuration we find in Bordeaux—Cabernet Sauvignon, Merlot, Cabernet Franc, Petite Verdot, Malbec, Sauvignon Blanc, Sémillon—while others have local grapes seen nowhere else. The southwest is an interesting mix.

We start in the **Dordogne** region, the back door to Bordeaux. Here the **Côtes de Duras** borders Bordeaux's Entre Deux Mers section, producing wines from red and white Bordeaux grapes. **Bergerac** further east is a similar Bordeaux mirror. Nearby **Montravel** is more varied, producing sweet white wines from Sémillon and dry whites from Sauvignon Blanc, sometime with oak aging. Bordeaux's third white grape Muscadelle is also grown. Red Montravel is largely Merlot. **Saussignac**, **Monbazzilac**, and **Rosette** produce sweet wine from the three white Bordeaux grapes. In the case of Monbazzilac, the wine might be botrytis influenced, depending on the weather and climate in any particular year. The **Côtes du Marmandais** is bisected by the River Garonne. North of the river, adjacent to Bordeaux's Entre Deux Mers, Merlot grows on clay and chalk soils. South of the river, abutting Bordeaux's Graves region, Cabernet Sauvignon and Cabernet Franc prosper on alluvial silt.

Cahors is the original home of Malbec (called Côt here), but one hundred and fifty years of geographical separation make this wine nothing like its Argentinean offspring. The Malbec is fuller and more rustic than it would be in Bordeaux. Vines here are planted on alluvial terraces looking down on the River Lot.

Way inland, **Marcillac** glories in the local Fer Servadou grape, making a light peppery red wine. This appellation is a final vestige of a once-vital wine region in France's Massif Centrale. **Gaillac** to the south is another red wine appellation using Fer Servadou, Syrah, and some Gamay, as well as the Bordeaux red grapes. North of the city of Toulouse, **Fronton** produces the red and rosé wine, from the local Negrette grape with perhaps some Syrah or Gamay, favored by the Toulousians. **Lavilledieu** and **Brulhois** are similar to Fronton. Brulhois may see some Tannat. On the banks of the Garonne, just north of the Armagnac region, **Buzet** produces Bordeaux varieties.

Haut Armagnac, **Ténarèze**, and **Bas Armagnac** grow the grapes used to make the wine that is distilled into Armagnac. These include Baco22A, Colombard, Folle Blanche and Ugni Blanc. South of Armagnac, **Tursan** is known for light, fruit-driven red and rosé wines from Cabernet Franc and Tannat, as well as some complex, aromatic white wines from Baroque and Gros Manseng. The full-bodied tannic wines of **Saint-Mont** are made from Tannat blended with Cabernet Franc and Fer Servadou.

Madiran's red wines are rich and tannic, the better to cut through the region's rich cuisine (think magret de canard and cassoulet). The tannic grape here is Tannat, which comprises 60 to 80% of the mix. The rest is Cabernet Sauvignon, Cabernet Franc or Fer Servadou. The white **Pacherenc du Vic-Bilh**, a distinct appellation, is nevertheless identical in scope to Madiran. Pacherenc du Vic-Bilh is made in both sweet and dry styles and is considered the perfect companion for the local foie gras. Bring your cardiologist along if you visit here.

Béarn around the town of Pau includes two parts that are not contiguous. The appellation makes big tannic red wines primarily from Tannat and white wines from the almost extinct Raffiat de Moncade grape.

Jurançon is a white wine specialist, producing distinctive sweet and dry wines from the local Petit Manseng and Gros Manseng grapes. The wines, which have been produced since the Middle Ages, show aromas of fresh passion fruit in the dry wines, mango in the sweet wines and dried bananas, vanilla and beeswax in the late-harvest wines.

Irouleguy in the Basque country by the Spanish border, produces fruity, tannic red wines from Cabernet Franc and Tannat, full-bodied, tangy whites from Courbu, Petit Courbu, Gros Manseng and Petit Manseng, and intensely fruity and deeply colored rosés from Cabernet Franc and Tannat.

The Wine Regions of France

Savoie

Wine Map of Savoie

Savoie is an alpine area, attracting phalanxes of tourists in both summer and winter. Most of its crisp white wine is produced as Savoie AOC.

The high yielding Jacquere is the most prevalent of the white grapes. Altesse, called Roussette in Savoie, makes some of Savoie's best wines under the **Roussette de Savoie** and **Roussette de Bugey** appellations. Roussanne (Bergeron) has its own appellation **Chignin-Bergeron**. Chardonnay is on the rise in Savoie, for still and sparkling wines, especially under the appellation of Bugey Cerdon.

Mondeuse is the red grape of note in Savoie for deeply-colored, peppery wines with a bitter edge. Gamay and Pinot Noir are grown to produce mainly light single varietal wines.

The Wine Regions of France

Jura

Wine Map of Jura

The Jura region is quite small, a narrow strip of land sandwiched between Burgundy and Switzerland. Five grapes predominate. Three are traditional local varieties. Poulsard is a red grape used mostly in dry reds and sparkling rosés. Red Trousseau needs a lot of sunshine to ripen and only grows in the warmest parts of this cool climate region. White Savagnin (called Nature here) is used in all the region's appellations for the idiosyncratic **vin jaune** ('yellow wine'). The other two grapes are the better known Pinot Noir and Chardonnay (called Melon d'Arbois and Gamay Blanc here). They are used to make dry wines in a fresh fruity international style.

Vin Jaune, like dry fino Sherry that is aged with the yeast called flor resting on its surface, is matured in a barrel under a film of yeast, known as the *voile*. Vin Jaune shares certain aromas with Sherry, but it is not fortified. Jura is also known for its sweet Vin de Paille (straw wine), from grapes that have been dried on mats of straw, thus concentrating the sugars and flavors. Both Vin Jaune and Vin de Paille are made under the **Arbois**, **L'Etoile** and **Cotes du Jura** appellations. The best Vin Jaune is produced under the **Chateau Chalon** appellation.

The Jura makes sparkling wines under the appellation Crémant du Jura.

The Wine Regions of France

Those Blank Spots on the Map

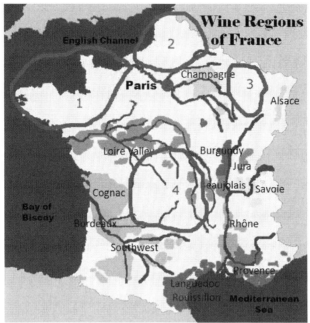

Wine map of France with circled and numbered blank spots

The blank spots on the map of France, circled and numbered above, require some explanation (beyond the fact that every inch of France produces some kind of interesting **food**).

Blank Spot 1, representing Normandy and Brittany, is France's main production center for **apples**. The French eat apples of course, but they also ferment them into delightful **ciders** both sweet and dry. Being ambitious, they take the process an extra step and distill apple wine into the **apple brandies** called **Calvados** in Normandy and **Lambig** in Brittany. It is not unheard of for one of these brandies to use juice from more than a hundred different species of apples: tart apples, sweet apples, and even some scarcely edible bitter apples.

Blank Spot 2 is the Lille Nord-Pas-de-Calais area, the center of France's **beer** industry. Brittany and Alsace also produce beer.

Blank Spot 3 is Lorraine. Before the two world wars, Lorraine was a thriving wine region, but these wars obliterated nearly every vineyard, and the region never recovered. The Champagne region west of this blank spot was also in the middle of these wars, but somehow it recovered.

Blank Spot 4 is as essential to world wine as are vineyards. Here you find France's most renowned **oak forests**, from which the wood for **oak barrels** is harvested on a fully sustainable basis. Plant an acorn, wait 150 years, and…viola… you get the perfect oak for aging wine.

Chapter Seventeen

World Wine Regions
Italy

Wine Map of Italy

We finished France by explaining the apparent blank spots on the map, those regions where wine is *not* produced. We do not have to do this with Italy. Italy has twenty regions. Out of these twenty regions, twenty produce wine. The Italian wine map has no blank spots. Grapes grow along highway dividers, in back yards, behind supermarkets, any place that has not been paved. The diversity of growing environments, wine styles, and indigenous grape varieties in Italy is matched nowhere else on the sphere we call earth.

Italy lacks the tradition of consistent appellation configuration and wine nomenclature so distinctive in France. Yes, it has a structure. The equivalent to the French AOC (Appellation d'Origine Contrôlée) is the Italian DOC (Denominazione di Origine Controllata), but then again the equivalency is not exact. Italy also has a senior form of DOC, the DOCG (Denominazione di Origine Controllata e Garantita), supposedly with more stringent requirements as to vineyard yield, appellation boundaries, grape varieties allowed and wine production methods (but elevation to DOCG status may just depend on political considerations.) The DOCG system could make up for the fact that Italy has no Grand or Petit Cru special quality status as do a number of French regions, but the parallel is not exact, since DOCGs extend to entire regions and French Grand Crus apply to individual vineyards.

Layered on this system are three label designations that tend to connote quality.

- The term *Classico*, used in regions such as Chianti, Soave, Valpolicella, Bardolino, Gambellara, and Orvieto, refers to the "original" core of a region. During the 20th century, many regions were expanded for economic and political reasons, diluting the brand equity of the original region, which was often on hillier terrain. By delineating a classico area, the growers are indicating that "this is the good stuff."

- The term <u>Riserva</u> refers to a wine that has undergone an extra period of aging, in cask, bottle or both. Rules for this vary from region to region. Spain has a *reserva* system (note the slight difference in spelling) in many of its regions also, but the American term "reserved" has no legal meaning.

- The term *Superiore* connotes that the wine has been created using more stringent vineyard and winery techniques than a wine that is merely *normale*. Superiore wines usually must have a higher level of alcohol than normale wines. That's not just to give drinkers a headache or make them drive in an unsafe manner. The higher alcohol indicates quality. If a wine has higher alcohol than normal, it means yeast had more sugar in the grape must (juice) to turn into alcohol in the first place. The extra sweetness in the grapes is usually the result of later harvesting, a tricky procedure given the possibility of autumn rains, and the vagaries of labor availability.

Like France, Italy has a lower rung for names covering whole regions rather than their constituent parts: the IGT (*Indicazione Geografica Tipica* or "Indication of a typical geographical region") wines. In Italy, one cannot make the assumption that these wines are inferior to wines with narrower geographical focus, or that they will command lower prices. The rise of the "Super Tuscan" wines is one instance in which producers have chosen to use the regional name instead of the local denomination because the rules for allowed grapes are less strict. These wines command high prices.

IGT is gradually being replaced by the new European Union term *Indicazione Geografica Protetta* (IGP) meaning "Protected Geographical Origin". The lowest level is Vino (simply, wine) or Vino d'Italia, replacing the old Vino da Tavola.

Yes, Italy has its DOCs and DOCGs, but it is not consistent in how these designations are named.

> In some regions, the DOC or DOCG is named after a **place**, as in France: Barolo, Barbaresco, Valpolicella, Bardolino, Soave, Chianti
> In other regions, the DOC or DOCG is named combining a **grape name with a place**: Barbera d'Asti, Dolcetto d'Alba, Vernaccia di San Gimignano, Brunello di Montalcino
> In other regions, the DOC or DOCG is named after the **wine type** only: Prosecco, Lacryma Christi, Est! Est!! Est!!!
> Some wines carry a **brand name**: Super Tuscans are one example

The Wine Regions of Italy
Valle d'Aosta

We will cover the twenty wine regions of Italy starting in the northwest, moving south along the "boot," and finishing with the two island regions Sicily and Sardinia.

The **Valle d'Aosta** is Italy's smallest region, bordering France, Switzerland and the Italian (major wine-producing) region of Piemonte to its south. The French language is widely spoken here. French grape varieties coexist with Italian. Nebbiolo, called Picotentro, is the leader in terms of reputation, Petit Rouge, which makes fruity red wines akin to Beaujolais, the most prolific. Chardonnay, Petite Arvine (white), Fumin (spicy red), Prie Blanc (white), and Pinot Noir, Vien de Nus (blending red), Dolcetto, Gamay, Moscato, and Pinot Grigio are also important. The wine growing region here centers on the valley of the Dora Baltea River, a tributary of the Po, which runs north to south. The vineyards cling to the lower slopes. The Alps act as a rain shadow, bringing warm, dry summers but with chilly nights. The chill is good to a point as it preserves acidity, but at this climate extreme it can damage the vines. Many vines are trained onto high pergolas to most effectively absorb heat rising upward from the ground at night. On the thin rocky soils here, vines work hard to reach water and nutrients. Winemakers work equally hard.

Valle d'Aosta has seven DOCs and no DOCGs. **Nus DOC**, near the town of Aosta produces a red wine made from Petit Rouge and Vien de Nus, and a white Pinot Grigio. Just to the east of Nus, **Chambave DOC** produces an herbaceous red from Petite Rouge and whites from Moscato Bianco in both dry and sweet versions. Tiny **Enfer d'Arvier DOC** in the west of the region makes a rustic red from Petite Rouge. **Morgex et de la Salle DOC** in the extreme north, near Mont Blanc, is, at up to 4200 feet, probably Europe's highest vineyard area. The stone walls around the small individual plots here help to insulate the vines. **Morgex** makes a delicate white wine from the Prie Blanc grape. Valle d'Aosta's easternmost area, the **Donnas DOC**, produces a Nebbiolo as does the **Arnad-Montjovet DOC**. In both these cases the Nebbiolo is a little less demanding than, say, a Barolo from Piedmont. The largest area, **Torrete DOC**, makes a medium-bodied floral red from Petite Rouge.

The Wine Regions of Italy
Piemonte (Piedmont)

Wine Regions
of Piemonte

Boca

Ghemme

Gattinara

Sizzano

Carema   Lessona   Fara

Erbaluce
di Caluso

Barbera del
Monferrato

Turin   Barbera
d'Asti   **Asti**

Freisa di Chieri

Roero   Nizza   Colli
Tortonesi

Barbera d'Alba   Gavi

Nebbiolo d'Alba   Brachetto
d'Acqui

Barolo   Barbaresco

Diano d'Alba

Wine Map of Piemonte

The name Piemonte derives from Medieval Latin *ad pedem montium*, meaning "at the foot of the mountains." The reference is to the region's location at the foot of the Alps. Located in northwest Italy, Piemonte borders both Switzerland and France. In addition to Italian, over a million people in the region speak Piedmontese, a romance language with similarities to both Italian and French. Piemonte produces a greater number of DOCG and DOC wines than any other wine region in Italy. It has no IGT classification. Piemonte has a continental climate, but one in which summer rainfall is limited because the Alps act as a rain shadow. Piemonte is characteristically hilly (less than 5% of its vineyards are classified as "flat"). The Alps and the river Po combine to create the characteristic fog, which often blankets the region.

A Piemontese vineyard in Monferrato shrouded in fog. Photo by Elliot Essman.

The fog gives us the name for Piemonte's greatest grape (perhaps Italy's greatest), the red **Nebbiolo** (*nebbia* means fog in Piemontese). Nebbiolo produces lightly colored red wines that are highly tannic when young. The wines often see long aging, which turns them brick orange at the rim of the glass. They have high acidity. With proper aging, Nebbiolo wines take on aromas and flavors of violets, tar, wild herbs, cherries, raspberries, roses, truffles, tobacco, and prunes. The grape does not travel well, despite some efforts to give it a second home in California

Red dots indicate Piemonte's Nebbiolo denominations.

Except for the **Nebbiolo d'Alba** denomination, which has the grape + place configuration, all the Nebbiolo denominations in Piemonte have names that refer to places only. The most famous, and expensive, are **Barolo** and **Barbaresco** in the south. These are 100% Nebbiolo, and require patient aging to ease their tannins to smoothness. Barbaresco, the junior partner, is the more accessible. The broader **Langhe Nebbiolo DOC** encompasses both the Barolo and Barbaresco areas, and allows up to 15% blending of local varieties like Barbera and Dolcetto, for a less expensive, earlier drinking wine. Further north, two popular Nebbiolo denominations known for less expensive wines are **Ghemme** DOCG (requiring a minimum of 75% Nebbiolo) and **Gattinara** DOCG (90% Nebbiolo). Other Nebbiolo denominations in Piemonte include **Carema**, **Fara**, **Boca**, **Sizzano**, and **Roero**,

The red grape **Barbera** accounts for considerably more production than Nebbiolo, for a very different type of wine. Barbera produces medium-bodied, fruity wines, deeply colored, high in acidity, and characteristically low in tannin. The grape's four major Piemonte denominations include

- **Barbera d'Asti DOCG**: Minimum 90% Barbera, with Freisa, Grignolino or Dolcetto. Rich, full-bodied, and age-worthy.
- **Barbera d'Alba DOC**: Minimum 85% Barbera, the rest may be Nebbiolo from the Langhe. Best aged several years in bottle, to integrate, oak, tannins and acidity.
- **Barbera del Monferrato DOC**: Minimum 85% Barbera, with Freisa, Grignolino or Dolcetto. Deep ruby, aromas of ripe plum and cherries, with black pepper. More aromatic and less robust than Asti or Alba
- **Nizza DOCG**: 100% Barbera, a new DOCG that used to be a sub-zone of Barbera d'Asti (and considered its finest expression).

Wine Regions of Piemonte

Boca
Ghemme
Gattinara
Sizzano
Carema
Lessona
Fara
Erbaluce di Caluso
Barbera del Monferrato
Turin
Barbera d'Asti
Asti
Freisa di Chieri
Roero
Nizza
Colli Tortonesi
Barbera d'Alba
Gavi
Nebbiolo d'Alba
Barbaresco
Brachetto d'Acqui
Barolo
Diano d'Alba

Red dots on the map indicate Barbera denominations in its home region of Italian Piemonte.

Dolcetto is Piemonte's third major red grape. Although the name means "little sweetie," Dolcetto wines are dry, with a pleasantly bitter edge. Dolcetto denominations include **Dolcetto d'Asti, Dolcetto d'Alba, Dolcetto di Diano Alba, Dolcetto di Dogliani, Dolcetto di Ovada** and **Dolcetto d'Acqui**.

Other reds include **Brachetto**, the base for sweet sparkling red wines from **Brachetto d'Acqui DOCG**, a grape normally vinified as a single varietal. **Freisa** is a workhorse grape that supports dry, sweet, still and sparkling wines (and is a blending grape in several of the Barberas). Freisa has two DOCs: **Freisa d'Asti** and **Freisa di Chieri**. The Piemontese native **Grignolino** produces light colored red wines and rosés with bold fruit aromas that have strong acidity and pushy tannins. **Grignolino d'Asti DOC** and **Grignolino Monferrato Casale DOC** are the two local denominations. An even less well known local grape, produced nowhere else on the planet, is the fruity and spicy **Ruchè di Castagnole Monferrato**, which has its own DOCG northeast of Asti.

Img198 Caption: "Piemontese Winemaker Dante Garrone produces Barbera, Grignolino, and Ruchè. Photo by Elliot Essman."

Piemonte is not red only. **Gavi DOCG** is the world class still white wine of Piemonte, made from the Cortese grape in the region's southeast, flinty, minerally, crisp and bone dry. The obscure local grape Erbaluce of **Erbaluce di Caluso DOCG** is used for a sweet wine made from dried grapes and an aromatic still white. In addition to its red Nebbiolo, **Roero** produces a crisp, dry white wine from the Arneis grape

Piemonte also produces two extremely popular sparkling wines from Moscato grapes grown around Asti. **Moscato d'Asti DOCG** is the sweeter of the two, more serious, and only lightly sparkling. **Asti Spumante DOCG** (now called just Asti) is fully effervescent and has more alcohol.

The Wine Regions of Italy
Liguria

Narrow **Liguria** is shaped like an upside down boomerang, with the great maritime city of Genoa in the east-west center. Heavily ensconced with the Mediterranean to its south, Liguria bridges the coastline between France and Tuscany, poignantly preventing Piemonte from having a seacoast. This is the Italian Riviera, a craggy area known for its steep seaside cliffs, where vines have to compete with resort developers for their dollop of sunshine. Soils here are rocky and infertile, which is good for wine if you combine it with a lot of work. Ligurians have done this for two millennia. They are not averse to taking risks (one of them discovered America). Liguria's mostly small wine growers produce a hundred varieties, but these add up to relatively small production.

Fortunately, the soils in Liguria are limestone-rich, which augurs well for white grapes, lending minerality to the wines. Fragrant white Vermentino is a popular wine here. The local Rossese supports spicy, fruity reds as does Ormeasco, the local version of Dolcetto.

Liguria's most renowned wine area is the **Cinque Terre DOC** (Five Lands), at the eastern end near Tuscany. Cinque Terre (named after a cluster of five villages) is known for its dry aromatic white wine, a blend of Vermentino, Bosco, and Albarola. **Colline di Levanto DOC** makes a similar white and a red with Sangiovese and local Ciliegolo. **Golfo del Tigullio DOC** produces a number of wines, including Passito (from dried grapes) using strictly Ligurian grape varieties like Bianchetta Genovese. The hills of the moon—**Colli di Luni DOC**—is partly in Tuscany. Here are found the great quarries of Carerra marble. The red blend must be 50% Sangiovese, but then a flood of local reds can contribute: Canaiolo, Pollera Nera, Ciliegiolo, Barsaglina. White wines form from Vermentino and Trebbiano.

Val Polcevera DOC, smack dab in the middle of Liguria, produces a range of wines in three colors, still and sparkling, including Passito dried-grape wines. White wines look to the local varieties of Vermentino, Bianchetta Genovese and Albarola, reds Dolcetto, Sangiovese and Ciliegiolo,

Ormeasco di Pornassio DOC sits at high altitude in Liguria's northwest. Ormeasco is the Ligurian name for Dolcetto. The altitude results in a brighter Dolcetto than in Piemonte, more perfumed, with ripe tannins.
Rossese di Dolceacqua DOC is a brightly colored, full-flavored soft red made from the local Rossese grape. The wine is tangy with notes of herbs and black currant.

The Wine Regions of Italy
Lombardy

Lombardy is the largest and most populated region in Italy, its industrial heartland and location of its second city, Milan. Even so, the region has a great deal of rural land, covering diverse climates. In the north, the alpine foothills have a continental climate. The sun bakes the slopes and then the vineyards cool rapidly with the alpine evening. In the plains of the south, temperature and humidity are much higher. The stretch of large lakes in the north — Lake Como, Lake Iseo, Lake Maggiore and Lake Garda — gives some water-based cooling effect even though the region is landlocked. Most of the wine from its 22 DOCs and five DOCGs is consumed locally, but several have international repute.

One of Italy's most highly regarded sparkling wines is northern Lombardy's **Franciacorta DOCG**, made in the traditional method (that is, Champagne style, including lees aging), using Chardonnay, Pinot Noir and Pinot Blanc, in both vintage and non-vintages styles. Unlike the centuries-old Champagne industry, Franciacorta is only about fifty years old, however.

Another northern denomination of note is **Valtellina**, the product of a high alpine valley, and unquestionably Lombardy's most highly regarded still wine. The signature grape here is Chiavennasca, the Lombardian term for Nebbiolo, but these mountain wines are lighter in body that the formidable Barolo and Barbareseco from Piemonte, with aromas of rose water and dried cherries. The regular Rosso di Valtellina is DOC, but the Superiore version has its own DOCG. Valtellina also has DOCG status for its dried grape **Sforzato di Valtellina**, fermented to dryness just like Amarone, and also Chiavennasca-based.

In the lower-lying south of Lombardy, **Oltrepo Pavese DOC** (it means "Pavia across the Po") produces more than half of all Lombardy wine and is considered a Pinot Noir (Pinot Nero) specialist. The region is more than Pinot Nero, however, producing twenty wines. Reds, primarily from Barbera and Bonarda, appear in still, rosé, and as Sangue di Guida (" Judas's Blood") a semi-sweet Frizzante. Whites from Malvasia and Moscato come in sweet and sparkling versions with Moscato also supporting Liquoroso (fortified) and Passito (dried grape) wines. This productive region also makes a range of still and Spumante wines from international varieties. The traditional method **Oltrepo Pavese Metodo Classico** qualifies as a DOCG.

San Colombano al Lambro DOC is a small producer, also in Lombardy's south. The denomination takes climatic advantage of some of the few hills available in the otherwise flat Po valley. Reds are a blend of Croatina and Barbera, with some Uva Rara (called Bonarda sometimes, but not the same Bonarda grown in Argentina). Whites, which include some sparkling wine, use the dynamic duo of Chardonnay and Pinot Noir (without skin contact).

Lambrusco Mantovano DOC is Lombardy's region for the production of the red sparkling wine Lambrusco, most of which is produced in Emilia-Romagna, on the other side of the River Po. No international grapes here—eight to ten indigenous grapes make the mix. Lombardy Lambrusco is usually made in a dry version, but some off-dry is produced. It has a ruby red color, aromas of flowers (violets), and a generally low alcohol level. It is of note that the sweet version of Lambrusco, largely from Emilia-Romagna, was the most popular Italian wine in the United States during the 1970s and 1980s, especially under the popular Riunite brand. (More on Lambrusco in the section on Emilia-Romagna.)

We cover the wine area of **Lugana**, which is split between Lombardy and the Veneto, in the next section on the Veneto.

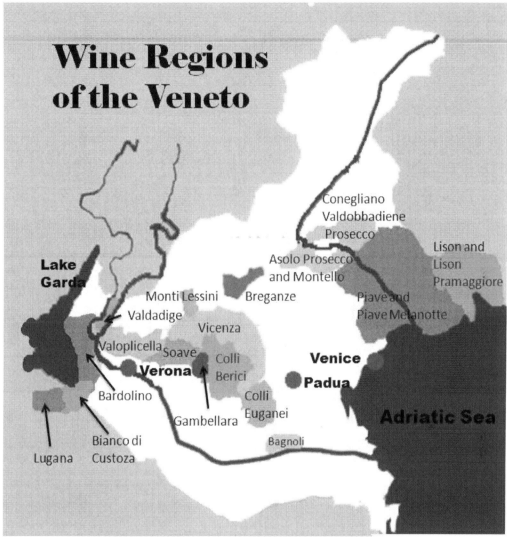

Wine map of the Veneto

The Veneto in Italy's northeast produces more wine than any other region, and a great deal of it is DOC and DOCG wine. Its most important wine is **Valpolicella** (the land of many cellars), which itself breaks down into a fine hierarchy of styles that includes Recioto, Ripasso and Amarone. The Valpolicella region is one of gravel soils east of Lake Garda, north of the city of Verona. Valpolicella is always a blend. The leader is Corvina, known for its bright cherry flavors and light color. Rondinella adds herbal flavors and aromas. Valpolicella is Italy's second most produced wine after Tuscany's Chianti.

- Garden variety **Valpolicella DOC** is a light wine, reminiscent of Beaujolais, showing the bright sour cherry notes of the Corvina contribution, with hints of blueberry and bananas.
- **Valpolicella Classico DOC** is made from grapes harvested in original section of the appellation, the hilly westernmost third.
- **Valpolicella Superiore DOC** is aged at least a year and has an alcohol content of at least 12%.
- **Amarone della Valpolicella DOCG** is a powerful, concentrated dry red wine made from dried grapes.
- **Recioto della Valpolicella DOCG** is a sweet dessert wine made from dried grapes, extremely rich and concentrated.
- **Valpolicella Superiore Ripasso DOC** is made with the grape skins that remain from the fermentation of Amarone or Recioto.

Bardolino sits between Lake Garda and Valpolicella, with the foothills of the Alps directly to its north, benefitting from cooling influence of both mountains and lake. This generally light wine is similar to Valpolicella in that its major grapes are Corvina and Rondinella. Bardolino has both Classico and Superiore designations.

Soave DOC, to the east of Valpolicella, is the Veneto's major white wine, produced from the Garganega grape (with up to 30% Chardonnay and Verdicchio). Soave is crisp, dry and fruity. It is produced in huge quantities and hence has had reputation problems. The Soave Superiore DOCG designation is an attempt to change this image problem. A classico zone exists. Neighboring **Gambellara** produces dry and sweet recioto white wines, also made from Garganega.

Bianco di Custoza DOC overlaps with the southern reaches of Bardolino, producing still white wines as well as the sparkling Bianco di Custoza Spumante, and sweet Bianco di Custoza Passito. All these wines are made from Trebbiano Toscano, Garganega, and the obscure Trebbianello, with possible additions of Cortese, Malvasia Bianca, Riesling Italico, Pinot Bianco, Chardonnay and Manzoni Bianco.

The vineyards of **Lugana** straddle the border between the Veneto and Lombardy. The region makes fruity, floral, spicy white wine from the Verdicchio grape, which thrives in its cool clay soils. Lugana also makes a red wine called Chiaretto with Groppello, Marzemino, Sangiovese and Barbera grapes.

Vicenza produces red wines from Merlot, Cabernet Sauvignon, Cabernet Franc, and Carménère (all French grapes), and whites from Garganega, Sauvignon Blanc, Riesling, Chardonnay, and Moscato, truly an international mix. Sub-alpine **Monti Lessini** to the north of Vincenza makes reds, whites, blends, Spumante (both white and pink) and sweet Passito from dried grapes. Single varietals include Garganega, Pinot Noir, Pinot Grigio, Pinot Bianco and Chardonnay. The still blends lead with either Merlot of Chardonnay. **Colli Berici** makes still wines from the same grape as Vicenza, and a bottle fermented *Spumante* sparkling wine from Chardonnay, Pinot Gris and Pinot Noir. It also uses Garganega as the base for *Frizzante*, *Spumante* and sweet *Passito* wine from dried grapes.

The **Colli Euganei** lies southwest of Padua on volcanic soil. The denomination produces a range of sweet Moscato-based wines, as well as whites and reds in still, Frizzante, and Spumante styles. Among red grapes, the Bordeaux varieties, including Carménère (rare in its home of Bordeaux), are planted. Whites include the internationals Sauvignon Blanc and Chardonnay. Nearby, the wines of **Bagnoli** include sparkling wines made from the local red Raboso grape, red wines from Raboso and Merlot, and rosés from Bordeaux blends.

Breganze stands by itself, conforming to no other Veneto regional heritage. The climate here is cool and the growing season short. Blended red wine here is led by Merlot, blended white by the grape that used to be called Tocai but is now called Friulano (also Tai) to differentiate it from the Hungarian Tokaji. Varietal reds are made from Pinot Nero, Marzemino, Merlot and Cabernet Sauvignon, each with a Riserva form, aged at least two years. Varietal whites are made from Vespaiolo, Chardonnay, Sauvignon, Pinot Grigio, Pinot Bianco and Friulano.

The **Prosecco** region, known for its light sparkling wine, stretches across a large area of northeastern Italy in the Veneto and the neighboring region of Friuli-Venezia Giulia. Prosecco is made from the grape now called Glera, but which many persist in calling Prosecco. Still Prosecco exists, but it is not exported. Sparkling Prosecco is made using the bulk charmat (or tank) method, resulting in two levels of fizz: Frizzante, which weighs in at a pressure level of about 2.5 atmospheres, and Spumante, with perhaps three atmospheres. By contrast, French Champagne generally has up to six atmospheres and Italian sparkling wines bottle fermented using the traditional method varies from three to six. Prosecco must be at least 85% Glera. The remainder may be the locals Bianchetta Trevigiana, Perera, Verdiso and Glera Lunga and the internationals Chardonnay and the three Pinots (Nero, Grigio, and Bianco). Following EU nomenclature, sweetness levels, from driest to sweetest, are Brut, Extra Dry, Dry and Demi-Sec.

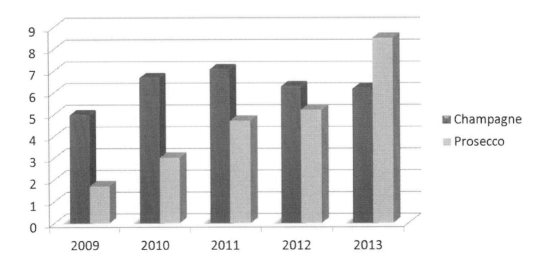

Annual Sales, Millions of Liters

The less expensive, less fussy Prosecco is successfully competing against Champagne in the sparkling wine market.

Given the huge area that may produce Prosecco, quality and consistency is always a concern. **Prosecco di Conegliano-Valdobbiadene DOCG** is a highly regarded Prosecco sub-district, as it the **Asolo Prosecco DOCG** (also known as **Colli Asolani**).

In addition to Prosecco, the **Montello e Colli Asolani** region produces still red and white wines from Chardonnay, Pinot Blanc, Cabernet Sauvignon, Carménère and Merlot as well as the locals Bianchetta and Manzoni Bianco. Montello (little mountain) also makes a foaming Spumante wine from Chardonnay and Pinot Bianco that we must distinguish from the same region's Glera-based Prosecco.

The **Piave DOC** is geographically the largest wine area in the Veneto, producing both blends and varietals. The lead red blend is Bordeaux style: both Cabernets and Carménère. Merlot, Carménère and the local Raboso are also produced as single red varietal wines. White varietals are Chardonnay, Verduzzo, Tai (Friulano), and the local Manzoni Bianco. Dried-grape Passito wines are made with Verduzzo and Raboso grapes. The **Piave Melanotte DOCG** was created in 2011 to promote varietal Red Raboso, which here must be 95% Raboso and be aged a minimum of three years.

Lison DOCG shares a corner of eastern Veneto with part of western Friuli-Venezia Giulia, and produces white wines from Friulano. The DOCG has a classico sub-zone. The **Lison-Pramaggiore DOC** offers still white wines from Chardonnay, Friulano, Pinot Bianco, Pinot Grigio, Sauvignon Blanc, and Verduzzo, as well as reds from Cabernet Franc, Cabernet Sauvignon, Carménère, Malbec, Merlot, Pinot Nero, and Refosco. Dessert wines made from the dried grape *Passito* method include Refosco (red) and Verduzzo (white). A sparkling Spumante wine is produced from Chardonnay, Pinot Bianco, and Pinot Nero.

The Wine Regions of Italy
Trentino-Alto Adige

Trentino-Alto Adige is the northernmost wine region in Italy. Northern reaches of the region have a significant German speaking population, the result of territorial accessions from Austria. The Trentino portion to the south is largely Italian, Alto-Adige in the north German. The Adige river system flows south through the region and accounts for most vineyard lands. The configuration of the mountain valleys encourages better sun exposure than one would expect for an alpine region.

Alto-Adige in the north, called SüdTirol by German speakers, has an extremely complex system of wine names, made all the more complex since each denomination has both a German and an Italian title. The **Alto Adige DOC** is an umbrella for them all, allowing a broad range of white grapes for the Valadige Bianco: Pinot Bianco, Pinot Grigio, Riesling Italico (Welschriesling), Müller-Thurgau, Chardonnay, Trebbiano, Nosiola, Sauvignon and Garganega. Red and rosés avail themselves of the local Enantio, Schiava, Lagrein and Teroldego varieties and international varieties Merlot, Pinot Noir, Cabernet Franc and Cabernet Sauvignon.

In Trentino, the **Trentino DOC** covers the region with a range of largely varietal wines made from local Schiava, Teroldego and Lagrein, as well as Chardonnay and Pinot Noir. One wine blends Cabernet Sauvignon, Cabernet Franc and Carménère. Cabernet and Merlot blends pay homage to Bordeaux. The white Trentino Bianco is majority Chardonnay and Pinot Bianco, with additions of Sauvignon Blanc, Müller-Thurgau and Manzoni Bianco.

Casteller DOC makes soft reds based on Merlot, Schiava, Lambrusco and Lagrein. **Teroldego Rotaliano DOC** in Adige specializes in red wine from 100% Teroldego.

Valdadige Terradeiforti DOC in Trentino produces three varietal wines: The deep red Enantio, the rustic red Casette and the ubiquitous Pinot Grigio. The reds, if aged, may be labeled Riserva, and the Pinot Grigio has a Superiore category.

Lago di Caldaro DOC (**Kalterersee DOC** in German), straddles Trentino and Alto-Adige surrounding Lake Caldaro. The region produces a prominent red from variants of the Schiava grape, which may see some minority participation by Pinot Noir and Lagrein. A sweet late-harvest version is produced.

Wine Regions of Friuli-Venezia Giulia

Austria

Prosecco

Ramandolo   Slovenia

Friuli Grave

Collio Orientali
del Friuli

Udine

Rosazzo   Collio Gorziano

Friuli Latisana   O Collio

Friuli
Aquileia

Lison-Pramaggiore   Friuli   Friuli Isonzo

Annia

Lison   Carso

Trieste

Gulf of Trieste

Wine Map of Friuli-Venezia Giulia

Friuli-Venezia Giulia encompasses the far north-eastern corner of Italy bordering Austria on the north, Slovenia to the east, the Veneto to the west and the Gulf of Trieste to the south. The north of the region is alpine, the south more Mediterranean, but most of Friuli-Venezia Giulia qualifies as cool climate. Friulano, also called Tai (after its former name of Tocai Friulano) is the region's signature white grape. Other indigenous whites include Verduzzo and Picolit. These see competition from international white grapes Sauvignon Blanc, Pinot Bianco, Riesling, and especially the hyper-popular Pinot Grigio.

Colli Orientali del Friuli and its neighbor **Collio Goriziano** have some of the most highly regarded hillside vineyards in the region. Sauvignon Blanc is the star grape here, in company with the local whites Friulano, Ribolla Gialla, Verduzzo and Picolit. The Picolit has its own denomination, **Colli Orientali del Friuli Picolit DOCG**. Refosco (a grape Friuli shares with nearby Slovenia and Croatia) is the lead red, followed by local Pignolo, and then the French invaders Merlot and both Cabernets. Within Colli Orientale del Friuli is the sub-zone **Rosazzo DOCG**, created in 2011 primarily for Friulano.

The **Friuli-Grave DOC**, named after its gravel soils, covers a large portion of the region, making white wines from Friulano, Chardonnay, Pinot Grigio and Sauvignon Blanc. **Friuli Aquileia DOC** and **Friuli Isonzo DOC** are similar.

Friuli Annia DOC produces red varietals from Cabernet Sauvignon, Cabernet Franc, Merlot and the local Refosco dal Peduncolo Rosso, and whites from Friulano, Pinot Bianco, Pinot Grigio, Verduzzo, Traminer and Chardonnay, as well as rosés and sparkling wines.

Friuli Latisana DOC makes varietal reds from Cabernet Sauvignon, Merlot and the local Refosco dal Peduncolo Rosso, whites from Pinot Grigio, Sauvignon Blanc, Chardonnay, Riesling, Pinot Bianco, Verduzzo, and Traminer, dried grape Passito wines and sparkling wines from both colors.

Carso DOC hugs the border with Slovenian Istria, producing floral reds from the Refosco grape and herbaceous whites from Malvasia.

Lison DOCG and **Lison Pramaggiore DOC** are discussed under Veneto, which shares the denomination. It should also be noted that Friuli-Venezia Giulia produces a great deal of **Prosecco**, also discussed under Veneto.

The Wine Regions of Italy
Emila-Romagna

Emila-Romagna has no problem proclaiming itself Italy's gastronomic hub (what with the wonders of Parma, Bologna, and Modena). The region takes up almost the full width of the Italian peninsula—just a thin bit of Liguria prevents it from having both an east and a west coast. The rolling hills of Emilia make up the western part, the flatter plains of Romagna the eastern. The region produces a great deal of wine to go with that Parmigiano Reggiano cheese, that Prosciutto di Parma, that Aceto Balsamico Tradizionale di Modena (balsamic vinegar), the endless varieties of cured meats (salumi), the tagliatelli Bolognese (and numberless other pastas), the local truffles, the chestnuts of Castel del Rio, the gelato, the pressed flatbread sandwiches called piadine—we could go on, but back to the wine.

About 15% of the wine in Emilia-Romagna comes under the DOC and DOCG designations. By contrast, in the Veneto, the proportion is 25%, and in Piemonte, it is 40%. Whites and reds are about equal here. We will look at the denominations of the region as they seem to slide in a great diagonal from, northwest to southeast.

Colli Piacentini DOC produces both red and white wines, as blends or single varietals from Cabernet Sauvignon, Pinot Nero, Barbera and Bonarda for reds, and Chardonnay, Malvasia di Candia, Pinot Bianco, Pinot Grigio and Pignoletto for whites. Colli Piacentini has four sub-zones: MonteRosso Val d'Arda, Trebbianino Val Trebbia, Val Nure and Vigoleno. All these zones produce both still and sparkling wine (Frizzante and Spumante), except for Vigoleno, which is known for is sweet Vin Santo style wines.

Colli di Parma DOC generates a range of still and sparkling wines from Cabernet Sauvignon, Cabernet Franc, Merlot, Pinot Nero, Barbera, Bonarda, Lambrusco Maestri and Sangiovese (for the reds) and Chardonnay, Sauvignon Blanc, Malvasia di Candia, Pinot Bianco, Pinot Grigio and Pignoletto (for the whites). Any of these grapes may be used for single varietal wines. Typical red blends are based on 25-40% Bonarda and Croatina. As for sparkling wines, *Spumante* and *Frizzante* styles are made from Malvasia, Chardonnay, Sauvignon Blanc and Pinot Bianco, or any of the red blends.

Colli di Scandiano e di Canossa DOC produces every style of wine, including four types of sparkling Lambrusco. The denomination makes varietal wines from the major international varieties and from locals Malvasia (di Candia), Spergola and Malbo Gentile.

Reggiano DOC makes sparkling red Lambrusco, dry reds from the local Ancellotta grape, and sparkling white wine. Reggiano is the largest of the five regions that produce Lambrusco. It has a reputation for sweet *amabile* and *dolce* versions of Lambrusco. These contain up to 15% partially fermented Ancellotta grapes for natural sweetness, with the remainder Maestri, Marani, Monstericco and Salamino Lambrusco grapes. The sweeter styles are lightly sparkling Frizzante, while the dry wines are darker and fuller bodied. A Bianco Spumante is also made from must fermented without stalks and skins. The rosato (rosé) style is made using some skin contact to let pigment ooze out into the juice.

Lambrusco Salamino di Santa Croce DOC makes wine from least 90% of the Lambrusco Salamino grape clone. The remainder can be Ancellotta and/or Brugnola. This is the most structured Lambrusco wine, made in dry and semi-sweet versions.

Lambrusco di Sorbara DOC is lightest in color among all Lambruscos and most delicate in aroma and flavor, with bright acidity and a strong mineral edge.

Lambrusco Grasparossa di Castelvetro DOC is produced from the Grasparossa Lambrusco grape that grows around Castelvetro di Modena. Darker than most Lambrusco, this wine has aromas of violets, black cherries, strawberries, and plums. It is fuller-bodied, more tannic, and higher in alcohol than most Lambruscos.

Reno DOC makes still and sparkling varietal wines from the local Montuni grape and from the better known Pignoletto. Its white blend is 40% Albana with Trebbiano, combined with an array of other local and international grapes.

Colli Bolognesi means literally "the hills of Bologna." This DOC makes varietal wines, defined as having at least 85% of the stated variety, using Merlot, Barbera and Cabernet Sauvignon for reds and Pignoletto, Pinot Bianco, Riesling Italico (Welschriesling), Sauvignon Blanc and Chardonnay for whites. **Colli Bolognesi Classico Pignoletto DOCG** applies to Pignoletto made in the delimited Classico zone.

Colli d'Imola DOC makes varietal wines from Barbera, Cabernet Sauvignon, Sangiovese, Chardonnay, Trebbiano and Pignoletto, with an 85% minimum rule.

Albana di Romagna DOCG is a white wine from the Albana grape. Sweetness levels are *secco*, *amabile*, and *dolce*. A sparkling version, *Romagna Albana Spumante*, can also be made but, only under the DOC classification. A dried grape Passito wine has quince and apricot notes, and many loyal devotees.

Colli di Faenza DOC produces reds from Cabernet Sauvignon, Merlot, Ancellotta, Ciliegiolo and Sangiovese, and whites from Chardonnay, Pinot Bianco, Trebbiano, Pignoletto and Sauvignon Blanc, both single varietals and blends.

Romagna DOC covers the eastern half of Emilia-Romagna for wines made from Albana, Cagnina, Pagadebit, Trebbiano and Sangiovese. The best quality, and for that matter quantity, is the Sangiovese, which comes in both Superiore and Riserva. The typical Romagna Sangiovese tastes of sour cherry, baked plum, herbs, and tobacco.

Colli di Rimini DOC has five major wine styles: a standard Rosso and Bianco, and three varietals. The Rosso wines are made from a blend of Sangiovese and Cabernet Sauvignon, similar to the 'Super Tuscans', while the Bianco counterpart is based on Trebbiano with Bianchello and/or Mostosa. The sparkling wines typical of Emilia-Romagna are not made in this easternmost denomination.

Bosco Eliceo DOC covers the coastal plains east of the city of Ferrara. Red varietals are made from Fortana (Brugnola) and Merlot. White blends are Bosco Eliceo Sauvignon (85% minimum Sauvignon Blanc) and Bosco Eliceo Bianco (70% or more Trebbiano Romagnolo).

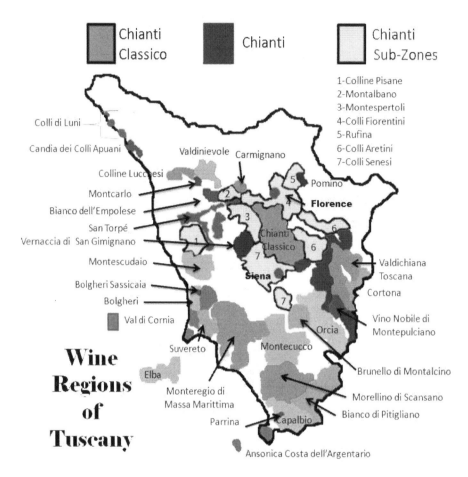

Wine Map of Tuscany

The map of **Tuscany** might seem a little daunting at first, but it becomes simpler if you consider than the vast majority of the colored spaces on the map grow some form of Sangiovese. The big three Sangiovese wines are Chianti, Brunello di Montalcino and Vino Nobile di Montepulciano. We view Tuscany as a romantic land of rolling hills dotted with picturesque villages, and it is just that. It is also a commercially important wine region, producing an array of fine wines, up to and including the so-called "Super Tuscans" (with which Cabernet Sauvignon is making major inroads). Tuscany is certainly not all Sangiovese and Cabernet—a number of white wines express themselves here, including Vernaccia di San Gimignano.

Tuscany has a range of climates. By the Tyrrhenian Sea the climate is Mediterranean and temperate, but inland, among the rolling hills, summer days are harsher and evenings cooler, a lovely environment in which to promulgate fine wine grapes.

The Sangiovese grape derives its name from the Latin sanguis Jovis, "the blood of Jove". In its epicenter of Tuscany, it tends to show sour red cherries, earthy aromas, and tea leaf notes, with medium-plus tannins, and high acidity. Sangiovese wine has two basic styles. One style is fruit forward, with red fruit like cherries and strawberries, a hint of tomato, spices like cinnamon and clove, bright acidity, medium to low tannins Another style is more rustic, showing dark chocolate and smoke with herbal notes like oregano and thyme, dried flowers, tomato, gripping tannins, highly acidic. Sangiovese has multiple clones (sub-varieties) and goes by a number of different Italian names.

We start with **Chianti**, the most widely produced wine in Italy (Valpolicella from the Veneto is number two). The center of all the fuss on the map, in terra cotta, is the Chianti Classico zone, a DOCG. This is the quality area originally delineated by Cosimo Medici III in the early 18th Century, which was in turn developed into a world-class wine by Barone Ricasoli in the late 19th century. Chianti quality fell in the late twentieth century, however, causing lowered standards and especially a drastic expansion of the Chianti regions. The stereotypical straw-covered flask of Chianti, called a *fiasco* in Italian, made a colorful candle holder, but the wine was not always that good. Chianti has dramatically improved and become more consistent in recent decades, rejecting the fiasco in favor of tall Bordeaux style bottles with high shoulders.

Note that Chianti Classico DOCG, although surrounded by Chianti DOCG, is a separate region and not a sub-zone of Chianti DOCG. That means that if a wine does not meet the standards of Chianti Classico DOCG it will not have the option of a demotion to Chianti DOCG, but must be labeled as IGP Toscana, the regional wine. The Chianti Classico people are dead serious about upholding their standards.

On the map, the numbered sections in yellow with black rims are the seven Chianti sub zones. Zone number 5, Chianti Rufina, is the most highly regarded but least represented on international wine store shelves because of its small production. Wines from the zones may label themselves as Chianti (zone) or just Chianti DOCG. The names of the zones are geographical descriptors. "Chianti Colli Fiorentini" as one example, simply means "Chianti from the Florentine Hills," Chianti Colli Senesi (from Siena), Chianti Colline Pisane (from near Pisa), etc. The maroon areas in the east of Tuscany denote plain old Chianti DOCG, regions of one time over-expansion. Note that Vino Nobile di Montepulciano (in green) is sandwiched in between two clumps of maroon, indicating that the denomination is also within the Chianti DOCG. In the same way, that other Sangiovese wine, the incomparable Brunello di Montalcino, is also part of the Chianti Colli Senesi sub-zone.

Riserva on a **Chianti** means that the wine spends a minimum of **two years** in oak and **three months** aging in the bottle, and has at least 12.5% alcohol.

Chianti does not have to be 100% Sangiovese (although it may be). The rule is 80% with up to 10% red Canaiolo and up to 20% of approved red grape varieties such as Cabernet Sauvignon, Merlot or Syrah. White grapes were once allowed, even mandated, in the Chianti blend, but they are no longer permitted.

Brunello di Montalcino DOCG is one of the most prestigious wines in all Italy, produced around the village of Montalcino near Siena in southern Tuscany. The wine is elegant, meant to age, garnet in color, with notes of berries, sweet vanilla and baking spices. "Brunello" means little dark one, and refers to the dark, big-berried clone of Sangiovese grown here, the Prugnolo Gentile. Sangiovese from this clone must account for 100% of the wine. The denomination rules are quite strict, not only for the type of grape but also regarding hillside vineyard placement, and other grape growing and winemaking procedures. Brunello must be aged four years, with at least two years in oak. The rules make for an exceptional wine, and an expensive one. **Rosso di Montalcino** is a less strictly produced (and less expensive) red wine requiring a shorter aging period.

In 2008, a scandal broke when prominent wine writers claimed that some Brunello producers were blending in other wines to make Brunello drinkable without the long wait (or to save money). An investigation followed. Although there was no health risk (as in the Barbera methanol scandal of 1985), Brunello took a reputational hit. Much Brunello had to be de-classified as table wine or IGT, commanding barely a fraction of its usual price. No one seems to have done any hard time because of this fraud...so far. The Italians called this episode "Brunellopoli" a reference to Tangentopoli, or "Bribesville", an Italian political scandal of the 1990s. American writers, of course, call it "Brunellogate."

Vino Nobile di Montepulciano DOCG is named after the *village* of Montepulciano and should not be confused with the *grape* called Montepulciano, to which this Sangiovese-based wine has no relation. (We will discuss the Montepulciano grape when we cover the region of Abruzzo.) The denomination is in southeast Tuscany, within the Chianti zone. Wine here has been produced since the age of the ancient Etruscans, before Rome, leading to a heyday of reputation during the late Middle Ages and early modern era. After a period of reputational suspended animation in the 19th and early 20th century, the DOC system brought this noble wine back into the limelight.

The same Prugnolo Gentile clone of Sangiovese used in Brunello must be used for Vino Nobile, but the wine need only be 70% Sangiovese, with allowed blending in of up to 20% Canaiolo and other local varieties. The wine must be aged at least 24 months, with at least a year in large oak casks rather than smaller barrels, to prevent too much oak influence. The medium-bodied wine is reddish brown, turning to brick over time, with plenty of red fruit—cherry, strawberry, plum—and a pleasant tannic tea-leaf finish.

Rosso di Montepulciano is a usually less expensive Sangiovese-based wine made under more relaxed rules.

The area also produces **Vin Santo di Montepulciano**, a sweet wine, in a white version from Malvasia Bianca, Trebbiano Toscano and Pulcinculo, and in a rosé from at least 50% Prugnolo Gentile (the same clone that produces the red wine).

Morellino di Scansano DOCG is a Sangiovese wine of Tuscany that is fighting for attention in the face of all the big players. The relatively large denomination sits in southern Tuscany, in the rolling hills overlooking the coast. Scansano is the village, and Morellino means "little dark one" referring to the Sangiovese grape. (Right—from another root word, "Brunello" has the same meaning). Viticulture here dates back to Etruscan times. The Sangiovese here is riper than the Chianti grapes further north, creating a crisp, fresh red wine with plum, cherry, pomegranate, leather, cedar and spice. The blend must contain 85% Sangiovese.

Carmignano DOCG sits north of the Chianti region, next to the Montalbano Chianti sub-zone on the eastern slopes of Monte Albano. This was one of the first regulated names in Italy, way before the DOC system came into being. Despite this, Carmignano spent decades as a Chianti Montalbano variant before winning its own non-Chianti denomination in 1975, becoming a full-fledged DOCG in 1990. Sangiovese must constitute at least 50% of the Carmignano blend, with up the 20% Canaiolo Nero and up to 20% each of Cabernet Sauvignon and Cabernet Franc. Uncharacteristically, the use of at least some of the Cabernet (either Sauvignon or Franc) is *mandated*—this is Cabernet that has thrived in the region for two hundred years.

Pomino DOC is a speck of a denomination in northwestern Tuscany nestled next to the Rufina Chianti sub-zone. Red Pomino accesses Canaiolo, Cabernet Franc, Cabernet Sauvignon and Merlot and must be aged for a year (two years for the Riserva). Pomino Bianco uses Pinot Bianco, Chardonnay and Trebbiano, bringing aromas of acacia, green apples and peaches.

Valdinievole DOC in the north produces a Rosso (red) from a minimum of 35% Sangiovese and Canaiolo Nero, and a white (Bianco) from a minimum of Trebbiano Toscano, as well as a sweet Vin Santo from a blend of Malvasia and Trebbiano.

The **Colline Lucchesi DOC,** takes its name from the hills to the north and east of the town of Lucca, in northwestern Tuscany. Its basic red blend is comprised of 45-70% Sangiovese with up to 30% Canaiolo and/or Ciliegiolo and up to 15% Merlot. It also produces varietal reds from Sangiovese or Merlot. The Bianco blend avails itself of Trebbiano Toscano, Greco Bianco, Vermentino and Malvasia Bianca, and white varietal wines depend on Vermentino or Sauvignon Blanc. The denomination also produces a sweet Vin Santo from dried grapes.

The **Candia dei Colli Apuani DOC** lies in northern Tuscany in the foothills of the Alpi Apuane. Vines here grow on the wind-sheltered lower slopes of the Apuani hills. Wine is produced in the towns of Massa, Carrara and Montignoso. The Ligurian grape Vermentino, said to originate in Spain, is grown here in both white and (rare) black forms. The black Vermentino is used for varietal red and rosé wines while the white Vermentino, at 70%, supports a blend with other Tuscan whites. Red and rosé blends are also produced from Sangiovese and Merlot. The **Colli di Luni DOC** to the immediate north of the Candia dei Colli Apuani is discussed in our section on Liguria, which shares the DOC with Tuscany.

Both **Montecarlo DOC** and the famous Monte Carlo in Monaco have the same meaning: the hill of Charles, but the Italian hill of Charles is named after 14th century Holy Roman Emperor Charles IV, while Monte Carlo refers to the 19th century Charles III of Monaco. The Italian hill makes wine. No surprises as to the grapes vinified here: the red blend must be 60% Sangiovese, to which may be added local grapes Ciliegiolo and Colorino, as well as Cabernet Franc, Cabernet Sauvignon and Merlot. White blends are 60% Trebbiano Toscano with additions of Sauvignon Blanc, Sémillon, Pinot Grigio, Pinot Bianco, Vermentino, or Roussanne. A Vin Santo is also produced from grapes allowed to dry on the vine.

Bianco dell'Empolese DOC (on our map, just to the left of the Montalbano Chianti subzone) is known for dry and Vin Santo white wines from the region's ever-popular Trebbiano Toscano. The dry whites are lightly aromatic, with notes of peach, apricot and white flowers. The tradition here is to drink the sweet golden Vin Santo with biscotti.

The squiggly **San Torpe DOC** near Pisa is relatively new to Tuscany. San Torpe makes rosé wines based on Sangiovese, and also white varietal wines from Trebbiano Toscano, Vermentino, and the French Sauvignon Blanc and Chardonnay. The Vin Santo is produced from Trebbiano Toscano and Malvasia Bianca Lunga.

North of Siena, the **San Gimignano DOC**, which produces the usual Sangiovese red blends, can also boast of Tuscany's only DOCG for white wine, the **Vernaccia di San Gimignano DOCG**. Vines here are planted on chalky sandstone soils at a minimum of 1700 feet above sea level. The delicious result is a dry, full-bodied, deeply-golden wine with seductive floral aromas, persistent acidity and a characteristic bitter finish. The local Vernaccia grape rules here. The Riserva version must be cellar aged (in oak or stainless steel) for at least one year. San Gimignano makes a white Vin Santo dessert wine from a blend of Vernaccia and Trebbiano Toscano, and a rosato (rosé) from Sangiovese.

Moving a shade to the south, the **Montescudaio DOC** produces varietal Sangiovese and Sangiovese-led blends, as well as varietal Cabernet Franc, Cabernet Sauvignon, Merlot, Chardonnay, Sauvignon Blanc and Vermentino wines. These varietals are a relatively new concept here. Trebbiano Toscano-based Vin Santo is also on the wine list here.

We move further south to the great disruptor of Tuscan vino-tranquility, the **Super Tuscans**, associated closely with the coastal **Bolgheri DOC**, and the enclave within it, the single vineyard **Bolgheri Sassicaia DOC**. The coast here is known as **the Maremma**. In the late 1960s the Super Tuscan came into being, especially the red wine called Sassicaia, "the place of many stones," referring to the region's gravel soil. These winemakers ignored local DOC regulations and began to make wines out of French grapes: Cabernet Sauvignon, Cabernet Franc and Merlot. Initially this prevented from their using prestigious DOC labeling on the wines, but the wines were of such quality that they commanded exceptional prices nonetheless. Knowing a good thing when it looked it in the face, the authorities created the two DOCs specifically allowing this wine style in 1994. The standout reds are deeply colored, age-worthy, concentrated with ripe fruit, elegant, with velvety tannins, lasting acidity, and memorable finishes. They are their own being, but one could rightly call them Bordeaux heritage with a Mediterranean soul. They do not in any way "taste French."

The Bolgheri DOC rules are broad. Bolgheri Rosso and Bolgheri Rosé may be made from 10 to 80% Cabernet Sauvignon, up to 80% Merlot, Sangiovese up to 70%, and other reds up to 30%. The Rosso must be aged two years.

For the Bolgheri Bianco blend, Trebbiano Toscano, Vermentino, and Sauvignon Blanc may comprise between 10 and70%, other local white grapes up to 30%. Sauvignon Blanc and Vermentino may also be released as single varietals following an 85% rule. The pink Vin Santo is made from Sangiovese, the white Malvasia, and other local red grapes, aged for 36 months.

The Bolgheri Sassicaia DOC rules are stricter: up to 85% Cabernet Sauvignon and a minimum of 15% Cabernet Franc, aged for 26 months.

Val di Cornia DOC has sections both south and east of Bolgheri. Val di Cornia Rosso qualifies for DOCG status. The wines have the fairly standard Tuscany configuration. Sangiovese must make up at least 40% of the Rosso and rosato wines, with Cabernet Sauvignon, Merlot and a number of other red grapes. Val de Cornia Bianco wines must be made up of least 50% Vermentino with Ansonica, Viognier, Trebbiano Toscano and Malvasia. The DOC allows varietal wines for its main red and white grape varieties. **Suvereto DOCG** was split off from Val di Cornia in 2011. Suvereto makes dry reds from Cabernet Sauvignon, Merlot, and Sangiovese. Both these denominations show the influence of nearby Bolgheri.

The coastal **Monteregio di Massa Marittima DOC** benefits from clay soils and sea breezes to produce a number of wine styles. Vermentino supports a single varietal and leads the Bianco blend with Trebbiano Toscano and Malvasia Bianca. These whites in turn are used for the white Vin Santo. The rosé Vin Santo is made from Sangiovese. Sangiovese accounts for a minimum of 80% of the rosato (rosé) and the Rosso (red) wines, with the usual addition of Cabernet Sauvignon.

The **Elba DOC** has been producing wine on the island of Elba since Roman times. It was the site of Napoleon's first brief exile, and his liked the wine. The top wine is a varietal white from the Ansonica grape, which also makes a sweet Passito version. The Elba Aleatico Passito red version merits its own DOCG, rare or sweet wines. The Rosso and Bianco blends are led by the usual Sangiovese and Trebbiano Toscano respectively. In addition, Elba makes a white varietal Muscat and a red varietal from Aleatico.

Montecucco DOC gives us rich wines with a ripe southern Tuscan flair from both Sangiovese and Trebbiano Toscano.

Capalbio DOC in the far south of Tuscany has many styles, including Spumante and Vin Santo as well as Rosso, Bianco and rosato, based on Sangiovese, Trebbiano and Vermentino. Capalbio overlaps most of the **Ansonica Costa dell'Argentario DOC**, which makes varietal wines from the white Ansonica grape.

Bianco di Pitigliano DOC also benefits from its southern location, growing grapes on extremely hilly land on porous volcanic soils. This Bianco starts with the unsurprising Trebbiano Toscano, with the local varieties Greco Bianco and Malvasia Bianca, as well as Sauvignon Blanc, Chardonnay and Viognier. Sparkling Spumante and sweet Vin Santo is also produced.

Moving up the eastern side of Tuscany, we find **Cortona DOC**, whose most prominent grape is — no, not Sangiovese, but the international variety Syrah. Most wines are varietals, either Syrah or Cabernet Sauvignon, Gamay, Merlot, Pinot Nero, and, of course, Sangiovese for the reds, and Chardonnay, Sauvignon Blanc, Riesling Italico (Welschriesling) and the natives Grechetto and Pinot Bianco for the whites..

Adjacent to Cortona is the **Valdichiana DOC.** Valdichiana Bianco must be at least 20% Trebbiano Toscano, with Chardonnay, Pinot Bianco, Pinot Grigio and Grechetto. Its Valdichiana Rosso must be at least 50% Sangiovese, with Cabernet Sauvignon, Merlot and Syrah, same for the rosato (rosé). Sparkling Valdichiana Spumante is made from the same grapes as the Bianco. The sweet Vin Santo is a joint effort of Trebbiano and Malvasia Bianca, a common combination in Tuscany.

Marche is pronounced Mar-Kay, with the stress on the first syllable. It is usually referred to as "the" Marche or **Le Marche** in Italian. It faces the Adriatic Sea to its east and is otherwise wedged between the regions of Emilia-Romagna and Abruzzo to the north and south respectively with Umbria to the west over the Apennine mountains. The vast majority of Marche wines sell as Vino di Tavola or as regional Indicazione Geografica Tipica IGT Marche, but the region does boast 15 DOCs and four DOCGs. Marche is best known for its whites from various sub-varieties of Trebbiano and from Verdicchio, which it claims as its own. **Verdicchio dei Castelli di Jesi DOCG** and **Verdicchio di Matelica DOCG** are two of its finest expressions, lively and herbaceous. Both are included in the much larger zone of **Esino DOC**, which produces a range of reds and whites from Sangiovese and Montepulciano for the reds and Verdicchio for the whites.

The local white grape Bianchello makes up at least 95% of the wine from the **Bianchello di Metauro DOC** in the Matauro river valley. Pecorino, Pinot Bianco and Malvasia Toscana are also widely planted.

Sangiovese and Montepulciano are Italy's top two producing red grapes, and Le Marche produces them both in abundance, the most prominent denomination being **Rosso Conero DOC** and **Rosso Conero Riserva DOCG**, where they blend with Ciliegiolo, Pinot Nero, Lacrima di Morro and Vernaccia Nera, the "black" Vernaccia to produce full-bodied tannic wines. This black Vernaccia is used for the red sparkling wine **Vernaccia di Serrapetrona DOCG**, which, unusually, undergoes three fermentations: the first of regularly harvested grapes, the second of dried grapes, the third in tanks using the Charmat (Martinotti) method. The result is mouth-watering intense red fruit. **Terreni di Sanseverino DOC** also makes wine from Vernaccia Nera (at least 50%) blended most commonly with Sangiovese and Montepulciano.

Lacrima di Morro d'Alba DOC produces dry and sweet Passito wine using the red Lacrima di Morro, meaning "teardrops from the town of Morro d'Alba." These wines undergo a second fermentation in which the must (or juice) of partially dried grapes is added to the mix. Most are 100% Lacrima grapes, but they are allowed up to 15% Montepulciano or Verdicchio (yes…a white grape).

The **Colli Maceratesi DOC** is a vast region producing white wines from the local Maceratino grape and reds primarily from Sangiovese.

The **Offida DOC** around the town of Offida produces reds (from mostly Montepulciano, with Cabernet Sauvignon), and Vin Santo (from the Passerina grape). Two varietal white wines qualify for the higher level **Offida DOCG**: Pecorino and Passerina, both Marche natives. The Pecorino is gaining a reputation for dry, mineral-rich wines, with floral aromas of jasmine and acacia, a certain spiciness, and firm acidity that is friendly with food.

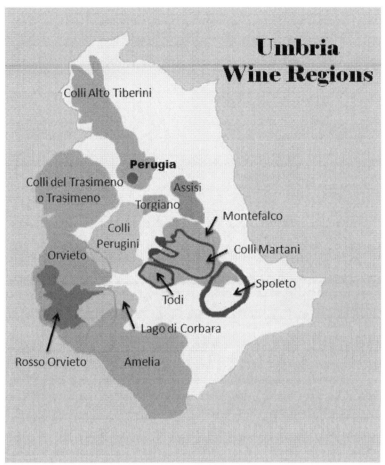

Wine Map of Umbria

Umbria is Italy's only region that does not border either a foreign country or a sea. This is the heart of Italy, a country of rolling hills among craggier heights. Long a second fiddle to the vinous magnificence of its Tuscan neighbor to the west, Umbria has in recent years seen an upswing in quality wine production, largely as the result of modern winemaking techniques and equipment. Sangiovese is the principal red here, but the local Sagrantino, Cabernet Sauvignon, Merlot and Pinot Noir are making inroads. Among whites, a cutting edge Chardonnay is barrel fermented with Umbria's own white grape Grechetto.

Assisi DOC is most famous not for its wine but as the birthplace of Saint Francis of Assisi, the patron saint of Italy itself. Production is small here. The white Assisi Bianco blend is 50-70% Trebbiano, with 10–30 Grechetto, and a maximum or 40% from other white grapes. Assisi also has a varietal Grechetto, requiring a minimum of 85% of that grape. The Rosso (red) blend is Sangiovese blended with Merlot.

The **Todi DOC** is a 21st century creation. Bianco blends are 50% Grechetto, Rosso blends led by Sangiovese. Sangiovese, Merlot, and Grechetto are also released as varietals following an 85% content rule. These varietals each have a more formidable Superiore version, as well as a dried grape Passito version.

Lago di Corbara DOC benefits from its namesake lake, created artificially when the Tiber River was dammed in the 1950s. The resulting reservoir proved beneficial for viticulture, the area having been previously too dry. Unbound by convention, the new winemakers here took to producing Cabernet Sauvignon, Merlot, and Pinot Noir. The denomination is red wine only.

The **Orvieto DOC** is Umbria's best known, and it is white wine only. The area is characterized by volcanic tufo rock, out of which wine cellars are dug. Trebbiano Toscano and Grechetto must make up 60% of the Bianco finished blend, finished primarily with Canaiolo Bianco and Malvasia Toscana. Like Chianti, Soave, and Valpolicella, the DOC has a *classico* zone around the town of Orvieto.

Orvietano Rosso DOC is a separate DOC representing the reds from the Orvieto region, which produces both blends and single varietals from an extremely broad array of Italian grapes (Montepulciano, Sangiovese, Aleatico, Canaiolo Rosso and Ciliegiolo) and their French rivals (Cabernet Franc, Cabernet Sauvignon, Merlot and Pinot Nero).

Colli Altotiberini DOC means "high hills over the Tiber." As usual, Trebbiano and Sangiovese lead the blends, with varietal wines from Grechetto, Trebbiano, Cabernet Sauvignon, Merlot and Sangiovese.

The **Colli del Trasimeno DOC** is east of Perugia around Lake Trasimeno. Wines here come in every style and color, blends and single varietals. The same can be said for the **Torgiano DOC** just south of Perugia and west of Assisi.

The **Colli Perugini DOC** south of Perugia takes its name from that major Umbrian city, producing the full range of wines, still, sweet, and sparkling, including a highly regarded Vin Santo from semi-dried, pressed Grechetto or Malvasia grapes. Sangiovese leads the red and rosé wines. The Spumante must be at least 80% Grechetto, Chardonnay, Pinot Bianco, Pinot Nero and/or Pinot Grigio.

Montefalco DOC produces no varietals, and just two blends. The Rosso is composed of 70% Sangiovese, helped by the region's own red grape, Sagrantino. The dry Bianco is a minimum of 50% Grechetto, up to 35% Trebbiano Toscano, finished with up to 15% other local varieties. **Sagrantino di Montefalco DOCG** was established in 1992, to support and recognize the powerful tannic Sagrantino grape. The wines must be 95% Sagrantino. The dry Sagrantino must be aged at least 30 months, at least 12 months in oak barrels. The denomination also produces a sweet Passito Sagrantino, made from dried grapes, also subject to the thirty month aging requirement.

Colli Martani DOC blazes no new trails: its Bianco is based on Trebbiano and Grechetto. These can be made into varietal wines as can Chardonnay, Sauvignon Blanc, Riesling and Vernaccia. Sangiovese leads the reds. This, Montepulciano and Merlot can be single varietal red wines. A sub-variety of Grechetto called **Grechetto di Todi** is known for its low yield and concentrated flavors, and is so highly regarded that when it is used as a blending component or single varietal its name may be added to wine labels from the region.

Amelia DOC, formerly known as the Colli Amerini DOC, is so well known for its olive oil that viticulture was neglected for many years. Local wines were rustic and consumed within the area. The awarding of a DOC in 1989 changed all that. Principal white grapes here are Grechetto, Malvasia, and Trebbiano. Reds are the local Ciliegiolo, Merlot, and Sangiovese.

Spoleto DOC in the south east of Umbria is known for its white wines, principally from Trebbiano Spoletino. Spoleto produces a Bianco blend, varietal Trebbiano, sparkling Spumante and sweet dried grape Passito.

The Wine Regions of Italy
Lazio

Lazio is Rome's region, once the center of empire, and heir to a wine tradition that goes back millennia. Over 200 grape varieties call Lazio home. Lazio's volcanic hills feature tufo and lava soil that is rich in potassium, an excellent environment for white wine production. Major white grapes include Trebbiano and Malvasia di Candia. The light, acidic wines are designed to drink young, the acidity cutting through the rich meats and sauces characteristic of the substantial local cuisine. Reds are made from the ubiquitous top two of central Italy—Sangiovese and Montepulciano—as well as Cesanese, Merlot, Nero Buono di Coro, Canaiolo and Ciliegiolo.

Est! Est!! Est!!! di Montefiascone DOC north of Rome has perhaps the most unusual wine name in the country. The story behind it is this: in the 12th century, a German bishop on his way to Rome to meet the Pope would send his prelate up ahead to scout out the best inns for wine. The prelate would chalk the Latin word "Est," meaning "it is," on the doors of the most promising inns in this regard. At Montefiascone the prelate liked the wine so much that he wrote *Est! Est!! Est!!!* on the door, giving the wine its present name. Or so the story goes (they did not have CCTV in those days so it is hard to substantiate). Most critics give this high acid, apple-tasting white wine low points beyond its touristic value (which accounts for nearly all its consumption). It is mostly Trebbiano Toscano with Malvasia Bianca and the local Trebbiano Giallo.

In the north, Lazio shares the **Orvieto DOC** with Umbria for white Trebbiano Toscano and Grechetto. **Aleatico di Gradoli DOC** is a red wine denomination producing wines from the Aleatico grape, as well as white grapes destined for Est! Est!! Est!!! **Colli Etruschi Viterbesi DOC** (known locally as Tuscia) produces Rosso blends from Sangiovese and Montepulciano, Bianco blends from Trebbiano and Malvasia, and varietal wines from Merlot, Sangiovese, Montepulciano, Trebbiano and Moscato Bianco. Growers here also contribute to Est! Est!! Est!!!

The **Cesanese del Piglio DOCG** is Lazio's only DOCG wine. The red Cesanese grape, native to Lazio, ripens quite late, but if the grower sees the long season through, the reward is an earthy red wine with bright red cherry fruit, floral notes and some red pepper. Cesanese del Piglio must be made from at least 90% Cesanese grapes. Most of these wines are dry, but semi-sweet and fully sweet versions are also produced. The **Cesanese di Affile DOC** nearby produces Cesanese wines on less prestigious terrain.

Castelli Romani DOC stretches over the fourteen villages in the hilly region southeast of Rome. The area has a cooler climate than the plains below it. Vines here grow in high-yielding and fertile volcanic soils. Whites, mostly still and dry, are made from the classic blend of central Italy: Trebbiano and Malvasia, reds from the equally classic Sangiovese and Montepulciano combination.

Frascati DOC is one of the fourteen Castelli Romani villages. The wine dates back to ancient Rome, it was extremely popular during the Renaissance, and became the "with it" wine for the *La Dolce Vita* people in the 1960s. Quality gave way to quantity after that, but the wine is once again on an upswing with the application of modern techniques. The basis for Frascati is the familiar Trebbiano and Malvasia, with dollops of indigenous Greco Bianco and Bombino Bianco. Additional grapes, including Chardonnay and Sauvignon Blanc, are permitted up to 30%. The Frascati Superiore and the Cannellino di Frascati, a sweet dessert wine, both qualify for DOCG labeling.

Marino DOC, although next to Frascati, has a climate better influenced by the sea. Its white wine is produced in a manner similar to Frascati, but it has a more concentrated quality.

The Wine Regions of Italy
Abruzzo

Abruzzo covers a chunk of central Italy between across the Apennines from Lazio to the west with the Adriatic Sea to the east. Sixty percent of this region consists of national parks, in which the intrepid explorer can find Gran Sasso, at 9500 feet, one of Italy's highest mountains. From the sea into the mountains, climate and terrain vary a great deal. Cool air from both the mountains and the sea accounts for excellent diurnal temperature swings, beneficial for the region's two dozen species of olives as well as for Abruzzo's grapevines. The gently tannic red Montepulciano grape is king here, accounting for two thirds of production, followed by the two whites Trebbiano and Pecorino, which together account for a further quarter. Cooperatives make 80% of Abruzzo's wine.

Montepulciano d'Abruzzo Colline Teramane DOCG is the region's sole DOCG. The Teramo hills are located between Gran Sasso National Park and the Adriatic. This is a complex red wine that combines earthy-ness with a smooth delivery, reminiscent of a good red Burgundy. Montepulciano must be at least 90% with a possible 10% Sangiovese. The wine must be aged two years, three for Riserva. This area offers a rather special treat. A local winery maintains a wine fountain for pilgrims taking the Cammino di San Tommaso, a trek from Rome to Ortona on the Adriatic where the bones of St. Thomas are said to be housed.

The **Montepulciano d'Abruzzo DOC** covers the entire coast of Abruzzo to a depth of twenty miles inland, a vast area that supports much production. A good deal of this deeply colored gently tannic low acidity easy drinking wine is exported. The wine must be 85% Montepulciano. The most common blending partner is Sangiovese. In the dead center of this DOC, the **Villamagna DOC** specializes in Montepulciano.

Trebbiano d'Abruzzo DOC, as the name implies, specializes in white wine made from the Trebbiano grape. The zone covers exactly the same area as the Montepulciano d'Abruzzo DOC. A combination of Trebbiano Toscano or Trebbiano d'Abruzzo must make up 85% of this wine. The remainder may be the locals Cococciola, Passerina and the more international white Malvasia.

Controguerra DOC is an area in northern Abruzzo that sees innovation in the face of so much tradition. The DOC produces (85%) varietal wines from Cabernet Sauvignon, Chardonnay, Ciliegiolo, Malvasia, Merlot, Trebbiano Toscano, Moscato Amabile, Passerina, and Pinot Nero. The tannic Rosso blend leads with Montepulciano and usually rounds it out with Cabernet Sauvignon and Merlot. The dry fruity Bianco blend is largely Trebbiano Toscano and Passerina, with little international element. The sparkling whites vary in composition depending on their intensity of bubbles. The Bianco Frizzante is similar to the Bianco blend, while the more forceful Spumante mixes Trebbiano Toscano (60–85%) with Chardonnay, Verdicchio and/or Pecorino. Controguerra red Passito from dried grapes is often 100% Montepulciano. The white Passito relies on Trebbiano Toscano, Malvasia, and Passerina. If either red or white Passito is barrel aged at least 30 months it earns the title of "Annoso,"

The **Cerasuolo d'Abruzzo DOC** creates a cherry-colored wine (cerasuolo means cherry), lighter in color than standard Montepulciano, by limiting grape skin contact during fermentation. The resulting wines are also fruitier and less tannic. While other grapes are allowed, most Cerasuolo d'Abruzzo is 100% Montepulciano. Theoretically, this wine can be made anywhere in Abruzzo, but most is produced in the low-lying south east of the region.

The Wine Regions of Italy
Molise

Small, mountainous **Molise** does not get much attention as a wine region (even though it has a wine history as old as any other on the peninsula). Located on the Adriatic coast between major producers Abruzzo and Puglia, it was politically part of Abruzzo until 1963. Molise has three DOCs, all of which overlap to some extent.

The **Biferno DOC** makes white blends with Trebbiano Toscano (65–70%) accompanied by Bombino (25–30%) and Malvasia (5–10%). The reds and rosés are largely the familiar Montepulciano.

The **Pentro di Isernia DOC** produces whites from similar constituents as Biferno but uses up to 55% Sangiovese for reds and rosés, as well as the local Tintilia.

The **Tintilia del Molise DOC** was approved only in 2011 (30 years after the other two), producing a varietal red from the local Tintilia grape.

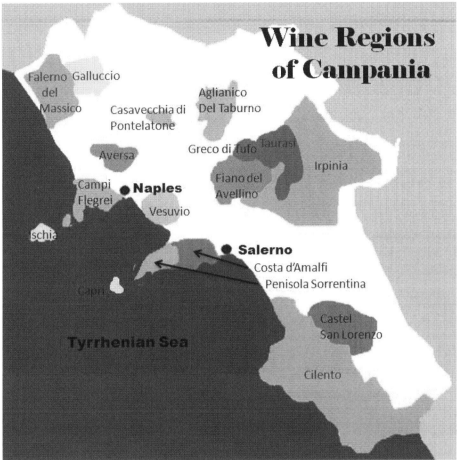

Wine map of Campania

Campania signifies that we are coming to the south of Italy. Centered around the great city of Naples, Campania is Italy's most densely populated area. Campania's wine roots pre-date Rome, stretching back to the Greek colonial period, where the region was part of *Magna Graecia*. The name Campania derives from the Latin term *Campania felix*, meaning fertile countryside. Many of the soils are richly volcanic—from the same volcanic activity that buried the storied city of Pompeii in 79 AD. Agriculture and food are the major industries of Campania. Fruit, vegetables, and flowers are prominent, as well as the two often-found Mediterranean partners, the olive tree and the grape vine.

Now that we are in Italy's south, the grapes change. The big central-Italian trio of Sangiovese, Montepulciano and Trebbiano starts to appear more sparsely, as do international varieties like Cabernet Sauvignon and Merlot. From this point on, indigenous southern Italian grapes speak their wisdom in the wine. One of the most impressive is the tannic red Aglianico (originally a Greek grape), found in the denominations Taurasi and Aglianico del Taburno. There is the white Fiano, grown for two millennia, in Fiano di Avellino. The white Greco di Tufo means, literally, "A Greek of the volcanic soil called tufo." Many other local grapes of both colors express themselves in Campania's numerous districts. We shall cover the denominations of Campania starting in the north and working our way south.

Falerno del Massico DOC claims a link to Falernum, the most prestigious wine of ancient Rome. We do not have samples of the Roman beverage, but know that it was a sweet white wine produced from the grape we call Greco (Greek) today. The Falerno of today is produced in a white version, from the aromatic Falanghina grape, and a red version, vinfiied from Aglianico and PiediRosso with help sometimes from Barbera and Primitivo (the Italian version of the Zinfandel grape). **Falerno del Massico Primitivo** is a single varietal wine made from 85% Primitivo.

Galluccio DOC stands on volcanic soils, producing Rosso and rosato wines from Aglianico. The grape ripens late, and is sometimes harvested as late as November, by which time its insistent tannins have relaxed. It thrives, however, in this distinctly southern climate. The Bianco is made from a minimum of 70% Falanghina.

Aglianico del Taburno DOCG is a tannic red wine from the mountains of Taburno, in the northern section of the Campanian interior. The growing season is long enough for Aglianico, with elevation and mountain breezes slowing down ripening and preserving acidity.

Casavecchia di Pontelatone DOC is a fairly new DOC, created in 2001, producing wines from the red Casavecchia grape. The grape (whose name means "old house") is extremely rare. Today's few acres of vines are said to be the offspring of a single cutting, rescued from the ruins of a vineyard in the town of Pontelatone. This tannic wine, redolent of dried herbs, black fruit and leather, began its resurrected life as a blending component, but winemakers are starting to produce it as a varietal wine, aged a minimum of two years, one year in barrel.

Aversa Asprinio DOC produces white wines only from the Asprinio grape, also called Greco Bianco, on the northwestern side of Naples. The growing area used to be larger but the city has swallowed chunks of it. The still white wine must be 85% Asprinio, the sparkling wine, which predominates, 100% Asprinio.

Campi Flegrei DOC, on the breathtaking Campanian coast just north of Naples, is closely associated with the Falanghina grape. Here the soils are volcanic, well draining, and mineral rich, resulting in a fragrant white wine, full bodied, with delicate fruit and layers of texture. The lead red is the interesting PiediRosso grape, bringing wine with plenty of dark fruit, lasting tannins balanced with equally ambitious acidity.

Ischia DOC refers to the island of Ischia, most of whose vineyards sit on terraces at altitudes of 600 plus feet. Ischia has its own white variety, Biancolella, which accounts for nearly half of production. Unusually, these vines are harvested using a special trolley that ruins on a monorail, moving up and down the steep slopes from terrace to terrace. The Bianco blend is primarily Biancolella and Forastera, while the red blend is led by Guarnaccia and PiediRosso. Biancolella, Forastera, and PiediRosso are released as single varietals, as is a PiediRosso Passito. A sparkling wine is made from Biancolella and Forastera. The vineyards here are menaced by resort development.

Vesuvio DOC bears the name of the volcano that destroyed Pompeii and Herculaneum and that still threatens modern day Naples (they have—good luck with this—evacuation plans). Soil here is understandably volcanic. The denomination has an additional designation **Lacryma Christi del Vesuvio DOC**, meaning "the tears of Christ on Vesuvius," applying to wines with higher levels of alcohol. White wines lead with a local grape called Coda di Volpe (fox's tail) or the more widely planted Verdecca grape, with possible contributions from Falanghina or Greco di Tufo grapes. The same grapes are used for a fortified white liquoroso wine, which has dry and sweet versions. Reds are primarily PiediRosso helped by Aglianico. The term "Tears of Christ" refers to the tears Jesus shed (one possibility) over Lucifer's fall from heaven, or (another possibility) because of the sheer beauty of the area. The tears fell to earth and animated the vines.

Fiano di Avellino DOCG, one of Campania's quality leaders, refers to the white Fiano grape that grows in the vicinity of Avellino. The ancient name for the region is "Apianum" (realm of the bees), which may appear on the label. The flagship wine here is a dry white varietal (85%) Fiano, with possible partnering from Greco, Coda di Volpe Bianca and/or Trebbiano. The mineral-rich wine is nutty and citrusy, with persistent acidity that allows it to age well for up to a decade.

Greco di Tufo DOCG is the modern equivalent of a wine that has been extant in Campania since well before the time of Christ. This is high altitude wine (1300 to 1600 feet), grown on sulfur-rich volcanic soil, which brings out a fine minerality. The grapes get a break from the hot summer sun every evening at this altitude, retaining their acidity over a long ripening season. Both still and Spumante wines must be a minimum 85% Greco di Tufo, with a maximum of 15% Coda di Volpe. The Spumante is metodo classic (second fermentation in bottle), and lees aged for 36 months.

Taurasi DOCG is a high altitude red from a minimum of 85% Aglianico (with PiediRosso, Sangiovese and/or Barbera). Soils here are mixed volcanic, calcareous, and limestone, all combining to give many layers to this richly tannic wine, with characteristic notes of red berries, plums, coffee and leather, all of which fan out into subtle layers with age.

Irpinia DOC includes within its borders the three prestigious DOCGs of Greco di Tufo, Taurasi and Fiano di Avellino. Irpinia in its own right produces white wines from Coda di Volpe, Falanghina, Fiano, and Greco, and reds from Aglianico, PiediRosso, and Sciascinoso.

Costa d'Amalfi DOC covers red, white and rose wines produced along the incomparable tourist haven of the Amalfi Coast. Vineyards in this steep terrain are widely terraced and need to be maintained with specialized equipment. White grapes include Biancolella, Chardonnay, Cococciola, Falanghina, Montonico Bianco, Passerina, and Pecorino, reds Aglianico, PiediRosso, and Sciascinoso. The villages of Furore, Ravello and Tramonti are the most widely esteemed (and have the right to add their village names to wine labels). The region has consistently resisted the call for adding international grapes, despite its international tourist clientele.

Penisola Sorrentina DOC (the Sorrento Peninsula) has a temperate maritime climate. The area has three distinct sub-zones. Gragnano and Lettere produce sparkling red wines largely from PiediRosso (with Aglianico and Sciascinoso). Sorrento is known for dry reds (from the same grapes as the others) and whites led by Falanghina (with Biancolella and Greco Bianco).

Capri DOC is the wine personality of that famous island. All its grapes are Campania natives. Capri Rosso must be 80% PiediRosso. Bianco is a mix of Falanghina and/or Greco. Tourist development is rapidly bulldozing much of Capri's vine growing areas.

Castel San Lorenzo DOC in southern Campania breaks the local grape tradition, producing Rosso and rosato wines from Barbera (60-80%) and Sangiovese (the remainder), and whites from Trebbiano and Malvasia. The denomination also makes sparkling Spumante and dessert wines from the Moscato grape.

Southerner **Cilento DOC** produces whites from Fiano (with Greco, Malvasia, and Trebbiano) and reds from Aglianico and Sangiovese, with some Primitivo. A poor region without a tourist economy, Cilento puts more effort into olive groves than into vineyards.

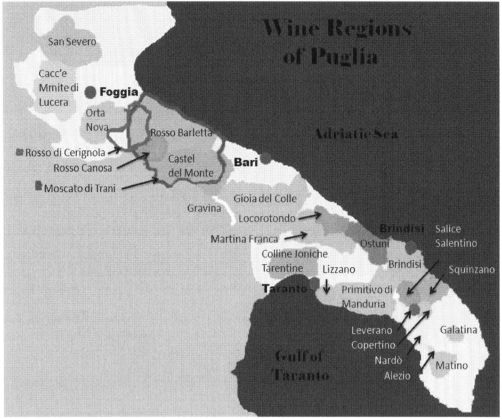

Wine Map of Puglia

Puglia is often called the heel of the Italian boot, but if we take a look we see that this large region is more fittingly called the heel and the spur. North-south oriented Puglia looks out to the Adriatic Sea on its entire eastern length and to the Gulf of Taranto on part of its west, giving it the longest coastline of any of the Italian regions. In English it is sometimes referred to as "Apulia." Puglia is flatter than most of the rest of Italy. Although only the seventh largest of the twenty regions in Italy, it stands number two in both grape and wine production (after the Veneto), but leads the country in olive oil production. A cursory look at our Puglia wine map would lead to the conclusion that grapevines and olive trees necessarily coexist, as they often do in the Mediterranean. As to the wine, for generations it was cheap and red, but the international market is demanding better quality, and the Puglians are listening. Puglia has 28 DOCs and four DOCGs.

Puglia's two leading red grapes, Primitivo and Negroamaro (also written as Negro Amaro), account for a solid two-thirds of all plantings. Primitivo is genetically identical to California's Zinfandel grape, but the sub-varieties (clones) differ from hundreds of years of separation. Both derive from the Croatian Crljenak Kaštelanski grape. Primitivo and Zinfandel also differ greatly in how they are handled. Californians let Zinfandel ripen to high sugar levels, bringing high alcohol, low acid and riper, gentler tannins, for a smooth fruity wine. The Puglians pick the grapes earlier, at lower sugar levels, bringing lower alcohol, higher acidity and more expressive tannins, an entirely different wine style. Nevertheless, given the popularity of Zinfandel, you will see Puglian wine labels with "Zinfandel" emblazoned under the "Primitivo." Note that Primitivo does not mean "primitive," but rather refers to the fact that the grape ripens early.

We will begin at the spur and work our way down to the lower heel.

San Severo DOC was Puglia's first. It looks north for its grapes, basing its Rosso on a minimum 70% Montepulciano with Sangiovese, Malvasia Nera, and Merlot. Whites (in this red wine learning area of the world) are based on Trebbiano and Bombino Bianco.

In looking at **Cacc'e Mmitte di Lucera DOC**, we must first explain its odd name, but we cannot, due to the fact that too many stories exist and none are able to be substantiated. The robust, highly tannic red wine here comes to us from the very local (and very obscure) Uva di Troia grape, which leads blends, helped by Malvasia Nera, Montepulciano and/or Sangiovese as well as a number of permitted white grapes : Trebbiano Toscano, Bombino Bianco and/or Malvasia del Chianti

The wines of **Orta Nova DOC**, all red or rosé, are produced from Sangiovese helped by Uva di Troia and Montepulciano, with up to 10% from the white grapes Lambrusco Maestri and Trebbiano.

Rosso di Cerignola DOC and **Rosso Barletta DOC** both produce red wine from the local Uva di Troia with partners Negroamaro, Sangiovese, Montepulciano and even some Malbec. The nearby **Rosso Canosa DOC** is similar.

The red wines of **Castel del Monte DOC** are based on Uva dei Troia, this time with Aglianico for support and some Bombino Nero. Three wines in this promising area have been nominated for DOCG status: Castel del Monte Bombino Nero, Castel del Monte Nero di Troia Riserva and Castel del Monte Rosso Riserva.

Moscato di Trani DOC produces white wines from Moscato Bianco, the Italian version of Muscat Blanc à Petit Grains.

The rolling hills of the **Gravina DOC** give it an excellent climate for producing some of Puglia's best white wines from Malvasia Bianca, Greco Bianco and Bianco di Alessano.

Robust red wines are the calling card of the **Gioia del Colle DOC**. Primitivo leads the blend with at least 60% with up to 40% Negroamaro, Sangiovese and Montepulciano, individually or as a blend, and up to 15% Malvasia Nera.

The **Locortondo DOC** is one of the oldest in Italy, a karst region with limestone soils. This is primarily white wine territory from the hyper-local Verdecca and Bianco d'Alessano grapes. These two grapes plus Fiano can be single varietal wines. Wines are both still and sparkling. The nearby **Martina Franca DOC** produces similar white wines.

Colline Joniche Tarantine DOC is an up and coming region trying its hand at international varieties, creating a Cabernet Sauvignon-led red blend and a Chardonnay-led white blend, with varietals from Primitivo and Verdeca.

Lizzano DOC is a coastal region just south of Taranto. It is completed enclosed in the larger Primitivo di Manduria DOC. Lizzano makes whites, reds, rosatos, and sparkling wines. The leading red grape is Puglia's own Negroamaro, which gets support from Bombino Nero, Montepulciano, Pinot Nero, Sangiovese, and Malvasia Nera. Whites are Trebbiano based. Varietal wines may be made from Malvasia Nera and Negroamaro.

Primitivo di Manduria DOC is Primitivo's core area. This is dark, tannic wine that needs some aging to precipitate out some of the grape's characteristic bitterness. The vine-dried sweet **Primitivo di Manduria Dolce Naturale DOCG**, Puglia's first DOCG, weighs in at 8% sugar.

The **Brindisi DOC**, part of which is urban, specializes in the tannic red Negroamaro for full-bodied wines with baked dark fruit. Up to 30% Malvasia Nera or Montepulciano and up to 10% Sangiovese may factor into the mix.

The **Ostuni DOC** leads its Bianco blend with the local Impigno grape, filling it in with the equally local Francavilla for a light aromatic wine that does best in cooler vintages. Ostuni has a red side also, producing floral and spicy rosés from Ottavianello, the local name for the Cinsault grape of France.

We move to the southern realm of Puglia's other red grape, Negroamaro, meaning literally "bitter black."

Salice Salentino DOC is the flagship Negroamaro specialist. Rosso and rosato are minimum75% Negroamaro with Malvasia Nera or Aleatico as usual partners in the blend. Aleatico (85%) and Negroamaro (90%) are produced as varietals. The white blend is 70% Chardonnay with varietal Chardonnay, Pinot Bianco, and Fiano also offered. Spumante can be made from any of the whites or from Negroamaro. Several Aleatico-based sweet and fortified wines are also produced. **Leverano DOC** is similar. **Squinzano DOC** makes wines similar to Salice Salentino and Leverano, but with no sweet or fortified wines. **Copertino DOC** has a simple structure: just reds and rosés from minimum 70% Negroamaro, maximum 30% Malvasia Nera, Montepulciano, and/or Sangiovese (maximum 15% Sangiovese). **Nardò DOC** makes reds and rosés from minimum 80% Negroamaro; maximum 20% Malvasia Nera di Brindisi, Malvasia Nera di Lecce, and/or Montepulciano. In **Alezio DOC** the proportions are minimum 80% Negroamaro; maximum 20% Malvasia Nera, Sangiovese, and/or Montepulciano. **Matino DOC**: 70% Negroamaro; maximum 30% Malvasia Nera and/or Sangiovese. Our final DOC, **Galatina DOC**, broadens out into some white wines with a Chardonnay-led blend and varietal Chardonnay. The Galatina red and rosé blends are a minimum 65% Negroamaro with a varietal Negroamaro at 85%.

The Wine Regions of Italy

Basilicata sells 98% of its wines as either the country-wide vino or the regional *Indicazione Geografica Tipica* IGT. It nevertheless has four DOCs, and one astonishing tannic red wine, **Aglianico del Vulture DOC**, grown on the slopes of around Monte Vulture, an extinct volcano. The soil here is richly volcanic. The climate is hot here in the far south, perfect for the late ripening Aglianico grape. The high altitude of the vineyards, over 1000 feet, assures those cooler, acid-retaining nights winemakers dream about. The 100% Aglianico wine when young has dark fruit, but as it ages, it takes on essences of earth, tar, dark chocolate, leather. An Aglianico Spumante is also produced.

Grottino di Roccanova DOC gives us Bianco primarily from Malvasia Bianca di Basilicata, Rosso and rosato from 60–85% Sangiovese; 5–30% Cabernet Sauvignon; 5–30% Malvasia Nera di Basilicata; and 5–30% Montepulciano.

Matera DOC makes a Rosso from Sangiovese, Aglianico and Primitivo, white varietals from Malvasia Bianca and Greco, a rosato from Primitivo, a blend called Moro from 60% Cabernet Sauvignon; minimum 20% Primitivo; minimum 10% Merlot, a varietal (90%) Primitivo, a Spumante from 85% Malvasia, a rosato Spumante from 90% Primitivo, and dried grape Passito wines from both Primitivo and Malvasia.

The Wine Regions of Italy

Calabria is the mountainous toe of the Italian boot. The region's olive industry far eclipses the wine grape here. Vineyards are widely dispersed, and cooperatives have never taken hold. Calabria's twelve DOCs (no DOCGS) account for only five percent of its wine.

The **Cirò DOC** is one of the oldest wine names in the world. Bianco is a minimum 80% Greco, rosato and Rosso minimum 80% Gaglioppo; maximum 20% Barbera, Cabernet Franc, Cabernet Sauvignon, Merlot, and/or Sangiovese. Gaglioppo is local to Calabria (75% of production), making spicy red wines with berry and cherry flavors. The denomination has two classico sub-zones: Cirò and Cirò Marina DOC. The **Melissa DOC** overlaps Cirò, producing white wines from Greco and reds from Gaglioppo.

Bivongi DOC makes rosato and Rosso from 30–50% Gaglioppo and/or Greco Nero; 30–50% Castiglione, Nero d'Avola, and/or Nocera, and whites from Greco Bianco, Malvasia Bianca, and Ansonica.

Greco di Bianco DOC produces a golden colored dessert wine from dried grapes. The "Bianco" in the DOC title refers to the town of Bianco, not to the color of the grapes, called, confusingly, Greco Bianco.

Lamezia DOC specializes in reds from the Sicilian red varieties Nerello Mascalese and Nerello Capuccio, with local reds Gaglioppo, Greco Nero, Nocera and Calabrese (Nero d'Avola). Whites are composed of Greco Bianco, Malvasia Bianca, and Ansonica grapes.

The **S.Anna di Isola Capo Rizzuto DOC** is on Calabria's eastern coast. Is applies exclusively to red and rosato wines made primarily from Gaglioppo.

Savuto DOC in western Calabria is red and rosato only from Gaglioppo, supported by Malvasia Nera, Greco Nero and Sangiovese,

Terre di Cosenza DOC takes up the whole of Cosenza province. It produces its Rosso from the local Magliocco Canino grape, and varietal wines from Cabernet Sauvignon, Nero d'Avola,
Gaglioppo, Greco Nero, Magliocco, Merlot and Sangiovese. The white blend is Greco, Guarnaccia, Montonico Bianco and/or Pecorello. White varietals include Greco Bianco, Chardonnay, Guarnaccia, Malvasia Bianca, Mantonico Bianco and Pecorello. A full run of sparkling, dessert and specialty wines is on the list.

Wine map of Sicily

Sicily is the largest island in the Mediterranean, a continuous producer of wine for over 2500 years. For years known just for sweet Marsala and Moscato wines, and high volume dry wines both red and white, richly diverse Sicily is making a name for itself with well-structured reds and whites. Private wine estates are on the rise in Sicily, although 75% of Sicily's wine is still in the hands of co-operatives. Growers have been reducing yields and trying new vine training methods and fermentation techniques, and much investment has come to the island from central and northern Italy.

Sicily has one DOCG, Cerasuolo di Vittoria, and 23 DOCs.

The product of Sicily's southeast, **Cerasuolo di Vittoria DOCG** has the light red color that gives the wine its Cerasuolo name, but aromatic and flavor notes are intense, with bright cherry, adding prune, chocolate, leather, and tobacco with age. The wine is 50–70% Nero d'Avola (aka Calabrese); 30–50% Frappato, and is gaining world renown as the flagship wine of the new Sicily. **Eloro DOC** next door, although less prestigious, produces standard reds and rosés from the same range of grapes.

Between Eloro and the city of Siracusa, the **Noto DOC** uses 100% Moscato to produce white, sparkling, Passito and Liquoroso wines. Red blends are 65% Nero d'Avola, and the Nero d'Avola varietal is 85%. The **Siracusa DOC** is similar, except that the whites add a minority of other grapes to the Moscato, and the red offerings include a varietal Syrah.

In northeastern Sicily, the **Etna DOC** covers the slopes of the still-active volcano that gives the DOC its name. Vineyards on the eastern side of the volcano stand as high as 4000 feet above sea level, while others grace lower slopes. The high climes guarantee a long growing and ripening season. The soil is rich and, of course, volcanic. The Rosso and rosato here is 80% Nerello Mascalese, maximum 20% Nerello Cappuccio. The Bianco: minimum 60% Carricante; maximum 40% Catarratto; maximum 15% Trebbiano, Minella Bianca and other authorized non-aromatic grapes. Spumante is made from Minimum 60% Nerello Mascalese.

The **Faro DOC** covers the wines of the Messsina area, in Sicily's extreme northeast. Faro is exclusively Rosso: 45–60% Nerello Mascalese; 15–30% Nerello Cappuccio; 5–10% Nocera; maximum 15% Gaglioppo, Nero d'Avola, and/or Sangiovese.

Malvasia delle Lipari DOC covers white wine made from Malvasia Bianco (with up to 5–8% Corinto Nero) in the volcanic Aeolian Islands, off the northeastern coast of Sicily. Lipari is the largest of the eight Aeolian Islands, and sees the greatest level of plantings. The wine goes back to antiquity, but relatively little is produced today. These Malvasia wines run the gamut of sugar levels, and include Passito and Liquoroso, which both must have at least 60 grams per liter (or 6%). The Passito can be up to 15% abv, the Liquoroso has 20.0% potential.

Pantelleria DOC is located on the island of Pantelleria just 45 miles from the coast of Africa. It was formerly known as **Moscato di Pantelleria DOC**. The Bianco here is minimum 85% Zibibbo (Moscato di Alessandria), the sweet Zibibbo Dolce and the varietal Moscato are both 100% Zibibbo. All sparkling and dessert wines here are 100% Zibibbo. These include a sparkling Spumante, a dried grape Passito, a wine called Moscato Dorato, a Moscato Liquoroso and a Passito Liquoroso. The Moscato Dorato has a minimum sugar level of 100 grams per liter (10.0%)

Contea di Sclafani DOC from central Sicily produces just about every form of wine known to the human species. The Bianco (as well as the Spumante and the sweet dessert wines) are minimum 50% of Ansonica (called Insolia here), Catarratto, and/or Grecanico, while the Rosso and rosato are produced from Nerello Mascalese and/or Perricone. Varietal wines are produced from Ansonica, Catarratto, Chardonnay, Grecanico Dorato, Grillo, Pinot Bianco, Sauvignon Blanc for whites, and Cabernet Sauvignon, Merlot, Nerello Mascalese, Nero d'Avola (Calabrese), Perricone, Pinot Nero, Sangiovese, and Syrah among the reds. The denomination makes a late harvest Vendemmia Tardiva from grapes that must dry on the vine until at least October 1, as well as a Dolce and a Dolce Vendemmia Tardiva.

We move to Sicily's western prong. Here the **Contessa Entellina DOC** produces a Bianco from Ansonica, varietal whites from Catarratto, Fiano, Chardonnay, Greciano, Sauvignon Blanc and Viognier, a Rosso and rosato from Nero d'Avola and Syrah, varietal reds from those two grapes and Cabernet Sauvignon, Merlot and Pinot Noir, and a Vendemmia Tardiva wine from Ansonica. Given that Sicilian grapes here founder in the swells not only of grapes from France, but from three prime regions of France—Bordeaux, Burgundy, and the Rhône—it is difficult to ascribe either character or philosophy to Contessa Entellina

Sambuca di Sicilia DOC has no connection to the Italian liqueur also called Sambucca. Sambuca makes a Bianco from Ansonica, varietal whites from Ansonica, Chardonnay, and Greciano, a Rosso and rosato from Nero d'Avola, varietal reds from Nero d'Avola, Cabernet Sauvignon, Merlot, Sangiovese and Syrah and a Vendemmia Tardiva wine from Ansonica blended with Grillo or Sauvignon Blanc.

Sciacca DOC offers what seems to be a typical Sicilian mix of local denizens with international colonizers. Rosso and Bianco are led by Nero d'Avola and Ansonica respectively. The rosato allows a possible mix from Ansonica, Cabernet Sauvignon, Catarratto, Chardonnay, Grecanico Dorato, Merlot, Nero d'Avola, and/or Sangiovese. Varietal possibilities are Chardonnay, Ansonica, Greciano, Cabernet Sauvignon, Merlot, Nero d'Avola and Sangiovese. No sweet or sparkling wines are made here.

Santa Margherita di Belice DOC inland from Marsala has a relatively simple structure. Bianco blends Grecanico Dorato and/or Catarratto Bianco Lucido with Ansonica. Varietal whites are Ansonica, Catarratto, and Greciano. Rosso combines Cabernet Sauvignon, Sangiovese, and Nero d'Avola. Varietal reds are authorized from Nero d'Avola and Sangiovese but not Cabernet. No rosato, sweet or sparkling wines.

Delia Nivolleli DOC is an enclave within the larger Marsala DOC. Its wine range is nevertheless wide. Varietal wines are made from Perricone, Nero d'Avola, Sangiovese, Cabernet Sauvignon, Merlot and Syrah, Ansonica, Chardonnay, Sauvignon Blanc, Damaschino and Müller-Thurgau (yes, a German variety). The Rosso is a mix of Cabernet Sauvignon, Merlot, Nero d'Avola, Perricone, Sangiovese, and/or Syrah, the Bianco Ansonica, Greciano and Grillo. A sparkling Spumante is made from Ansonica, Chardonnay, Damaschino, Grecanico, and/or Grillo in any proportion.

Erice DOC in the northwest corner overlaps the Marsala area. Erice's Bianco is 60% Catarratto, Sicily's most widely planted white grape and a common Marsala component. The Rosso is led by Sicilian stalwart Nero d'Avola. The German Müller-Thurgau pops up once again among the numerous varietal possibilities.

Alcamo DOC produces varietal wines from Nero d'Avola, Cabernet Sauvignon, Merlot and Syrah for reds and Sauvignon Blanc, Chardonnay, Grillo, Catarratto, Ansonica and Greciano, and the German Müller-Thurgau for whites. Bianco is minimum 60% Catarratto; maximum 40% Ansonica, Chardonnay, Grecanico, Grillo, Müller-Thurgau, and/or Sauvignon Blanc; Rosso is minimum 60% Nero d'Avola; maximum 40% Cabernet Sauvignon, Frappato, Merlot, Perricone, Sangiovese, and/or Syrah. Rosato is Cabernet Sauvignon, Frappato, Merlot, Nerello Mascalese, Nero d'Avola, Perricone, Sangiovese, and/or Syrah in any proportions. Alcamo has a classico zone.

Monreale DOC produces the full range of Bianco, Rosso, rosato varietal wines and Vendemmia Tardiva wines from Ansonica, Catarratto, Chardonnay, Grillo, Pinot Bianco, Cabernet Sauvignon, Merlot, Nerello Mascalese, Nero d'Avola, Perricone, Pinot Nero, Sangiovese, and Syrah.

Marsala DOC produces Sicily's (and indeed Italy's) most well known fortified wine. Marsala is fortified with distilled alcohol either during or after fermentation depending on style desired. There are three styles (colors) – Ambra, Oro, Rubino. Ambra and Oro are made from white grapes, a blend of Grillo, Cataratto, Inzolia (Ansonia) and Damaschino. Rubino wines are produced from Perricone, Nero d'Avola, and Nerello Mascalese.

The Wine Regions of Italy
Sardinia

The island region of **Sardinia** is our last among Italy's twenty. The island has a long history of conquest by other Mediterranean countries and forces. It has been, and still feels, apart from the rest of Italy, and it lacks the pervasive wine culture of the other nineteen regions. French and Spanish grapes predominate here: the Spanish Garnacha (Grenache in France) is Cannonau here. While Sardinia has a number of localized DOCs, it also has several that apply throughout the island.

Cannonau di Sardegna DOC applies to red and fortified wines made from Cannonau, including a Riserva version aged two years. A sweet fortified Cannonau liquoroso is also produced.

Monica di Sardegna DOC applies to the unique Sardinian Monica grape, produced nowhere else in the world. Up to 15% of other red grapes may be blended in. Monica di Sardegna Frizzante is the lightly sparkling version.

Moscato di Sardegna DOC gives us a dry wine from a minimum of 90% Moscato Bianco (Muscat Blanc à Petite Grains), a Spumante, Vendemmia Tardiva, and Passito from the same grape.

Sardegna Semidano DOC avails itself of the white Semidano grape, unique to Sardinia, for Bianco, Spumante, and Passito wines

Vermentino di Sardegna DOC gives us whites and sparkling wines from the Vermentino grape, which inhabits much of the western Mediterranean (Rolle in French). The grape is widespread, and shows particular adaptability in Australia.

Chapter Eighteen

World Wine Regions
Spain

Wine Map of Spain

The Phoenicians—before the Greeks—brought winemaking to Spain by 1000 BC. Spain has extremely varied climates and terrains, from the arid central plateau, northeast to the sea spray of Rias Baixas in Galicia, south to the sunny climes of Andalucía. Although Spain lies at a lower latitude than wine powerhouse France, 90% of the country's vineyards enjoy altitudes higher than any of the major French regions—this gives grapes cool evenings in which to rest and marshal their acidity.

Spain's major rivers define a number of wine regions. The Duero flows west toward the Atlantic, becoming Portugal's great river of port grape production, the Douro. The Ebro is Spain's most important, flowing from the Cantabrian mountains in the Basque country through Castilla y Leon, Navarra, Rioja and Aragon, and finally emptying into the Mediterranean coast in Catalonia. Lack of water can be a problem in Spain's vineyards, but irrigation is now largely allowed.

Spain has a system of quality designations that largely matches that of France, but with some distinctive Spanish twists. The EU's standard Protected Denomination of Origin (DOP) category, AOC in France, DOC and DOCG in Italy, centers around the Spanish DO, for Denominación de Origen. There are two appellations which qualify for the higher level DOCa Denominación de Origen Calificada: Rioja and Priorat. Priorat is in Catalonia, which is striving to break away from Spain, and calls the designation DOQ (Denominacio d'Origen Qualificada) in the Catalan language. Spain has an additional high quality designation called Denominación de Origen Pago used for exceptional single vineyard estates, of which there are about a dozen. The EU's IGP Indicación Geográfica Protegida is gradually replacing the old Spanish Vino de la Terra system of regional wines. The lowest level is Vino or Vino de España, plain old wine. French winemakers have recently hijacked a tanker truck of this red liquid and vented it out over one of their roads as a protest to its importation.

Spain is divided into seventeen Autonomous Communities that are more or less consistent with larger wine regions. Examples are Galicia, Castile and León, Aragon, and Catalonia in the north, Castile-La Mancha in the center, Andalusia in the South.

Major Spanish Red Wine Grapes

- Tempranillo accounts for a quarter of all grapes grown in Spain. It goes by many local names: Tinto Fino in Ribera del Duero, Tinta de Toro in Toro, Ull de Llebre in Catalonia, Cencibel in La Mancha, Tinto Roriz in Portugal. It has been grown in Spain since the Phoenicians settled in 1100 BC. Tempranillo has thick skin, it ripens early, hence the name (*temprano* means early), likes chalk soils and high altitudes, and is relatively neutral, taking well to blending with other varieties (Garnacha, Graciano, Cabernet, Merlot) and/or aging in oak.

- Garnacha (Grenache) is powerful and alcoholic, lacks tannins and acidity, is often blended, distinct in Priorat and vinified as a single varietal in Cariñena and Calatayud in Aragon.

- Cariñena (Carignan), distinct in Priorat and Montsant (both in Catalonia)

- Graciano – aromatic component of Rioja

- Monastrell (Mourvèdre) – popular tannic grape in Jumilla and Yecla in the southeast

Major Spanish White Wine Grapes

Albariño – Rías Baixas, rich, floral, with peach and apricot notes, or minerally, tart, and bracing, like green apples and lemon peels.

Garnacha Blanca – used in blends.

Godello – Valdeorras, and increasingly in Ribeiro – apples, pears, texture

Verdejo – citrus, melon, apple

Viura – white Rioja – versatile

Wine Map of Rioja

Rioja DOCa is the spiritual home of Tempranillo, and of Spain's flagship red wine, Rioja. Tempranillo here is rarely single varietal. It is blended with Garnacha (for body and alcohol), Graciano (additional aromas), and Mazuelo (a range of flavors). Aging in oak is important in Rioja, leading to several possible age statements:

- Rioja – no oak contact

- Crianza – one year in oak, another year in bottle

- Reserva – one year in oak, two years in bottle

- Gran Reserva – two years in oak, three in bottle

A number of other red Spanish wines have similar systems for age-designation.

Note the spelling here, Reserva with an E, compared to the Italian Riserva with an I. In both countries, these terms have legal significance to denote aging. The American label term "Reserve" has no legal significance.

Rioja has three sub-regions. **Rioja Alta** at higher elevations produces a light, fruitier, more acidic wine. **Rioja Alavesa** produces wines with fuller body. **Rioja Baja** is the warmest of the three sub-regions and may often produce deeply colored, high alcohol, low-acid wines. Producers often blend wines from all three sub-regions to attain their ideal mix. When you also factor in the different proportions of grapes and the aging choices, you get great variety.

Navarra, which hugs Rioja to the east, produces largely similar wines.

Wine Map of Northeast Spain

Priorat DOCa in Catalonia (Catalunia) is the other "one cut above" red wine on the Spanish horizon. It is known for its distinct slate-rich llicorella soil. The roots of these Garnacha and Cariñena vines have to slither their way through faults in the underlying slate to reach deeply entrenched sources of moisture, leading to extremely low yields and proportionately concentrated red wines. **Montsant** completely surrounds Priorat and is known for high quality red wines, also from Garnacha and Cariñena as well as Tempranillo, Cabernet Sauvignon, Merlot and Syrah.

Tarragona, which is divided into two sections, makes wine in a number of styles. It has long been known for its Garnacha-based late harvest sweet fortified wines as well as the lighter sweet Moscatel de Tarragona. Many of its grapes are destined for the production of Cava, whose region Tarragona overlaps. Dry varietal reds, whites and rosés round out the mix.

The **Penedès** region of Catalonia produces red wines from Tempranillo, Garnacha and Cariñena, but is much better known as the center of Spanish sparkling Cava production which is dominated by two giant producers, Codorniú and Freixenet. Cava is produced like Champagne but the grapes are Spanish: the strongly flavored Xarello, the floral and aromatic Macabeu, and the fresh acidic Parellada.

Costers del Segre, meaning in Catalonian "banks of the Segre river," is a harsh arid inland area that produces grapes for Cava as well as Garnacha, Cabernet Sauvignon, Tempranillo, Merlot, Monastrell, Syrah, and Pinot Noir among reds, Chardonnay, Riesling and Sauvignon Blanc among whites.

Somotano on our northeast map is in Aragon rather than Catalonia. The region is in the foothills of the Pyrenees, with a continental climate and relatively high altitude vineyards. This is a modern-leaning region producing white wines from Chardonnay, Macabeo and Gewürztraminer and red wines from Cabernet Sauvignon, Syrah, Merlot and Garnacha.

Also in Aragon are the two appellations of **Calatayud** and **Cariñena** where some very old Garnacha grows on bush vines at high altitudes under arid circumstances. Large cooperatives see to the winemaking here, giving us big bold varietal Garnacha wines at often astonishingly low prices (thanks in part to significant EU subsidies). **Campo de Borja** just to the north has a number of cooperatives producing Garnacha and Tempranillo.

Wine Map of Northwest Spain

Moving west into Castile and León on Spain's northern plateau, **Ribera del Duero** follows the Duero river. The appellation has a number of similarities with Rioja, and is its reputational rival. Tempranillo, called Tinto Fino here, is usually blended with Cabernet Sauvignon, Malbec and Merlot, following the lead of the renowned *Vega Sicilia* winery. The aging requirements for Ribeira del Duero (Crianza, Reserva, Gran Reserva) are identical to those of Rioja. We should note that Vega Sicilia has no connection to Italy's Sicily. The *Vega* part refers to the river's green vegetation and the *Sicilia* refers to Saint Cecilia, the patron saint of music, who is revered in the region.

Further down the Duero, **Rueda** is making a name for itself with white wines from the Verdejo grape, considered by many to be Spain's finest white, and a value as well.

Further downstream **Toro** specializes in 100% varietal Tempranillo, called Tinta de Toro here.

Cigales to the north has specialized in clarets and rosés since medieval times, producing today similar wines from Tempranillo, Garnacha Tinta, and Garnacha Gris as well as the whites Verdejo and Albillo.

Still in Castile and León, **Bierzo** is a bridge between the cool humid climate of Galicia and the hot dry climate of Continental Spain. Bierzo has great variety, producing whites from Doña Blanca, Godello and Palomino grapes, and reds from the Mencia grape with floral overtones, some unaged, some Crianza and reserva level.

Valdeorras, whose name means "Valley of Gold", is in the Autonomous Community of Galicia. These are gentle rolling hills. Godello, Donna Branca and Palomino Fino are the white grapes, Mencia, Merenzao, Sousón, Brancellao, Alicante Bouschet, Gran Negro, Tempranillo and Negreda are the reds. The deeply savory and full-bodied white Godello has been gaining many international fans lately, some commentators likening it to fine white Burgundy. A few decades ago, Godello was obscure and nearly extinct. Nearby **Ribeira Sacra** also produces Godello, and the Galician white Albariño. **Ribeiro** specializes in the local white Treixadura grape, so often found over the border in Portugal.

The jewel of Spanish Galicia must be **Rías Baixas**, a cool wet region hard by the ocean. Albariño leads here. The vines are trained on granite posts called *parrales* to maximize sun exposure and ensure air circulation, thus mitigating the effect of the humidity.

Wee next move south, to the center of the Iberian peninsula. With nearly half a million acres under vine, the **La Mancha DO** in the Castile-La Mancha Autonomous Region is the world's largest continuous vine growing area. A continental climate applies here, with cold winters and long hot summers. La Mancha grows Tempranillo (called Cencibel here), Garnacha, Moravia, Cabernet Sauvignon, Merlot and Syrah among reds, Airén, Macabeo (also called Viura), Chardonnay and Sauvignon Blanc.

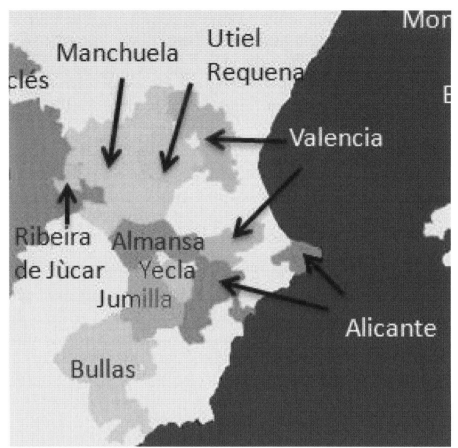
Wine Map of Southwest Spain

Southwest Spain has its own wine personality.

Manchuela in Castile-La Mancha, gives us Bobal, Cabernet Sauvignon, Tempranillo, Garnacha, Merlot, Monastrell, Moravia Dulce, Syrah and the whites Albillo, Chardonnay, Macabeo, Sauvignon Blanc, and Verdejo. **Utiel Requena** next door in the Valencia Autonomous Region is a specialist in the red Bobal grape, which produces fruity wines that are low in both acidity and alcohol.

Valencia DO is divided into two different zones. The signature white wine of the region is Merseguera, but the region also produces Malvasía, Pedro Ximénez, Moscatel Romano, Planta Fina, Macabeo, Chardonnay, Planta Nova, Tortosí, Verdil, Sauvignon Blanc, and Sémillon.
Reds avail themselves of Monastrell, Garnacha, Cabernet Sauvignon, Pinot Noir, Merlot, Forcayat, Bobal, and Syrah. Because of the hot climate here, aging requirements are shorter. Also, the DO has a rule that allows Bobal from neighboring Utiel Requena to be added to Valencian reds.

Alicante has two separate and distinct sub-zones: in **Vinalopó**, along the banks of the River Vinalopó in the southern area of the province, Monastrell leads the local red wines. Along the coast in the north, La Marina, concentrates on the white Moscatel grape. Alicante is most renowned for the sweet dessert wine Fondillón, made from overripe grapes.

Yecla, **Jumilla**, and **Bullas** (all in Murcia) specialize in the tannic red Monastrell (Mourvèdre), here vinified as a single varietal.

Wine Map of Southern Spain

In the south of Spain, **Montilla-Moriles** is best known for sweet dessert wine from the white Pedro Ximénez grape. Its variants are classified like Sherry, but they are not fortified. **Jerez-Xérès** is the main Sherry appellation. Manzanilla de Sanlúcar is the home of Manzanilla Sherry. **Malaga** is a sweet fortified wine from Pedro Ximénez and Moscatel grapes. **Condado de Huelva** produces heavy, full-bodied wines from the local white Zalima grape.

Wine Map of Portugal

Portugal has lost its fair shares of wars, but one war it has most definitely won: the war against the French grapes. French grapes pushed their international way into Spain, Italy, Germany, Greece—all of Europe, except isolated backward-looking Portugal. As a result, Portugal's indigenous vine varieties pressed their own way into the 21st century, validating the country's grapevine and wine structure and even doing some international colonizing of their own. Some of the most important of these grapes are those used to make Port wine. The same Port grapes are now used to make some exciting still dry wines. Touriga Nacional has taken its place as Portugal's signature red grape. Touriga Franca is also leading red blends. In the world of white wines, Portugal is also making a statement, with Vinho Verde and the white grape Arinto of Bucelas, Bical of Bairrada, and Encruzado of the Dão. Even though Portugal is small, it enjoys great diversity region to region.

Portugal has three quality levels, almost identical to those of France. The lowest level wine is **Vinho** or **Vinho de Portugal**. The "H" is pronounced like an "I" in English. You then have IGP, **Indicações Geographicas Protegidas**. The highest level is **Denominação de Origem Controlada** (DOC).

The **Vinho Verde** region is in the northwest, mostly in Minho province. The title "the Minho" is sometimes used for the region. The "Verde" in Vinho Verde refers to the fact that the white wine is a young wine, released within six months after harvest. The Minho region, of course, actually *is* green, since this is Portugal's wettest landscape. The wine is characteristically low in alcohol (the percentage is often in single digits), with vibrant fruit and determined acidity. Alvarinho, with its peach and apricot, floral and citrus notes, and a mineral edge, is the most highly regarded grape used in Vinho Verde. Richly floral Loueiro is the most widely planted. Trajadura adds a certain delicacy. Avesso, Azal, and Arinto are also used.

Trás-os-Montes in the northeast, produces wine under the title of **Transmontano VR (Vinho Regional)**, but has smaller areas within the region that qualify as **Trás-os-Montes DOC**. The name means "across the mountains." The extreme continental climate here brings long hot summers and long cold winters. At high altitude and climate extremes, red wines of all styles are made from Bastardo, Marufo, Tinta Roriz (Tempranillo), Touriga Franca, Touriga Nacional and Trincadeira (Tinta Amarela), whites from Côdega do Larinho, Fernão Pires, Gouveio, Malvasia Fina, Rabigato, Síria (Côdega) and Viosinho.

The **Porto/Douro** region produces the red grapes that are used to produce the fortified wine Port (in the city of Oporto by the ocean), as well as still dry red wines. The five most widely used grapes for red Port wine are Touriga Franca, Tinta Roriz (Tempranillo), Tinta Barroca, Touriga Nacional, and Tinto Cão. This is difficult land, with very little soil, on steep slopes that usually need to be terraced. The region along the Douro river divides into three parts: **Baixo Corgo** on the western edge, **Cima Corgo** in the middle, and the highest altitude **Douro Superior** edging up to the Spanish border. In the past, dry wines were made for local consumption, likely from the grapes not deemed good enough for the major Port houses. This was before modern techniques like fermentation temperature control came into currency. Nowadays, the army of small growers here are likely to plant grapes specifically for still wines. High altitude vineyards that face north are the most highly prized.

The **Távora-Varosa DOC** is situated directly south of the Douro. In this mountainous region, white Malvasia Fina leads in production with Bical, Cerceal, Fernão Pires and Gouveio among the whites. Reds are Tinta Barroca, Tinta Roriz, Touriga Franca and Touriga Nacional. In these high altitude conditions, the tannic red grapes have a harder time ripening than the whites.

The granite hills of the **Dão** support vineyards at 1300 to up to 2600 feet above sea level. Mountains shield the region from Atlantic influence and from the hot African winds coming from the southeast. As in much of Portugal, the Dão produces a range of grapes, for fruity reds and aromatic age-worthy whites. Major red grapes are Touriga Nacional, Alfrocheiro, Aragonez, and Jaen e Rufete. Whites include Encruzado, Bical, Cercial, Malvasia Fina, and Verdelho.

Bairrada to the west of the Dão is a damper area closer to the Atlantic, benefitting from low rolling hills with clay-limestone soils for primarily red wine production. The indigenous high tannin high acid Baga grape is the leader. Bical leads the whites, and both varieties support traditional method sparkling wines.

Beira Interior is a mountainous region by the Spanish border. During the hot summers, sugar level and hence alcohol level can be excessive, leading often to harvesting before tannins have had time to ripen, but careful vineyard techniques can compensate for this. Red grapes, many from desirable old vines, are Bastardo, Marufo, Rufete, Tinta Roriz and Touriga Nacional. The signature white wine is the acidic Cova da Beira, made from the hyper-local Fonte Cal grape. Other white varieties include Arinto, Malvasia Fina, Rabo de Ovelha and Síria.

In contrast to the mountainous regions in northern Portugal, where small holders predominate, the vast arid region of **Alentjo** in the south is one of industrial sized estates. Much of the wine here is sold as Vinho Regional Alentejano. Aragonez (Tempranillo) is the most widely-planted red grape. Plantings of Cabernet and Syrah are appearing in parts. Other grapes supporting the region's usually easy drinking reds include Borba, Évora, Redondo and Reguengos. Antão Vaz is the major white grape of the region, showing firm acidity and tropical fruit. Other whites include Arinto and Roupeiro, both with impressive acidity.

Ribatejo's wine regions straddle the Tagus River, Iberia's longest. Two appellations apply: the **Do Tejo DOC** (formerly known as Ribatejano) and the less restrictive **Tejo VR** (formerly known as Ribatejo). The top wines from both appellations are red, blends of Portuguese and international varieties. The aromatic, gently spicy Fernao Pires leads the region's white wines.

The **Lisbon area** presents a long thin line of vine appellations that face two major menaces: the Atlantic winds and property development. The winds affect primarily the extreme western coastal areas. The eastern areas have some hill protection. **Alenquer** and its neighbor **Arruda** benefit from this wind protection. They are both red wine specialists using the classic Portuguese reds from Aragonez, Touriga Nacional, and Touriga Franca. **Torres Vedras,** east of Alenquer and cooler, produces similar wines. These three appellations now allow some international grape presence with Syrah, Sauvignon Blanc and Chardonnay.

Behind protective hills just south of Alenquer is the white wine region of **Bucelas**, which gives us a crisp, dry, mineral white, made with primarily Arinto, with Rabo de Ovelha and Sercial, in still and sparkling forms.

Palmela focuses on red wines, particularly from the Castelão Frances grape variety.

DOC Óbidos on the coast is windy and cool, perfect for some of the country's best sparkling wines. **Lourinhã** is even cooler, challenging ripening and yielding a high acid grape that does its best work in brandies.

Colares and **Carcavelos** were once renowned coastal appellations, but property development has compromised them badly. Carcavelos still makes a few cases of a sweet fortified wine from local grapes, both red and white. Colares makes high-acid, tannic wines from red Ramisco grapes, planted in sand dunes, and Malvasia–based aromatic whites.

Setúbal DOC on the Setúbal Peninsula is best known for its fortified Moscato. The grape, called Moscatel de Setúbal here, is better known as Muscat of Alexandria.

The far southern region of **Algarve** has four DOCs – **Lagos**, **Portimão**, **Lagoa** and **Tavira**. Wine here is mostly red from classic Portuguese varieties like Castelão and Touriga Nacional, with some international varieties like Syrah. At just 125 miles from Africa, Algarve has a warm climate, and a reputation for wines high in alcohol.

Chapter Nineteen

World Wine Regions
Germany

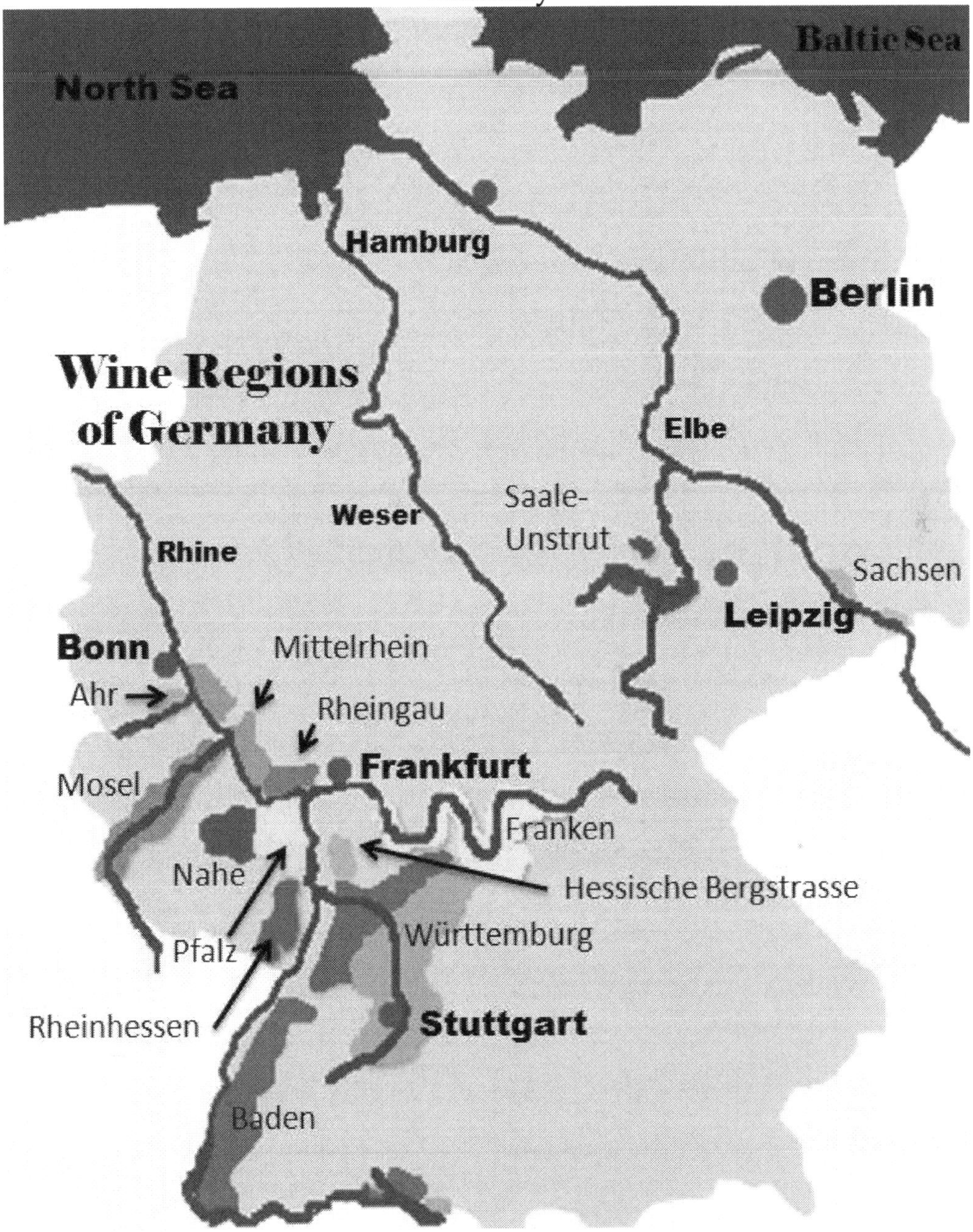

Baltic Sea
North Sea
Hamburg
Berlin
Wine Regions of Germany
Elbe
Weser
Saale-Unstrut
Rhine
Sachsen
Leipzig
Bonn
Mittelrhein
Ahr
Rheingau
Frankfurt
Mosel
Franken
Nahe
Hessische Bergstrasse
Württemburg
Pfalz
Rheinhessen
Stuttgart
Baden

Wine Map of Germany

Germany has thirteen regions, all closely associated with rivers. Eleven are in the old West Germany, two in the old German Democratic Republic.

German wines are poorly understood. A few key points should clear this up.

For years, oceans of sweet, poor quality white German wine were sold to generations of international drinkers, many of them labeled erroneously as Riesling, leading to reputation problems.

Germany sits at the northern reaches of European viticulture. Grapes here struggle to ripen. Growers use every trick in the book to promote ripening. One example is to plant vines on steep slopes overlooking rivers. The rivers concentrate the sun's rays and focus them back onto the vines. The rivers also retain heat and radiate it up to the vines at night. Even so, as a general rule, German grapes at harvest produce juice, called grape "must, that tends to be lower in sugar and higher in acidity than grapes from warmer regions. Germany does pay attention to its thirteen regions, but the "must weight," the potential alcohol in the grape juice, is the most important criterion for quality. For this reason, we look at the quality pyramid before we talk of any regions.

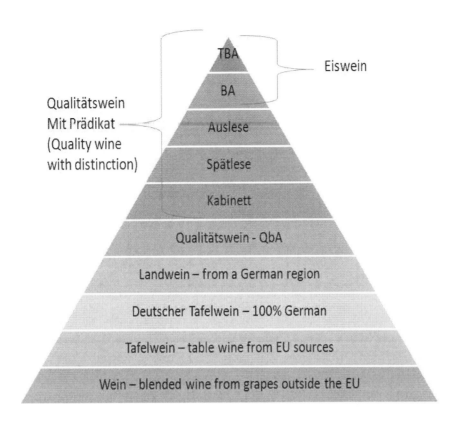

Qualitätswein
Mit Prädikat
(Quality wine
with distinction)

TBA

Eiswein

BA

Auslese

Spätlese

Kabinett

Qualitätswein - QbA

Landwein – from a German region

Deutscher Tafelwein – 100% German

Tafelwein – table wine from EU sources

Wein – blended wine from grapes outside the EU

German Wine Quality Hierarchy

The bottom four levels of the pyramid represent forgettable wines, mostly white, not from Riesling but from Müller-Thurgau, Silvaner, and other productive grapes. The fifth level, Qualitätswein (QbA), is of better quality but does not represent the best levels. This wine may be chaptalized, which means sweetening may be added (to the grape juice, not to the finished wine) so as to bring the alcohol level up to within accepted standards. In such a case, the wine must be fermented completely dry.

The next level up, Qualitätswein mit Prädikat, covers the top five rungs of the quality pyramid, applying primarily to Germany's signature grape, Riesling. Chaptalization is **not** allowed. The lower levels of these five, **Kabinett** and **Spätlese**, may be either dry or sweet, **Auslese** is usually somewhat sweet, and the top two, **Beerenauslese** and **Trockenbeerenauslese** are always sweet.

Spätlese means taken (harvested) late, a process which, barring autumn rains, lets the grapes ripen longer to get as sweet as possible. Auslese means taken out, referring to a process in which the best bunches of grapes are hand-picked for the wine. Multiple passes of the vineyard are often necessary for this and the two highest processes. For Beerenauslese, the best individual grape berries are selected. For Trockenbeerenauslese, the best grapes that have dried on the vine are selected. **Eiswein** (ice wine) is made from the frozen berries of the top two. The word "trocken" meaning dry in German, refers to the grapes, not the wine (which is extremely sweet, and highly concentrated in flavor).

All wines from cool climates tend to be high in acid, and Riesling as a variety is highly acidic. Sweetness compensates for this acidity. A Riesling Kabinett will usually *taste* dry, but it might have considerably more sugar that, say, a Marlborough Sauvignon Blanc or an Australian Clare Valley Riesling. If residual sugar is not high enough to compensate for the acidity, the grower may add unfermented grape juice, called Süssreserve, after fermentation. Acidity reduces the *perception* of sweetness. Beerenauslese and Trockenbeerenauslese have such concentrated sweet juice that the final result is invariably sweet. Riesling has the firm acidity to be able to handle such a sweetness level.

German Wine Grapes; White

- Aromatic **Riesling** is Germany s benchmark grape. It is high in acid, and takes a full 130 days to ripen.

- Müller-Thurgau is requires only 100 days to ripen, can be planted on more sites, and has higher yields. Its flavor is not distinctive like Riesling s however. It is the main ingredient in cheap German white wine like Liebfraumilch.

- Silvaner is also fairly neutral, but does well in the chalky soils of Franconia and Rheinhessen, making earthy and rustic dry wines.

- Other white wines are produced from Kerner, Bacchus, Scheurebe, Gewürztraminer, Grauer Burgunder/ Ruländer (Pinot Gris), and Weisser Burgunder (Pinot Blanc).

German Wine Grapes: Red

- Spätburgunder (Pinot Noir)

- Dornfelder, producing dark-colored, full-bodied, fruity and tannic wines

- Lemberger (Blaufränkisch)

- Portugieser

- Trollinger

- Schwarzriesling (Pinot Meunier)

The German Wine Regions

The best regions in Germany are those capable of ripening Riesling reliably, and even here the results are not consistent from year to year. The southern regions of Franken, Baden and Württemberg are warmer, and less Riesling-oriented.

Germany's number one producer, the **Rheinhessen**, two-thirds white, produces Müller-Thurgau, Riesling, Dornfelder, Silvaner, Portugieser, Kerner, Spätburgunder, Grauburgunder, and Scheurebe. Reds led by Dornfelder (a German crossing created in the 1950s) are on the upswing here.

Pfalz (the Palatinate) leads with Riesling, followed by Dornfelder, Müller-Thurgau, Portugieser, Spätburgunder, Kerner, Grauburgunder, and Weißburgunder. Climate is mild and sunny for Germany. Pfalz generally competes with the Mosel for the title of greatest Riesling producer.

Baden leans toward red wines, with Spätburgunder (Pinot Noir) accounting for a third of all plantings. The region is shielded by the Odenwald hills and the Black Forest on one side and the Vosges mountains on the other, giving it a warmer climate and more sun than any other German region.

Württemberg leads with light bodied, fruity reds from Trollinger, with Riesling and the reds Lemberger (Blaufrankisch) and Spätburgunder (Pinot Noir). It is Germany's largest producer of red wine.

The **Mosel** region covers its namesake river and two of its tributaries, the Saar and the Ruwer. This is prime Riesling country, producing many world-class wines on south and southwestern facing hillside vineyards, many of which need to be terraced.

Franken (Franconia) produces a range of wines, but the white Silvaner has the highest production, followed by Müller-Thurgau. Reds are produced from Domina and Pinot Noir. Many of the better wines here are sold in squat *bocksbeutel* bottles.

The Nahe along the Nahe River and a number of its tributaries, has a mild dry climate, and produces Riesling and other whites in its interior reaches, and Pinot Noir and other reds closer to its confluence with the Rhine at Bingen.

The Rheingau sits at a special point in the Rhine's progress where the river flows eastward for a stretch, and hence the Rheingau faces south, resulting in some of the world's finest Riesling. It is no coincidence that the German Center for Viticulture and Oenology is located here, in Geisenheim. Riesling accounts for seven out of eight vines here, Pinot Noir the remaining eighth.

Saale-Unstrut and **Sachsen (Saxony)**, the only two regions from the old East Germany, produce a variety of whites, from other than Riesling, in extremely cool climates. Much of this wine is consumed locally.

The Ahr specializes in Spätburgunder (Pinot Noir), grown on steep slopes above the winding Ahr river. The soil of slate, gravel, and volcanic rock absorbs warmth during the day and radiates it back to the grapes at night, somewhat mitigating this region's northern latitude.

The Mittelrhein covers about 75 miles of breathtaking Rhine River scenery between Bingen and Bonn, including the famous Lorelei Rock and a number of castles. Riesling accounts for 70% of the grapes, for still and sparkling Sekt wines. Pinot Noir and Dornfelder are used for the reds. Slate soils characterize the vineyards, and the major river moderates the climate.

Hessische Bergstraße is the smallest of Germany's 13 regions. Riesling accounts for just over half of production, with Pinot Noir next at 18 percent, and Pinot Gris, Pinot Blanc, Müller-Thurgau, and Silvaner. Protected from the elements by rings of hills, this region is known for its mild climate and long growing season.

Chapter Twenty

World Wine Regions
Europe

Austria

Wine Map of Austria

Austrian wine has changed a great deal over the last few decades—for the better. The improvement took place because of a terrible event, the Austrian diethylene glycol wine scandal of 1985. German wine laboratories discovered that some Austrian producers had added diethylene glycol, a substance used in some forms of anti-freeze, to bulk wines they shipped to Germany, ostensibly to give them better body and a sweeter feel. No one got sick, but a number of Austrians went to prison, and Austrian wine exports collapsed. The positive effect of this was a thorough house cleaning by Austrian wine authorities and a move by the industry away from sweet bulk wine toward upscale dry wines. The industry recovered and is making an array of impressive wines today. Austrian wines have a fresh energy to them.

Austria is no clone of Germany. It is situated further south, and the wine producing areas are tangibly warmer than Germany's. Wine is produced only in the eastern section of the country, the west being taken up by the alpine region. Austria grows over 30 grape varieties, primarily white, but red wines are on the increase, and now account for a solid third of production. The flagship white grape is the native Grüner Veltliner, accounting for a third of the country's plantings. Other whites include Neuburger, Rotgipfler, Zierfandler and Roter Veltliner. Reds include Zweigelt, Blaufränkisch, St. Laurent and Blauer Wildbacher. International varieties like Pinot Noir and Chardonnay also have their place.

Austria, like Germany, has a system of wine quality levels based on must weight (juice sugar content before fermentation). The system is slightly different.

- Kabinett, standard must weight for quality wines
- Spätlese: higher must weight
- Auslese: select grapes with higher must weight
- Beerenauslese: further selection of individual berries
- Ausbruch: grapes shriveled by botrytis (noble rot)
- Trockenbeerenauslese: completely botrytised grapes
- Eiswein
- Strohwein or Schilfwein: made from grapes dried on straw mats.

The **geographic classification** system in Austria takes some explaining. For starters, there are **four generic districts**, covering the whole country. Three are labeled in red on our map, the other is the capital Vienna, or Wien in German. From north to south, these are

1. Niederösterreich meaning "Lower Austria," the "lower" referring to its position downstream on the Danube River
2. Wiener Gemischter Satz, the capital city, Vienna
3. Burgenland
4. Steiermark

(If the German language is unfamiliar to you, take a second to note the placement of the I and E in "Wien," pronounced "VEEN," or Vienna. The word for wine is "Wein," pronounced VINE.)

Within the four generic regions are sixteen wine producing regions. Nine fit within the classification of DAC, meaning "Controlled District of Austria," roughly the equivalent of the French AOC or Italian DOC levels. Each DAC specifies the grape varieties or wine types that are allowed to use the DAC name on their labels. An additional seven regions (within two of the four generic regions) do not come within the DAC rules, for various reasons. In the case of Wachau, for example, the appellation has its own system of quality levels that pre-date the DAC system.

The nine DACs are:

1. Weinviertel DAC (Grüner Veltliner)
2. Mittelburgenland DAC (Blaufränkisch)
3. Traisental DAC (Riesling and Grüner Veltliner)
4. Kremstal DAC (Riesling and Grüner Veltliner)
5. Kamptal DAC (Riesling and Grüner Veltliner)
6. Leithaberg DAC (Grüner Veltliner, Weißburgunder, Chardonnay, Neuburger and Blaufränkisch)
7. Eisenberg DAC (Blaufränkisch)
8. Neusiedlersee DAC (Zwiegelt)
9. Wiener Gemischter Satz DAC (minimum of three white grape varieties of one vineyard, harvested and produced together) – the name means "Mixed Vienna Group."

If a producer makes wine from a grape that is not authorized in the DAC, the wine must be labeled under the name of the larger generic region. So a Pinot Noir from the Weinviertel (which only authorizes Grüner Veltliner) would be labeled "Pinot Noir, Niederösterreich."

The non-DACs are:

In Niederösterreich:
10. Wachau
11. Wagram
12. Thermenregion
13. Carnuntum

In Steiermark (all of Steiermark):
14. Weststeiermark
15. Südsteiermark
16. Vulkanlandsteiermark

Let us take a look at these sixteen regions. We will start in **Niederösterreich** and work our way down and around, through Vienna, through Burgenland, and finish in Steiermark.

Wachau is Austria's most prestigious wine appellation. A UNESCO world heritage site, it is a region of crystalline rock soils on steep terraces perched on gorges of the Danube. Summer is hot and dry here, but the river gives relief. Riesling and Grüner Veltliner are the major two grapes, both generating age-worthy wines. The indigenous white grape Neuburger is here, as well as Gelber Muskateller (Muscat Blanc) and Sauvignon Blanc. Before the DAC era (which Wachau opted out of), Wachau created its own quality code, the *Vinea Wachau*, dividing dry white wines into three categories: **Steinfeder,** aromatic, light-bodied wines up to 11.5% alcohol, **Federspiel**, with 11.5% to 12.5% alcohol by volume, and **Smaragd**, for rich late-harvest, dry wines.

Kremstal DAC has distinct growing zones. In the west, by Wachau, are the rocky soils of the Kremstal river valley and the historic town of Krems, producing mineral-rich Riesling and spicy Grüner Veltliner. East of Krems is an area of deep loess soil, the home of a softer, more elegant Grüner Veltliner.

Kamptal DAC to the east of Kremstal makes wine from Grüner Veltliner or Riesling in a classic medium-bodied style and a rich, opulent dry reserve style. Riesling here grows on steep south-facing slopes, producing powerful mineral wines. Further south, toward the Danube, wider loess and loam terraces support full-bodied Grüner Veltliner, Pinot Noir, Pinot Blanc and the red Zweigelt. These last three must be labeled under the generic regional term "Niederösterreich".

Traisental DAC authorizes Riesling and Grüner Veltliner for DAC labeling. This is a small area producing spicy Grüner Veltliner. Vines cling onto on narrow terraces with arid, calcareous gravel soils, giving the wines great concentration and full body. This is a climate transition zone, where the cool climate of the Alps meets the warmer stretches of the Pannonian plain, funneling in from neighboring Hungary.

Wagram, not a DAC, was previously known as Donauland (Danube-land). Vines here are planted on both banks of the river. A range of Grüner Veltliner styles are made, but the red Roter Veltliner is also popular (the two "Veltliners" are not genetically related). Red Zweigelt, Pinot Noir and Eiswein (Ice Wine) have their champions here.

Weinviertel's DAC is strictly for Grüner Veltliner, but it produces a range of other wines as Austria's largest wine region, stretching from the Danube in the south to the Czech border in the north, and all the way to the border of Slovakia in the east. The northeast concentrates on Grüner Veltliner, Welschriesling and Pinot Noir. The limestone cliffs in the north bring a mineral quality to the wines. Further to the south east, the warm Pannonian climate creates an optimal growing environment for Pinot Noir, Pinot Gris, and Pinot Blanc, and also Traminer, which supports a range of wines from dry through to dessert. On steep inclines in the south, approaching Vienna, Riesling basks in its aromatic glory.

Carnumtun, not a DAC, stretches from the borders of Vienna in the west to the border of Slovakia in the east. The vineyards are south of the Danube on three hilltops. Soil is dense loam, loess and sandy gravels, favoring red wine production from the indigenous Blauer Zweigelt, along with Cabernet Sauvignon, Merlot and Blaufränkisch.

Thermenregion, not a DAC, is so named because of its thermal springs. The northern part, by the Vienna Woods, makes white wine from the indigenous Zierfandler and Rotgipfler varieties (rarely seen elsewhere), either vinified separately or blended with each other. In the south, the red wines Sankt Laurent and Pinot Noir are predominant. The Pannonian effect come into play here in force, resulting in a dry climate with an average of 1,800 hours of sunshine during the year.

The **Wiener Gemischter Satz DAC** is a codification of the centuries-old tradition in the capital and its environs of producing wine designed to be consumed fresh in the city's traditional Viennese "Heuriger" wine taverns, amid much vivacious social interaction. The Vienna environs have over 1500 acres of vines. In the west of the City, carbonate-rich soils create ideal conditions for Riesling, Chardonnay and Weißburgunder (Pinot Blanc). In the southern parts of Vienna, calcareous, brown and black earth soils favor the production of full-bodied white wines and rich, supple red wines. Virtually all Viennese producers cultivate grapes for the traditional "Gemischter Satz," different varieties planted and harvested together, and then crushed and vinified all as one mass. Grapes include Grüner Veltliner, Riesling, Chardonnay and Pinot Blanc among whites, and reds like Pinot Noir and Zweigelt.

We move now south to **Burgenland,** where both climate and topography are radically different from the more northern regions. All four regions in Burgenland are DACs.

Leithaberg DAC is an all-rounder, authorized as a DAC to produce reds (from Blaufränkisch as the principal grape variety, with up to 15 percent Zweigelt, St. Laurent or Pinot Noir) as well as whites from Weißburgunder (Pinot Blanc), Chardonnay, Neuburger and Grüner Veltliner, either as single varietals of as blends. The soils on the east-facing slopes of the Leithagebirge mountain range are limestone and slate, creating a pure red Blaufränkisch, as well as complex white Weißburgunder, Chardonnay and Grüner Veltliner.

Neusiedlersee DOC refers to the large shallow Lake Neusiedl, which promotes a wet climate perfect for the development of noble rot (botrytis cinerea) during the autumn for wonderful Beerenauslese and Trockenbeerenauslese dessert wines from Chardonnay, Scheurebe, Traminer and Welschriesling, the latter having the potential to produce exceptional quality levels. These wines are labeled "Burgenland," since the DAC only applies to the red Zweigelt. The Zweigelt here is joined by its cousins Blaufränkisch and St. Laurent

Mittelburgenland DAC applies only to Blaufränkisch. This is the center of red wine production in Austria. The appellation also produces Zweigelt, Cabernet Sauvignon, and Merlot. Neighboring **Eisenberg DAC** is also authorized for Blaufränkisch.

Steiermark (Styria) has more in common with the Slovenian vineyards across the border than it does with the rest of the Austrian wine lands. The three Styrian wine-growing regions each have their own configurations. In the undulating hills of **Weststeiermark**, Schilcher Rosé dominates. In **Südsteiermark**, Sauvignon Blanc and Gelber Muskateller are mosty prominent. In **Vulkanland Steiermark**, named for an extinct volcano, the grape of note is Traminer.

Wine Map of Luxembourg

Wine has been produced in Luxembourg continuously since Roman times. Luxembourg wine production is centered in the country's southeast, where it is largely in the hands of cooperatives who sell the wine under the name of "Vinsmoselle". The cooperatives operate a sparkling wine plant in Wormeldange, which produces wines under the label "Poll-Fabaire." Müller-Thurgau (called Rivaner here) accounts for 30% of plantings, followed by Auxerrois Blanc (14%), Pinot Gris (13.7%), Riesling (12.8%), Pinot Blanca (11.0%), Elbling (9.5%), and Pinot Noir, the only red widely grown (6.8%). The single label for quality wines is *Moselle Luxembourgeoise*. Special wines can be awarded the designations *Vin classé*, *Premier Cru* or *Grand Premier Cru*, depending the vote of a tasting panel. The *Crémant de Luxembourg* designation is awarded for sparkling wine.

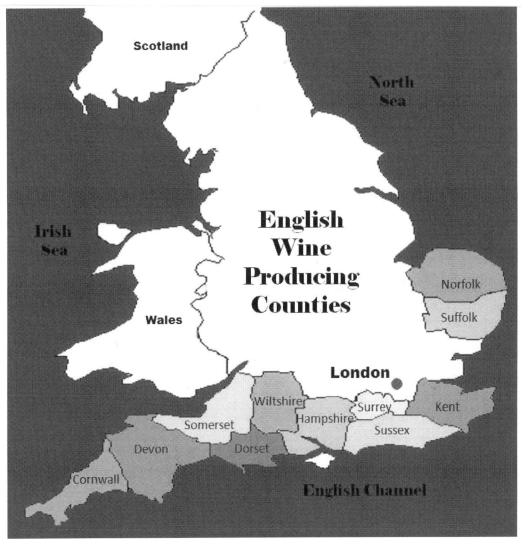

Wine Map of England

The English have always taken wine quite seriously, even if they have not been able to grow many vines because of their high latitude and wet rainy climate. Global warming is helping them, however. Growers are choosing their varieties with care, opting for climate-appropriate hybrids when necessary. Good wine, especially sparkling wine, is coming out of England.

The terms "English Wine" and "Welsh Wine" refers to wines from grapes grown in England and Wales, respectively. The term "British wine," on the other hand, refers to wine made in Great Britain from grape juice or concentrate that can originate anywhere in the world, which usually precludes its being wine of any quality.

England has over 450 vineyards. The limestone soil in Kent and Sussex is particularly favorable for quality wine production (if one can get the weather right). The hybrid Seyval Blanc is the most populous white grape, followed by the German Reichsteiner, the German Müller-Thurgau, the German Bacchus, Chardonnay, the French crossing Madeleine Angevine, the recently-created German early-ripening crossing Schönburger, the high yielding early ripening German crossing Huxelrebe and the German crossing Ortega. Red varieties include Dornfelder, Pinot Meunier and Pinot Noir.

Note here that Seyval Blanc is a *hybrid,* while all the other whites here other than Chardonnay are *crossings*. A hybrid crosses a vinifera grape with a non-vinifera grape, while a crossing crosses two vinifera grapes. Because Seyval Blanc contains some non-vinifera genes, it is outlawed by the EU authorities for quality wine production, but this is no longer an issue for England, since it is leaving the EU (Brexit).

Traditional method bottle-fermented sparkling wines, which have been beating out French competitors in recent blind tasting tests, are produced from Chardonnay, Pinot Noir, Pinot Précoce, Pinot Meunier, Pinot Blanc, Pinot Gris, Seyval Blanc, and Reichensteiner.

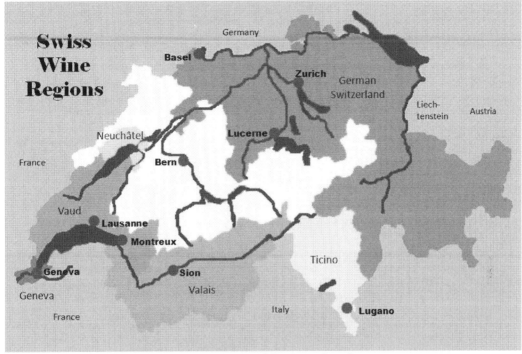

Wine Map of Switzerland

The landlocked European country of Switzerland is more than just watches, army knives, banks, and world-class tennis stars: it produces wine, and much extremely fine wine. The Swiss drink a great deal of wine, encompassing nearly all the wine they themselves produce and much more they import. Only two percent is exported, mainly to Germany, which is the reason the rest of the world knows very little about Swiss wine. The two major wine grapes are Pinot Noir, and the native white Chasselas, each of which account for about 30 percent of production. The reds Gamay and Merlot come next. Reds account for about sixty percent of Swiss production. Since Switzerland is not an EU member, they lack a quality appellation system. Instead, the local wine producing cantons each have their own labeling traditions.

The **Geneva** region, largely French speaking, produces reds, whites, and rosés in still, sweet and sparkling formats. Two Swiss crossings—Gamaret and Garanoir—accompany Pinot Noir and Gamay for the reds and rosés. Merlot is also widely planted. Cabernet Sauvignon and Cabernet Franc also have a small representation. Crisp whites are made from the Swiss Chasselas, and the two Burgundy grapes Chardonnay and Aligoté, as well as Pinot Blanc, Pinot Gris and Müller-Thurgau.

Lake Geneva here moderates the climate, warming the region in winter and cooling it in summer. The land here is relatively flat for Switzerland.

North and east of Lake Geneva is the **Vaud** region, also French speaking. Lake Geneva, which is part of the Rhône system, moderates the climate here as well. Chasselas is the key wine grape here in the Vaud, which unusually for Switzerland is a white wine specialist. Chasselas has many characters, because, like Riesling, it reflects subtle differences in growing conditions (*terroir*) more than most white grapes. The French influence is felt also, with increasing plantings of Chardonnay, Sauvignon Blanc, Pinot Gris, Pinot Blanc, and Viognier. Reds are from the same grapes as Geneva.

North of the Vaud, still in French speaking Switzerland, is **Neuchatel**, also called the Three Lakes region. Neuchatel is 55% red, almost all of it Pinot Noir. It also produces a range of whites, but Chasselas accounts for most of white wine production. The region has been producing a pale rosé wine called *Oeil de Perdrix*, meaning "Eye of the Partridge," for over 500 years.

Valais in the southwest is Switzerland's largest producer, accounting for half of all Swiss wine. Most vineyards are situated at between 1500 to 2500 feet above sea level, but these are dwarfed by the Alps, which act to shelter the region from extreme weather. Vineyards here are nevertheless steep. Pinot Noir rules here, with Chasselas second. Valais also grows varieties seen nowhere else, like the red Diolinoir, Cornalin and Humagne Rouge. It has numerous sub-regions, and over one hundred appellations.

Ticino is in the Italian speaking portion of Switzerland. It is more southerly and hence warmer than the rest of Switzerland and produces almost exclusively Merlot.

The large area of **German speaking Switzerland** in the north has, as can be expected, some similarities with Germany itself, especially Baden in southern Germany. Pinot Noir, called Blauburgunder, is the major grape, as it is in Baden. The minority whites are produced from Müller-Thurgau, Pinot Gris, Chardonnay, Sauvignon Blanc and Kerner. The region includes the canton of Thurgau, where Doctor Hermann Müller, the creator of the Müller-Thurgau crossing, was born.

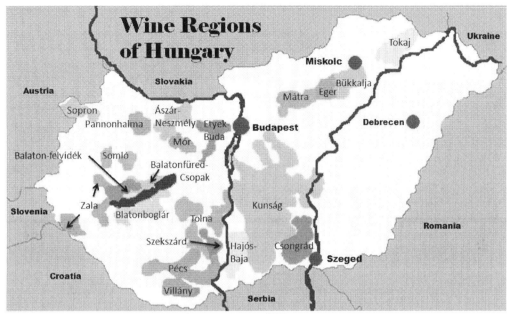

Wine Map of Hungary

Ask most wine drinkers what they know about Hungary, and the answer will likely be two wines: Tokaji and Bull's Blood. These two wines sit at opposite extremes of quality and price. **Tokaji Aszú**, from the northeast of Hungary, is the formidable sweet wine made from grapes affected by noble rot (botrytis). French King Louis XIV adored it, Beethoven was inspired by it. Tokaji is the pricey one. The cheap wine is Bikavér ("Bull's Blood"), a product of mass production on high yielding vineyards during the country's unfortunate Communist era. The story is similar for all the ex-communist wine producing nations: the fall of communism left a vacuum slowly filled by independent vine growers, wine makers (sometimes, but not always, the same), exporters, distributors, and so forth. Hungary has some large players, of course, but its particular strength is its growing legion of small artisanal winemakers, working in over twenty delimited regions.

The **Tokaj** region in the northeast (which juts into a bit of Slovakia) produces dry wines from the white Furmint grape, but its most famous product is the hyper-sweet **Tokaji Aszú**. To make it, the grower picks only those grapes that have been shriveled by noble rot, one grape at a time. The grapes go into a large vat, and are then trampled into a paste called Aszú dough. The winemaker then adds grape must or wine to the dough and lets it all steep up to two days. The winemaker then racks the liquid into casks or vats, and stores them in cool cellars. These vessels are not tightly closed, letting in oxygen, and encouraging a slow fermentation process that can last for years, for an ultimate wine that can last decades. The aroma, flavor, and feel of **Tokaji Aszú** cannot be described.

The **Eger** region, in the north produces the robust Bulls Blood Bikavér blends. Recent laws have created a Bikavér Superior label. Bikavér is a blend of mainly Kadarka and Kekfrankos (Blaufrankisch), with additions of Zweigelt, Blauburger, Kekmedoc, Cabernet Franc, Cabernet Sauvignon, Merlot and Pinot Noir. When Bikaver is good, it is medium-bodied, with soft tannins, plumy flavors, and spice. Eger is sandwiched between **Mátra** to the west and **Bükkalja** to the east, both mainly white wine producers.

The trio of **Kunság, Csongrád** and **Hajós-Baja** fill out the Great Plain (part of the larger Pannonian Plain) between the Danube and the Tisza Rivers. Half of all Hungarian wine is produced here, much of it average quaffing wine destined to bulk export to Germany and Austria.

The **Szekszard** wine region in southern Hungary is on the west side of the Danube, across from Hajós-Baja. It produces fragrant, structured red from Kekfrankos, Kadarka, Cabernet Sauvignon, Cabernet Franc and Merlot. White wines are also produced from Welschriesling, called Olaszrizling here, Chardonnay, and Sauvignon Blanc.

Tolna is a region of large producers of easy-drinking wines from Chardonnay, Welschriesling, Pinot Blanc, Rhine Riesling, Rizlingszilváni, Kadarka, Kékfrankos, Zweigelt, and Merlot.

Pécs has a long growing season. Because of the long hot summer, wines are usually full-bodied and either high in alcohol or residual sugar. The characteristic wine of the region is the white Cirfandli (Zierfandler in German), spicy and floral with high alcohol. Good Chardonnay and tart dry white Furmint are also produced.

Villány is Hungary's most southerly and hottest wine region, producing high quality full-bodied red wines from Cabernet Sauvignon, Merlot, Cabernet Franc and Portugieser.

Lake Balaton in the west is surrounded by wine appellations. The Pannonian Plain was once an ancient sea. Lake Balaton and Austria's shallow Neusiedlersee are its last aqueous remnants. The mild climate **Zala** region (also called Balatonmelleke) between the two lakes is humid. It produces table grapes. Wine grape varieties include Welschriesling, Rieslingszilváni, Zöld Veltelini, Piros Tramini, Chardonnay, Kékfrankos, Zweigelt, and Blue Portugieser.

Balatonboglar covers the southern shores of the lake. It is producing good sparkling wines from Chardonnay and Pinot Noir, reds from Pinot Noir, Merlot and Syrah, and dry whites from Sauvignon Blanc, Pinot Gris and Muscat Blanc. While the area to the north of the lake has produced wine for centuries, Balatonboglar itself is relatively new.

Balatonfured-Csopak sits on the northwest edge of the lake. It is renowned for its Olaszrizling (Welschriesling).

Balaton-Felvidek is mainly a white wine region. Olaszrizling leads production, followed by Chardonnay.

Etyek-Buda, just west of the capital city of Budapest, is known for the area's traditional grape Keknyelu, which produces full-bodied smoky white wines. The international bullies Pinot Gris, Chardonnay, Sauvignon Blanc and Riesling are in the process of nudging this rare traditional gem into obscurity

In **Mór** to the west, the white indigenous Hungarian Ezerjo, the most widely planted, is used mainly for sweet wines. It is followed in production level by Chardonnay, Rajnai Rizling, Rizlingszilvani, Sauvignon Blanc, Sztirkebarat, and Tramini. Mor wines tend to be on the aggressive side, and have the acidity to support long aging.

The **Ászár-Neszmély** produces white wines, mainly from Sauvignon Blanc, Pinot Gris and Olaszrizling (Welschriesling).

Pannonhalma in the northwest produces mainly French grapes: Cabernet Sauvignon, Cabernet Franc, Merlot, and Pinot Noir.

In the extreme west of Hungary, **Sopron** is essentially an extension of Austria's Neusiedlersee-Hugelland region. Sopron is a red wine producer. Its primary grape is Kekfrankos (Blaufrankisch), with plantings of Cabernet Sauvignon, Cabernet Franc, Merlot, and Pinot Noir.

The **Somló** appellation lies on the slopes of the Somló Mountain. Vineyards surround this dormant volcano rising from the plains of the Tapolca Basin. The appellation is white wine only, from Hárslevelű, Furmint, Juhfark, Welschriesling, Tramini and Chardonnay.

Wine Map of The Czech Republic

The **Czech Republic** is better known for beer than wine. Some wine is made in the western area of Bohemia, but 95% of wine production takes place in the southwest, Moravia, adjacent to the Austrian wine producing region of Niederösterreich.

Bohemia's wine areas are among the northernmost in Europe. The top five grape varieties are Müller-Thurgau, Riesling, St. Laurent, Blauer Portugieser, and Pinot Noir.

Moravia has four wine appellations, all hugging the southern border with Austria: Znojemská, Mikulovská, Velkopavlovická, and Slovácká. Grapes include Rivaner (Müller-Thurgau), Pinot Blanc, Grüner Veltliner, Welschriesling, Sauvignon Blanc, Pinot Noir and Blauer Portugieser. Cabernet Moravia, which is a truly indigenous variety, is a cross of Cabernet Franc and Zweigelt first bred in the early 1970's, and officially a new variety of grape as of 2001.

Wine Map of Slovakia

Slovakia produces its wine along most of its southern border with Austria and Hungary.

The **Malokarpatská**, "Lesser Carpathian" wine region, is in the west. Veltlínske Zelenéis is the most grown grape variety, producing light white wines. Rizling Vlašský (Welschriesling) is next, followed by Müller Thurgau. **Nitrianska**, the "Nitra wine region," concentrates on the same grapes.

Južnoslovenská, the "South Slovak" wine region, hugs the Austrian border. It is the warmest part of Slovakia, with vineyards planted on Loess uplands. Veltlínske Zelenéis is the most grown grape variety, producing light white wines. Rizling Vlašský (Welschriesling) is next, followed by the red Frankovka Odrá, the Slovakian name for Blaufrankisch. Small amounts of Cabernet Sauvignon and Chardonnay are produced.

Stredoslovenská. the "Central Slovak wine region," produces mainly whites from Veltlínske Zelenéis, Rizling Vlašský, Pinot Blanc, and standard Riesling.

Východoslovenská, the "East Slovak wine region," produces mainly whites from Rizling Vlašský (Welschriesling), Müller Thurgau, and Riesling. Ten percent of the wine is red from Frankovka modrá.

Tokajská is the Slovakian section of the adjacent and more famous Hungarian region of **Tokaji**. After much dispute, the Hungarians consented to Slovakia using the Slovakian term "Tokajské," which means "of Tokaji," on labels. Hungarian quality standards apply.

World Wine Regions
Europe
Slovenia

Just to put the next six (or seven) countries into perspective, each of them was once a part of the country that used to be called Yugoslavia—Land of the South Slavs. Yugoslavia was formed after World War One. After World War Two, Communist Marshal Josip Broz Tito took power, and through the force of his personality was able to keep the multi-ethnic federation together. Tito died in 1980, and by the time the Berlin Wall fell in 1989, the federation was in shambles. The subsequent civil war—actually several wars—left tens of thousands dead, and seriously disrupted the economy, including the wine producing economy. In 1991 Slovenia and Croatia, both major wine producers, declared independence. Macedonia followed the same year. Bosnia and Herzegovina declared independence in 1992, Montenegro and Serbia split into separate countries in 2006, and Kosovo declared independence from Serbia in 2008.

Wine Map of Slovenia

Even when it was a part of Yugoslavia, Slovenia exported its excellent wine to western Europe. Slovenia is in the northwest of the old Yugoslavia, bordering both Italy (next to the wine region of Friuli-Venezie Giulia) and Austria (next to the wine region of Steiermark). **Goriška Brda** is seamlessly integrated with the Italian appellation of Collio Goriziano DOC. Vineyards straddle the international border, producing the same grapes on either side. Wineries in Slovenia vinify Italian grapes and vice versa. Major grapes here are Merlot, Cabernet Sauvignon, Chardonnay, Sauvignon Blanc, Pinot Gris (Sivi Pinot), and Pinot Noir (Modri Pinot), as well as more local grapes like Rebula, Refosco (Refošk) and Friulano. Friulano used to be called Tocai on both sides of the border, but now the term is banned by the EU so as to avoid confusion with the famous Hungarian sweet wine Tokaji (pronounced Toke_EYE).

The wider Slovenian regional label here is **Primorje (Primorska)**, also referred to as "the littoral." A step south from Goriška Brda is **Vipavska Dolina**, the valley of the Vipava river, which specializes in light crisp whites from the local Pinela and Zelen grapes. The **Kras** (karst) plateau another step south, is an area of limestone hills and iron-rich soils, noted for a big high acid red wine called Teran made from the Refosco grape.

Slovenia's **Istrian peninsula** is its only bit of seacoast on the Adriatic. Here, Refosco and Malvazija are the most widely planted grapes.

In the **Posavje** region, the wines and many of the grapes are delightfully local. **Bela Krajina's** vineyards inhabit the alpine foothills, on limestone Karst soils. This is a region of blends. The most prominent is **Metliska Crnina** - traditionally a red blend of Modra Frankinja (Blaufrankisch), Modra Portugalka (Blauer Portugieser), Zametna Crnina (a Slovenian original), and Sentlovrenka (St. Laurent), highly extracted and velvety. **Belokranjski** is a dry rosé wine blended from Zametna Crnina and Modra Frankinja. Bela Krajina also produces high quality Modri Pinot (Pinot Noir).

In **Dolenjska** the signature wine is called **Cviček**, a blend of both white and red grapes. The red grapes Modra Frankinja and Zametna Črnina make up 70 per cent of the blend, the white varieties Kraljevina, Laški Rizling, Rumeni Plavec and Zeleni Silvanec, 30 per cent. Every year in the region a Cviček Queen is crowned. The wine is lightly colored, with fresh aromas and flavors of raspberry, cherry and red currant, and a low alcohol level.

Bizeljsko-Sremič is known for its still and sparkling white wines from Sauvignon Blanc, Chardonnay, and Laski Rizling. The acid rich indigenous Rumeni Plavec, is used for blending. Bizeljcan is an aromatic, dry blend of Laski Rizling, Sauvignon, Rumeni Plavec, and Sipon; white Sremican is a dry blend of Laski Rizling, Sauvignon, and Rumeni Plavec; red Sremican is a dry red wine blended from Modra Frankinja, Zametna Crnina, and Laski Rizling.

Podravje in the northeast, centers around the city of Maribor in the **Štajerska Slovenija** sub-region. Its wines are almost exclusively white. Laški Rizling (Welschriesling) is the major grape here, with Sipon (the Furmint grape of Hungary), Renski Rizing (Rhine Riesling), Sauvignon Blanc and Chardonnay, Pinots Noir, Gris, and Blanc. The warm climate **Prekmurje** sub-region near Hungary is known for its soft reds from Pinot Noir (Modri Pinot) and Blaufrankisch (Modri Franinja).

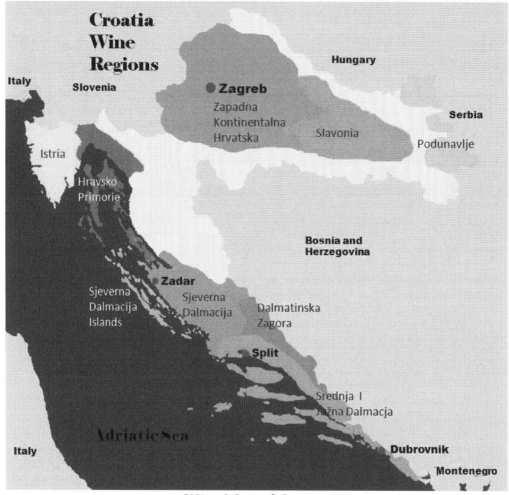

Wine Map of Croatia

The Dinaric Alps split Croatia into two widely different wine regions, both producing primarily white grapes. The **interior region**, with its continental climate, is home to the Slavonian oak forest, used for wine aging barrels as an alternative to both French and American oak. (Do not confused Slavonia, the section of Croatia, with Slovenia, a separate wine-producing country.) Croatia has over sixty indigenous grape varieties.

The **Croatian Uplands** are in the center of the country, not far from the capital of Zagreb. The region produces Pinot Noir, whites from Sauvignon Blanc, Chardonnay, Gewürztraminer, Riesling, Muscat, Silvaner and Pinot Gris, as well as sweet botrytised wines and ice wines.

East of the uplands is the region called **Slavonia and the Croatian Danube**. The big wine here is Graševina (Welschriesling), crisp and very clean from the volcanic soil. Sauvignon Blanc, Chardonnay, and Pinot Gris also support the whites here. Reds are made with Blaufrankisch.

Coastal Croatia lies across the Adriatic Sea from Italy and has a similar Mediterranean climate. Dotted with hundreds of islands and inlets, the coast attracts major resort and tourist attention, and so do its wines (and mention ought to be made of its fine olive oils). The math is in Croatia's favor—it has a population of just over four million and annually welcomes twelve million tourists.

On the northern reaches of the coast, **Istria (Hrvatska Istra)**, which Croatia shares with Slovenia, has Malvazija Istarska, its own Malvasia variant. Unlike most white wines, the skins are macerated in the juice (like red wine), bringing out a deep golden color and notes of rich honey and apple. The Istrians age their wine in acacia rather than oak, resulting in a full-bodied wine that can age. Istrian reds are generally Teran and Refosco.

The red Plavac Mali makes some waves (and a full-bodied, insistent red wine) on the **Croatian Coast (Hvratsko Primorje)**. Plavac Mali is the foundation of the popular wines Postup, Dingač and Zlatan Plavac. Crljenak Kaštelanski, related to Plavac Mali, at one time was an obscure black grape from a small island in the Split area. It is back and flourishing now that genetic tests have revealed it to be one and the same with California's Zinfandel.

The islands of the **central and southern Croatian coast** produce a great deal of white Malvasia, called Marastina here. Other white grapes include Zlahtina from the island of **Krk** (you need to imagine the vowel) in the north, Vugava form the island of **Vis**, Bogdanuška on the popular touirist island of **Hvar**, and Pošip and Grk (imagine that vowel again) on Korčula.

Croatian wines are classified by quality.

- Vrhunsko Vino: Premium Quality Wine
- Kvalitetno Vino: Quality Wine
- Stolno Vino: Table Wine

Wines may also qualify for a geographical origin stamp, and a varietal stamp, but no uniform DOP/AOC/DOC type appellation system exists yet.

Wine Map of Serbia and Kosovo

Wine in Serbia goes back to Roman time, but the twentieth century saw the near total destruction of Serbia's grapevines. First came the devastation of phylloxera, then two world wars, the post-war era of communist collectivization of agriculture in Yugoslavia, and finally a series of civil wars that shook Serbia to the core. Of course, wine will seek its own level, and the Serbia wine culture is reviving. The country has a handful of large wine companies, with some three hundred small producers, although it still imports more wine than it produces. The government has put money into equipment modernization, and has already promulgated wine appellation laws that comply with EU regulations.

In Serbia, the equivalent of PGI for larger appellations is covered by their Geografska Indikacija (GI). Like the Italians they have two equivalents for the EU's PDO: Kontrolisano Poreklo I Kvalitet (KPK) and the more exalted Kontrolisano i Garantovano Poreklo i Kvalitet (KGPK) .

In the north, bordering Hungary, is **Subotica-Horgoš**, which has sandy soils related to the Pannonian Plain. The region produces the whites Graševina (Welschriesling), and Riesling. **Srem** to the south near the capital of Belgrade is influenced by the Danube, producing whites from Graševina and Chardonnay, and reds from Portugieser and the local (for Serbia and Montenegro) Vranac. **Banat** near the border with Romania is the home of the rare indigenous white grape Kreaca.

In the center, **Šumadija-Great Morava** has large producers for its local red Prokupac. International varieties also grow here. The acidic white grape Smederevka is produced around its namesake town of Smederevo. The region also produces reds and good Cabernet Sauvignon.

In the west, the **Pocerina** region with its undulating hills around the mountain of Cer is a Pinot Noir specialist. **West Morava** gives us Prokupac, Vranac, and even some Cabernet Sauvignon and Merlot. Looking east toward Bulgaria, **Timok** produces Vranac, Cabernet Sauvignon, Muscat Hamburg, Chardonnay, Rheinriesling and Sauvignon Blanc. The large region of **South Morava** gives us a range of grapes, including the reds Prokupac, Vranac, and Cabernet Sauvignon, ands the whites Graševina and Chardonnay.

Kosovo declared independence from Serbia in 2008. More than half of the 193 member states of the United Nations, including the United States, have recognized its independence, but Serbia continues to claim the region as its sovereign territory. Serbia will have to recognize Kosovo as independent if it is to have any chance of joining the EU. War seriously hampered Kosovo's wine industry, but now it is rehabilitating its pre-war reputation for choice Pinot Noir, Merlot, and Chardonnay.

Wine Map of Montenegro

An ex-Yugoslav republic on the Adriatic coast across from Italy's Puglia, Montenegro is dry and mountainous, with a Mediterranean climate. Vines grow at up to 2000 feet above sea level. Its two regions are the **Lake Skadar Region** and the **Coastal Zone**. Red Vranac accounts for more than half of production, making a fresh, balanced, deeply-colored varietal wine. Kratošija, the local name for Zinfandel, is the number two red grape, followed by Cabernet Sauvignon, Merlot, Syrah, and Grenache. Among whites, the locals Kristač and Žižak lead the pack, which includes Chardonnay, the Georgian grape Rkatsateli, Pinot Blanc and Sauvignon Blanc.

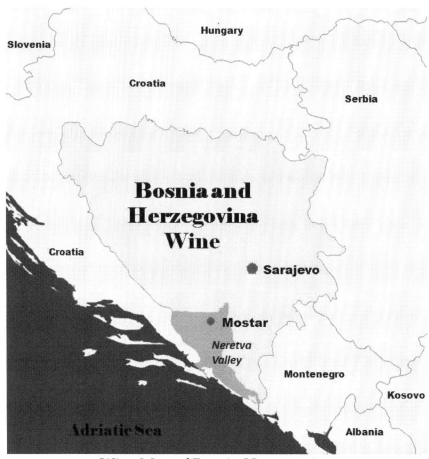

Wine Map of Bosnia-Herzegovina

The horrible 1992-1995 war in Bosnia-Herzegovina damaged much of the region's viticulture and it still has not recovered. The **Neretva Valley/Mostar** region is the most important production region. Slightly more than half of all plantings are white grapes, especially the local Žilavka, which makes an aromatic, full-bodied wine. The region produces the acidic white Serbian grape Smederevka, as well as local whites Krkošija and Bena. Blatina is the local red, usually blended with Alicante Bouschet. Vranac and Cabernet Sauvignon are also produced.

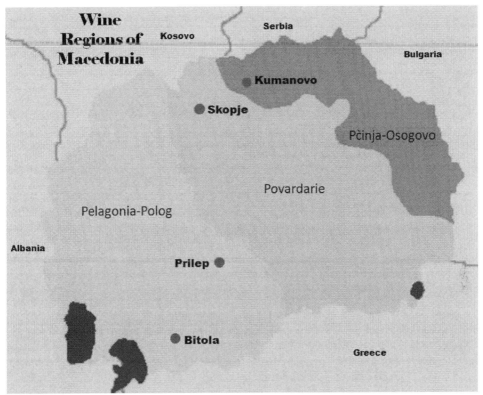

Wine Map of Macedonia

The geographic region called Macedonia stretches over northern Greece, part of Bulgaria, and the present-day landlocked country of Macedonia, which occupies the region's northern third. The Republic of Macedonia is inhabited by a majority of Macedonians, who speak a South Slavic language, and a sizeable Albanian minority of about 25%. Greece objected to the country's admission to the United Nations under the name of Macedonia, and therefore the country is often referred to as the Former Yugoslav Republic of Macedonia (FYROM) by the UN, the EU, and other organizations.

Red wines lead Macedonian production, largely from the local varieties Vranac and Kratosija, with the usual interlopers Cabernet Sauvignon and Merlot. The main wine-growing regions here are **Pcinja-Osogovo** in the north, **Povardarie** in the center, and **Pelagonija-Polog** in the south.

413

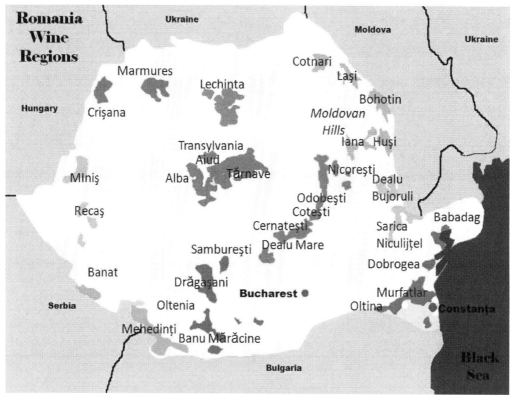

Wine Map of Romania

Romania has a romance language, deep connections with France, and a wine culture that dates back to the Romans from which the country's language, and name, derives. Although on the same latitudes as France, one cannot stretch the parallels too far. The Romanian climate and topographical configuration is quite different, and the French did not see their vine growing culture compromised by communist collectivization. The take on 21st century Romania is that it is adding quality to the quantity of wine it was known for during the 20th century.

Romania's climate is dominated by mountains. The Transylvanian Alps and Carpathian Mountains combine to bisect the country on the north-south axis, with various plains and elevated regions on either side. Climates are diverse, but generally favorable for viticulture, except in the highest of the mountains.

Romanian wine grapes are a mishmash. On the one hand, the country has its fair share of admirable indigenous grapes, and on the other it is still in the process of following an EU mandate that it eliminate the many American hybrid vines planted during the collectivization, quantity-over-quality era. Among white grapes, Fetească Albă and Fetească Regală are the most prevalent, producing wines in all levels of sweetness. Welschriesling (Italian Riesling) comes in at number three. Aligoté, Sauvignon Blanc, and Muscat de Ottonel round out the list. Cabernet Sauvignon and Merlot lead

the reds. The indigenous reds Roşioară and Băbeasca Neagră are in the

process of losing ground to Fetească Neagră. Pinot Noir and Blaufrankisch are also on the upswing.

Transylvania sits in the north center of Romania on a wide plateau surrounded on all sides by the Carpathian Mountains. The most important grapes here are Fetească Albă, Fetească Regală, Muscat Ottonel, Pinot Gris, Sauvignon, Pink Traminer, Italian Riesling, Neuburger, and Rhine Riesling. Grapevines are cultivated on wind-sheltered hills. White wines here are well balanced and dry. Within Transylvania, the **Tarnave** region is sandwiched between two rivers, Târnava Mica and Târnava Mare. Both the rivers and the altitude create a cool local climate, resulting in fruity white wines and with very good acidity. **Alba Iulia-Aiud** is to the west of Tarnave, producing Italian Riesling, Fetească Albă, Fetească Regală, Pinot Gris, Sauvignon, and Muscat Ottonel, on hillside vineyards. **Lechinţa** covers a small, fragmented area in northern part of Transylvania, producing still white wines, available as dry, semi-dry, semi-sweet and sweet, from Traminer Roz, Pinot Gris, Muscat Ottonel, Sauvignon Blanc, Neuburger (an Austrian crossing), Welschriesling, Fetească Regală, Fetească Albă, and Chardonnay.

Crisana and Maramures are in Romania's northwest. Crisana makes red wines from Cadarca, Cabernet Sauvignon, Pinot Noir, Merlot), while Maramures produces acidic white wines excellent for brandy.

Banat is situated in the west of Romania. Its best known region is Minis-Maderat, The most important grapes are Cabernet Sauvignon, Pinot Noir, Italian Riesling, Sauvignon, Burgund Mare, Fetească Regală, Merlot, Muscat Ottonel, and Cadarca.

Muntenia, Oltenia, the Danube Terraces and the Southern Lands. This region takes up the southern third of Romania, and includes its capital Bucharest. Vineyards here sit on the south-east facing slopes of the Carpathian Mountains, on the hills south of the mountains, along large rivers and in some locations near the Danube river. This is a warm south-oriented region with plenty of sunshine. In the east of the region, the well known **Dealu Mare** appellation makes sweet whites with firm acidity, and bright reds from Fetească Negara and Cabernet Sauvignon, two grapes that extend through this most productive region of Romania.

The **Moldovan Hills** in the northeast of the country produce the famous Grasă de Cotnari botrytised sweet wine, whose residual sugar content may approach 300g/liter (30%). Climate here is generally continental, with vineyards planted on south facing slopes in order to maximize sunlight. Grapes include Fetească Albă, Francusa, Grasa de Cotnari, Tamaioasa Romaneasca, Muscat Ottonel, Chardonay, Pinot Gris, Sauvignon, Fetească Regală, Fetească Negara, Babeasca Neagra, Aligoté, Busuioaca de Bohotin, Zghiara de Husi, Italian Riesling, Cabernet Sauvignon, Merlot, Pinot Noir, Alicante Bouschet, Oporto, Zweigelt, Sarba, Galbena de Odobesti, and Plavaie.

The Region of **Dobrogea** covers Romania's Black Sea coast and the Danube delta. **Murfatlar** here is known for concentrated dried grape wines. Production includes Cabernet Sauvignon, Chardonay, Pinot Gris, Pinot Noir, Columna, Merlot, Muscat Ottonel, Italian Riesling, Sauvignon Blanc, Fetească Negara, Fetească Regală, Aligoté, and Babeasca Negara. **Babadag** produces still red, white and rosé wines, available as dry, semi-dry, semi-sweet and sweet. **Nikulitel**, site of the renowned vineyard of Sarica Niculitel, growing the whites Aligoté, Riesling, Sauvignon Blanc, and Fetească Albă, and red varieties Merlot, Cabernet Sauvignon, Syrah, and Fetească Negara.

Wine Map of Bulgaria

As our map shows, most of Bulgaria is wine country. The country has a continental climate, with hot summers (somewhat mitigated by the Black Sea to the east and the Danube River to the north). In the latter part of the communist era, from the 1960s to the 1980s, Bulgaria began to move away from bulk wines, largely exported to Russia, and into quality wines, especially reds like Cabernet Sauvignon, with substantial exports to Great Britain. After decades of disarray, the 21st century is showing a greater cohesiveness in the Bulgarian wine industry, but Bulgaria's largest wine trading partner is still Russia. Except for the eastern region by the Black Sea, red grape varieties dominate Bulgarian viticulture, accounting for nearly two thirds of all grapes grown. Merlot has recently pushed its buddy Cabernet Sauvignon off the number one spot. The local red grapes Pamid and Melnik are in decline, but Mavrud, born in western Thrace, is gaining in importance as the major component in red blends. Prominent whites include the Georgian grape Rkatsateli, the Serbian Dimiat, the pink Misket grape, Muscat Ottonel, Chardonnay, Traminer, Trebbiano, Riesling, Sauvignon Blanc, Aligoté and Viognier.

Bulgaria has a modern EU-compliant system of controlled appellation. The country has two PGIs, the Thracian Lowlands and the Danubian Plain, and over 50 PDOs.

The **Thracian Lowlands** have a temperate climate ideal for the local Mavrud, as well as Merlot, Cabernet Sauvignon, Muscatel and Pamid.

The **Danubian Plain** in the north produces Muscat Ottonel, Cabernet Sauvignon, Merlot, Chardonnay, Aligoté, Pamid and the local Gamza (Kadarka) grape.

The **Valley of the Roses** sandwiched between the two PGIs is world-renowned for its rose-growing industry. It produces 85% of the world's rose oil. The characteristic wine grape is the Misket Cherven, or Red Misket, a pale pink grape that produces a white wine with floral aromas, vanilla, rose, citrus and tropical fruit. The wine has minerality, light body, and a clean finish.

The **Struma River Valley** in the southwest near the border with Greece grows the unique Bulgarian varietal Shiroka Melnishka ("Broad Leaved Vine of Melnik") used for dry and semi-dry wines. The grape likes oak from which it produces tobacco notes. Cabernet Sauvignon, Merlot and Pamid here also produce dry, spicy reds.

The **Black Sea Coast** is characterized by long and mild autumns, ideal ripening conditions for white wines from Dimyat, Riesling, Muscat Ottonel, Ugni Blanc, Sauvignon Blanc, Traminer, and Gewürztraminer.

Wine Map of Moldova

Moldova won its independence with the fall of the Soviet Union in 1991. Its people are ethnically similar to the nearby Romanians. Wine has been a significant part of Moldovan culture for many centuries. The Moldovan economy relies heavily on wine exports to a number of countries, and also from wine tourism. The Guinness Book of World Records lists one of Moldova's wine cellars, the Milesti Mici in **Codru**, as the world's largest (with approximately one and a half million bottles). Codru is the biggest wine producing center, known for Fetească, Sauvignon Blanc, Riesling, Traminer Rose and Cabernet Sauvignon, as well as sparkling wines and fortified wines.

The northern appellation of **Balti** produces mainly the white grape varieties Aligoté, Pinot Blanc, Pinot Gris, Fetească, and Traminer.

One of Moldova's distinctive wines is the red blend **Negru de Purkar** from the district of **Stefan Voda**, combining Cabernet Sauvignon, the Georgian grape Saperavi, and the local Rară Neagră.

Cabernet Sauvignon, Merlot, Pinot Noir, Chardonnay, Riesling and Pinot Gris are among the international grapes prominently used in Moldovan wines. Indigenous whites include Fetească Albă, Fetească Regală, Plavai, and Busuioacă Albă. Local reds include the Rară Neagră used in Negru de Purcari and Fetească Neagră.

Albania is small country on the Adriatic Sea wedged in between Montenegro on its northern border, Kosovo to the northeast, (the Former Yugoslav Republic of) Macedonia to its east, and Greece to the south.

Wine production in Albania goes back to the classical era, or even before — archaeological evidence of winemaking goes back at least six thousand years. Wine production was suppressed during the long Ottoman occupation, stagnated but survived during the communist era, and also survived the more recent transition to a market economy. In 2015, this small country had over 25,000 acres of vineyards, widely dispersed among mostly small family holdings.

Albania is known particularly for its indigenous grape varieties. Major whites include Shesh i Bardhe, Debin, e Bardhe, and Pules. Reds include Shesh i zi, Kallmet, Vlosh, Serine, and Debin, e Zeze.

The white and red forms of Shesh, Shesh i bardhe and Shesh i zi, respectively, account for more than a third of all plantings. The white Shesh has a fine floral element to it, while the red Shesh can benefit from aging.

Kallmet is Albania's noblest red grape, cultivated since the Roman era. The white Vlosh makes full-bodied astringent wines that are sometimes fermented with intentional oxidation, to bring on a sherry-like character.

Albania has four wine producing regions:

- The **coastal plains**, rising to about 1000 feet above sea level, including the capital city of Tirana
- The **central hilly region**, varying in altitude between 1000 and 2000 feet
- The **eastern sub-mountainous region**, 1800 to 2500 feet in elevation
- The **highlands**, where grapevines grow as high as 3,300 feet above sea level

Wine Map of Greece

Greece, as we have mentioned, has been producing wine for a long time, but in some way, it has not. It was only in the 1980s that Greece began to modernize its wine industry. Greek growers and enologists trained in places as diverse as Bordeaux or Napa, bringing back expertise and attractive investment. Ask many people their idea of Greek wine and they will quickly answer "Retsina," that pine resin wine. There is nothing wrong with Retsina, but Greek wine is so much more. Now with an international focus, the wines are making news, and even the grapes are colonizing other areas that previously thought of the grape as a French plant.

Greece produces international varieties like most other countries, of course, but it has an interesting stable of both red and white grapes that have the potential to, and often do, produce world class wine.

Most of Greece is rocky, on the mainland and its 3000 islands. The Mediterranean climate is dry to the east, wetter in the west. Soils are mostly limestone, alluvial near the rivers, and sandy by coastlines, with volcanic soils on islands.

Red Wine Grapes

- **Agiorghitiko** (Ay-Your-YEE-Tee-Ko, meaning the grape of Saint George) is a native grape of the Nemea in the Peloponnese, where Hercules slew the Nemean lion. It tends to be soft and fruity, and can be made into a drink me now wine or one designed to age a few years.

- **Xinomavro** (meaning sour black) is the predominant grape variety in Macedonia, especially around the city of Naousa. The X here is *not* pronounced like an English Z, but like a quick K-S: Ksee-no-MAV-ro. Xinomavro is tannic, savory, with notes of olives and tomatoes, full-bodied, and ought to age awhile.

- **Mavrodaphne** (meaning black laurel), grows in the Peloponnese and the Ionian Islands. It is the mainstay of the famous chocolate-tasting dessert wine Mavrodaphne of Patras.

- **Limnio**, or **Kalambaki** is indigenous to the island of Lemnos in the Aegean, where it has produced red wine for two millennia. Limnio is full-bodied, high in alcohol, herbaceous, with aromas and flavors of laurel (bay leaves).

- **Mandilaria** is a tannic grape grown on Rhodes and Crete. It is often blended with other grapes to soften the mouthfeel.

- **Kotsifali** is a variety mainly grown on Crete.

White Wine Grapes

- **Assyrtiko** is native to the volcanic island of Santorini, but it is now planted all over Greece. It maintains its acidity nicely as it ripens, even in unrelenting hot climates. The fruit can be warm and round, showing peach and apricot.

- **Savatiano** (the "Saturday" grape) is the predominant white grape in Attica, where it displays excellent heat resistance and shows a distinct floral and fruity aroma. It is quite versatile, and is one of the major grapes used to produce Retsina.

- **Robola** has a mouth-filling smoky mineral feeling, with warm round citrus. It is most closely associated with the Ionian Island of Cephalonia (Kefalonia).

- **Athiri** is a lower acid variety planted in Macedonia, Attica, and Rhodes.

- **Debina** is a white Greek wine grape primarily in the Zitsa region of Epirus. Because of its high acidity, it is used in sparkling wine production.

- **Lagorthi** is mainly cultivated on high slopes of the Peloponnese, fruit filled and acidic.

- **Malagousia** grows in Macedonia, making elegant full bodied wines, with medium-plus acidity and exciting perfumed aromas.

- **Moschofilero** is a Blanc de Gris variety from the AOC region of Mantineia, in Arcadia in the Peloponnese. Wines, both still and sparkling are crisp and floral. It is pronounced Mo-Sko-FEEL-err-o.

- **Roditis** (the "pink" or "rose" grape) produces elegant, light white wines with citrus flavors all over Greece. Also called Rhoditis.

Greek Wine Quality Designations

The highest level of Greek wines has two designations, the EU PDO (protected denomination of origin) much like the Italian DOC and DOCG system.

- Onomasia Proelefsis Anoteras Poiotitos (O.P.A.P.), Appellation of Origin of Superior Quality

- Onomasia Proelefsis Eleghomeni (O.P.E.), Controlled Appellation of Origin

Like most of the rest of Europe, Greece has regional wines, called "Topikos Oinos," equivalent to the French Vin de Pays or the Italian IGP/IGT. The EU designation is PGU, protected geographical indication.

The lowest level is Epitrapezios Oinos, basic table wine.

Retsina is its own category

The Greek Wine Regions

We will start in the northeast and work our way south.

Thrace also includes parts of Turkey and Bulgaria. This is the land where the cult of Dionysus is supposed to have begun. Thrace has three PGI zones, each producing wines from Cabernet Sauvignon, Chardonnay, Syrah and the Bulgarian Mavrud grape.

Macedonia in the cooler north is a large region. At one time, under Alexander the Great, it ruled a vast empire stretching east to what is now Pakistan. Xinomavro is widely planted here, in the three dispersed red wine regions of **Amyndaio**, **Goumenissa** and **Naousa**. These are big, tannic red wines. Further south, the Slopes of Meliton (Playes Melitona) appellation makes Cabernet Sauvignon, Cabernet Franc and Limnio. It is important not to confuse the Greek region of Macedonia with its northern neighbor, the Former Yugoslavian Republic of Macedonia.

Epirus takes up the Greek mainland's northwest corner. This is a rugged area where vines of the indigenous Debina, Vlachiko and Bekiari grapes cling to the side of mountains. Cabernet Sauvignon is also produced. Most vineyards are over two thousand feet above sea level. Appellations include **Zitsa** (the only PDO) and **Ioannina**.

Corfu is one of the Ionian Islands off the west coast of Greece. It is best known for white wines. There is no PDO, just a regional appellation requiring at least 60 percent Kakotrygis in the wine, with the rest Robola and Moschato (Muscat Blanc à Petits Grains). Tourism is more important on Corfu than winemaking.

Kefalonia (Cephalonia) is the largest of the Ionian island and the home to three PDO-level appellations. **Robola of Kefalonia** is the most important, producing light, fresh, citrusy, white wines from the Robola grape, grown at elevations up to 2600 feet on dry limestone soil. The island also has two sweet wine appellations: **Mavrodaphne of Kefalonia**, from the island's lower lying areas, as well as the neighboring island of Ithaca (Ithaki), and **Muscat of Kefalonia** is a white *vin doux naturel* made from the Muscat Blanc a Petits Grains grape variety.

The fertile valleys of **Thessaly** produce a range of crops, leaving the hillsides for grape vines. PDOs here include **Anchalios** for Roditis, **Messenikolas** for light reds from **Mavro Messenikola**, **Rapsani** – a blend of Xinomvaro and Krassato, and **Stavroto**, for Tyrnavos and Limniona.

Central Greece has a complex, mountainous topography. It is home to the nation's largest city, Athens and the birthplace of Retsina, which is mostly made from the Savatiano grape. More than twenty PGI zones call this region home. There are PDOs for **Attica** (the Athens area) and **Attalandi**. Prominent grapes are Roditis, Savatiano, and the international varieties.

The Peloponnese has the **Mantinia PDO** at 2100 feet altitude, known for its white Moschofilero, the **Nemea PDO**, at 800 to 2600 feet, known for Agiorghitiko, and **Mavrodaphne of Patras PDO**, a sweet fortified wine. The area also produces the sweet Muscat of Patras.

Crete, the largest island of Greece, has four PDOs, producing wines from the native varieties Liatiko, Vilana and Kotisfali and also from international varieties. Soils on the island are limestone-rich. The PDOs are **Peza**, **Arhanes**, **Dafnes** and **Sitia**, all in the eastern reaches of the island. Ridges shelter these northward looking vineyards from the hot African wind. Crete also has six regional appellations: Chania, Rethymno, Lasithi, Kissamos, Heraklion and one for the entire island.

Rhodes is a large island near the coast of Turkey, home to two PDOs. The **Rhodes PDO** authorizes red and white varietal wines made Morgiano and Athiri. **Muscat of Rhodes PDO** uses two different local varieties of Muscat for its *vin doux naturel* style.

Santorini is famous for its mineral-rich dry aromatic white wines from the Assyrtiko grape (often mixed with a little Athiri and Aidani). The island also produces red wines from Mandilaria and Mavrotragano. It is renowned for its **Vinsanto** wine (spelled here as one word and not "Vin Santo" as in Italy) from air dried grapes, from Assyrtiko, Athiri and Aidani. Tourist development is a threat to the exceptional wines of this unique island.

The island of **Samos** is renowned for its sweet **Muscat of Samos**, from the Moschato Aspro grape variety, the local name for Muscat Blanc a Petits Grains.

The island of **Lemnos** in the northern Aegean Sea has two PDOs, one for a VDN style sweet wine (**Muscat of Lemnos**) and the other for dry wines (**Lemnos PDO**), both from Muscat of Alexandria. Note that all the other Greek appellations that refer to the Muscat grape use the other variety, Muscat Blanc a Petits Grains.

The island of **Paros** in the central Aegean Sea is home to significant plantings of the Malvasia grape variety, used to make a crisp, dry white wine from 100% Malvasia and a red wine from one-third red Mandilaria softened by two thirds white Malvasia.

Winemaking on the Aegean island of **Chios** has been going on for several thousand years, although the island is better known for its anise-based spirit Ouzo. Assyrtiko and Roditis are the main grape varieties, grown at up to 1500 feet.

The heavily tourist-oriented island of **Mykonos** produces a small amount of wine from Assyrtiko, Cabernet Sauvignon and Syrah. Tourists consume it all on the island.

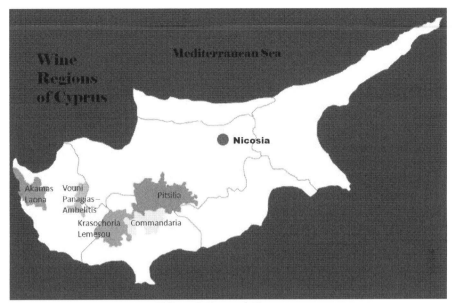

Wine Map of Cyprus

Recent archaeological evidence suggests that winemaking on the island of Cyprus dates back to 3500 BC, more than 5500 years ago. A mere thousand years ago the island's sweet wine Commandaria had a reputation second to none in Europe. Winemaking declined with the Ottoman conquests in the 16ᵗʰ century. The British took over Cyprus in 1878, winemaking resumed on Cyprus, but the industry concentrated on bulk wine that it would ship to bottlers abroad. Cyprus became an independent republic in 1960, but it was not until its membership in the EU in 2004, and the subsidies that followed, that winemakers there set their sights once again on fine wine.

Cyprus's major grape is the Mavro, which simply means "black" in Greek. It accounts for half of production, and is not where the potential quality lies. The imported grape Syrah has better prospects for red wine in this hot dry climate, as do the local reds Maratheftiko and the tannic Lefkada, The indigenous white Xynisteri grape accounts for a quarter of production and makes wine of notes from the higher altitude vineyards.

Cyprus evidently has some good wine in its future, but its real success now is the revitalization of the hyper-sweet Commandaria, made from dried red Mavro and white Xynisteri grapes in fourteen select villages on the slopes of the Troodos Mountains.

World Wine Regions
Europe
Malta

The Mediterranean island of Malta has no wine regions per se, but it does produce wine, with five producers on Malta itself and two on Malta's smaller island of Gozo. Malta has two indigenous varieties, the Gellewza which makes soft fragrant reds and rosé, and the Ghirgentina, the source of full-bodied white wines. Cabernet Sauvignon has also been successful here, as have Syrah and Mourvèdre. Malta began a quality labeling system in 2007 when it introduce the DOK designation, the equivalent to the EU PDO, and an IGT designation a little lower down.

World Wine Regions
Europe
Ukraine

Most of Ukraine is too cold for wine grape production, but its southern reaches near or along the Black Sea and the Sea of Azov have a long tradition of winemaking. When Ukraine was part of the Russian Empire, its wines from its Crimean peninsula were prized by the imperial court of the Tsar. Later, Ukraine became the USSR's largest wine producer. In 1986, Soviet Premier Mikhail Gorbachev decided that abuse of alcohol was ruining the country and began a veritable crusade against the grape, decimating Ukraine's vineyards (as well as those of the rest of the USSR). Five year later, in 1991, despite Gorbachev's temperance crusade, the Soviet Union dissolved, and Ukraine became an independent country. Its wine industry began to recover, only to see its prime vineyard region, the Crimean peninsula, annexed by Russia in 2014. In keeping with the nearly worldwide refusal to recognize the annexation, we include **the Crimea** as a Ukrainian wine region here. In addition to the Crimea, Ukraine's southern looking wine regions include the area called **Bessarabia** adjacent to wine-rich Moldova, **Carpathian Ruthenia**, and **Southern Ukraine**, covering the Black Sea coast west of the Crimea as well as the southern Dnieper River region. Major grape varieties include Aligoté, Muscat, Traminer, Chardonnay, the Georgian grape Rkatsiteli, and Pinot Gris among whites, Cabernet Sauvignon, Pinot Noir, and the American Isabella grape among reds. Sparkling wine is produced in Ukraine's large cities from Pinot Blanc, Aligoté, Riesling and Fetească.

World Wine Regions
Europe
Russia

If we do not count the Crimea as part of Russia—and we do not—Russia's vineyard area is pitifully small for the largest country on the planet. More than three-quarters of Russia's grapevines are planted in **Krasnodar Krai**, facing on both the Sea of Azov and the Black Sea. Most other regions of southern Russia are too cold in winter for vines to survive, forcing growers to bury them to protect against the cold—those grapes that do survive are generally used for brandy rather than wine. Krasnodar Krai grapes include the usual crew of international varieties, plus Burgundy's "other" white grape Aligoté, the Georgian white Rkatsiteli and red Saperavi, and some local varieties like the red Krasnostop.

World Wine Regions
Europe
Georgia

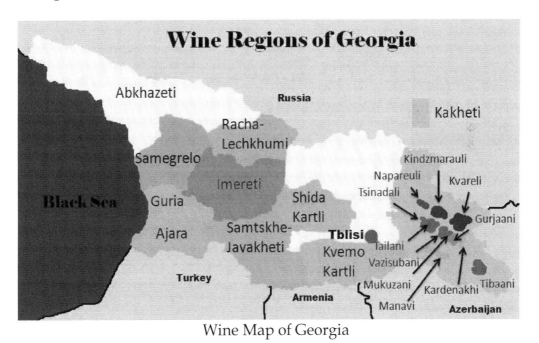

Wine Map of Georgia

The oldest evidence of human winemaking comes to us from the country of Georgia and dates to about 6,000 BC. Eight thousand years later, Georgia has a healthy wine industry and claims to be "The Cradle of Wine." Wine permeates every branch of human activity in the mountainous country in the Caucasus, at the far eastern edge of the Black Sea. The oldest archaeological evidence of wine making comes to us from Georgia, remains of pips (seeds) from cultivated grapes. What's more, the pips seemed to be sheltered in the remains of clay jars, evidently earlier versions of the *qvevri* clay fermentation vats that traditional Georgians use today. The idea is to push everything into the *qvevri*, grape bunches, skins, and stalks, and wait for nature to take its course. This is not the kind of thing you do with Cabernet or Pinot Noir, but with Georgian varieties like Rkatsiteli and Saperavi. These two varieties, white and red respectively, have colonized much of eastern Europe.

Georgian traditional clay fermentation vats called *qvevri*. Photo by Levan Totosashvili.

Georgia has much in the way of modern winery equipment, but a significant portion of its wines are still fermented in *qvevri*, partially because the mystique of tradition appeals to international markets. Small operations might have only a *qvevri* or two, but large winemakers maintain them in phalanxes, buried to their rims in the ground.

Georgian wines are most commonly blends of two or more grapes. Prominent white wines include:

- **Pirosmani** is a semi-sweet white wine made from a 40% Tsolikauri, 60% Tsitska blend.
- **Tsinandali**, a blend of Rkatsiteli and Mtsvane grapes from the sub-regions of Telavi and Kvareli in the Kakheti region.
- **Tvishi**, is a natural semi-sweet white wine made from Tsolikauri in the Lechkhumi region.
- **Mtsvani**, a dry white wine made from Mtsvani.
- **Alaznis Veli**, a white semi-sweet wine made from the Rkatsiteli, Tetra, Tsolikauri and other grape varieties.
- **Anakopia**, is a white semi-dry table wine made from the Tsolikauri grape in the Sukhumi and Gudauta districts in Abkhazia.
- **Tbilisuri**, a pink semi-dry wine produced from the Saperavi, Cabernet and Rkatsiteli grape varieties grown in east Georgia.
- **Khikhvi**, a vintage white dessert wine made from the Khikhvi grape variety grown in Kardanakhi.
- **Saamo**, is a vintage dessert wine from Rkatsiteli.
- **Gelati**, a white dry wine made of the Tsolikauri, Tsitska and Krakhuna grape varieties cultivated in Western Georgia.
- **Kakheti**, a white table wine made of the Rkatsiteli and Mtsvane grape varieties cultivated in Kakheti.
- **Bodbe**, a white from Rkatsiteli
- **Dimi**, a white made from the Tsolikauri and Krakhuna grape varieties grown on small areas in Imereti (Western Georgia) by the old local technique consisting in fermenting the grape pulp to which grape husks are added.
- **Gareji**, a dry white wine made of the Rkatsiteli and Mtsvane grape varieties cultivated in Kakheti.
- **Ereti**, a dry white dry wine made from Rkatsiteli and Mtsvane grapes
- **Shuamta**, a dry white dry wine made from Rkatsiteli and Mtsvane grapes
- **Alazani**, a mid-straw colored semi-sweet wine made from 100% Rkatsiteli.

Georgian red wines include:

- **Akhasheni**, a naturally semi-sweet red wine made from the Saperavi grape variety grown in the Akhasheni vineyards of the Gurdzhaani district in Kakheti.
- **Khvanchkara**, a high-end, naturally semi-sweet red wine made from the Alexandria and Mudzhuretuli grape varieties cultivated in the Khvanchkara vineyards in Racha, Western Georgia.
- **Kindzmarauli**, a high quality naturally semi-sweet wine made from Saperavi from the slopes of the Caucasian mountains in the Kvareli district of Kakheti.
- **Mukuzani**, a dry red wine made from 100% Saperavi in Mukuzani, Kakheti.
- **Ojaleshi**, a red semi-sweet wine made from the grape variety of the same name cultivated on the mountain slopes overhanging the banks of the Tskhenis-Tskali river
- **Pirosmani**, a naturally semi-sweet red wine from Saperavi
- **Saperavi**, a red wine made from the Saperavi grape variety grown in some areas of Kakheti.
- **Usakhelauri**, a naturally semi-sweet wine, produced from the Usakhelauri grape variety cultivated mostly in the Zubi-Okureshi district in Western Georgia.
- **Apsny**, a naturally semi-sweet red wine made of red grape varieties cultivated in Abkhazia.
- **Lykhny**, a naturally semi-sweet pink wine made of the Izabela grape variety cultivated in Abkhazia.
- **Mtatsminda**, a pink semi-dry wine produced from Saperavi, Tavkveri, Asuretuli, Rkatsiteli and other grape varieties grown in the Tetritskaro, Kaspi, Gori and Khashuri districts.
- **Aguna**, a pink semi-dry wine from Saperavi, Cabernet and Rkatsiteli grown in east Georgia.
- **Sachino**, a pink semi-dry wine from the Aleksandreuli, Aladasturi, Odzhaleshi, Tsitska, Tsolikauri and other grape varieties cultivated in west Georgia.
- **Barakoni**, a naturally semi-dry red wine made from the unique Alexandreuli and Mudzhuretuli grape varieties cultivated in western Georgia on the steep slopes of the Rioni gorge in the Caucasian mountains.
- **Salkhino**, a liqueur-type dessert wine made from the Izabella grape variety with an addition of the Dzvelshava, Tsolikauri and other

grape varieties cultivated in the Mayakovski district (western Georgia).

- **Alazani**, a light red, semi-sweet wine made from a 60% Saperavi, 40% Rkatsiteli blend.

Georgian fortified wines include:

- **Kardanakhi**, from Rkatsiteli.
- **Anaga**, a madeira-type wine made from the Rkatsiteli, Khikhvi and Mtsvane grape varieties.
- **Sighnaghi**, a port type wine made from Rkatsiteli grown in the Sighnaghi district in Kakheti.
- **Veria**, a fortified vintage white port made from Rkatsiteli, Mtsvane, Chinuri and other commercial grape varieties grown in Eastern Georgia.
- **Lelo**, a port-type wine made from the Tsitska and Tsolikauri grape varieties grown in the Zestaphoni, Terjola, Baghdati and Vani districts.
- **Marabda**, a port-type wine made from Rkatsiteli.
- **Kolkheti**, a fortified vintage white port made from Tsolikauri, Tsitska and other white grape varieties grown in Western Georgia.
- **Taribana**, a port-type wine made from Rkatsiteli cultivated in Kakheti.

Georgia in total has eighteen appellations registered with the EU. The region of **Kakheti** in the east produces 80% of the country's wine, mainly from Sapreravi, Rkatsiteli, and Mtsvane. It has a number of sub-regions. **Kartli** in the center is a cooler region than Kakheti, producing lighter wines, sometimes sparkling. **Imereti** and **Racha** in the west have their own characteristic light white grape varieties, most prominent being Tsitska and Tsolikouri, which may be blended with each other. Higher in elevation is **Racha-Lecdhkhumi**, with its local reds Mujuretuli and Alexsandrouli from which semi-sweet and sweet wines are made. The coastal trio of **Samegrelo**, **Guria**, and **Ajara** are minor producers.

Chapter Twenty-One

World Wine Regions
The Middle East

Turkey

Wine Map of Turkey

Turkey, a big populous country that straddles two continents, is one of the world's leading producers of grapes. Unfortunately, the Turks make wine from only two percent of their grapes—the rest they eat out of hand, dry into raisins, or use to produce their anise-flavored spirit *raki*. Turkey is a majority Moslem country, bringing on an ambivalent relationship between the government and the wine industry. Turkey goes back and forth between suppressing alcoholic beverages and encouraging their production. Taxes on wine are high in Turkey. When this author was in Istanbul, his tour guide stressed that he did not drink wine, but was very fond of "fermented grape juice." The comment highlights Turkey's schizophrenia on the subject. What is without question is that among the 75 million Turks, in a state that is on the face of it secular, a market for wine exists.

Turkey's wine grapes are largely indigenous, based on the judgment that sufficient Cabernet and Chardonnay are being produced in the rest of the world. The wine regions we show on the map are informal, since the country lacks defined legal appellations. Major grapes include:

- **Bornova Misketi**, a form of Muscat, grown in and around the Aegean city of Izmir. It produces aromatic, lively, light, white wines ranging from dry to lusciously sweet, with aromas of honeysuckle, basil, rose, mint, honey, bergamot, lemon balm, orange flowers, daisies, grapefruit and melon.

- **Boğazkere**, meaning "throat burner," is a tannic red grown in southeastern Anatolia. It prefers hot climates. The wine has medium acidity, and notes of black cherry, raspberry, blackberry, mulberry, pepper, clove, eucalyptus, tobacco, leather, pine forest, dark chocolate, and licorice.

- **Öküzgözü** is native to eastern Anatolia. It gets its name from the fact that it has large, black berries that resemble a bull's eye. The high acid wine is delicately flavored, with fruit and floral notes and a gentle color like Pinot Noir.

- **Kalecik Karası** grows in central Anatolia not far from the capital in Ankara. The dry wine is a light rose in color, with candy aromas on the nose, medium body, low tannins, and crisp acidity.

- **Çalkarası**, from the Aegean region, makes light fruity red and rosé wines, with peaches, strawberry, red and white fruit, and stimulating acidity.

- **Sultaniye**, the "Sultana," mainly grown for raisins, grows in the Aegean region, making light fruity white wines with notes of asparagus, pear, pineapple, floral, mango, lemon, golden and green apples, and hay.

- **Narince**, whose name means "delicate" in Turkish, comes to us from the Tokat area in mid-southern Anatolia. The grape makes straw-colored wines with floral notes, yellow fruit and citrus aromas on the nose. It is round, medium to full bodied, balanced with good acidity. Narince often sees oak, and may find itself in blends with Chardonnay.

- **Emir** is native to Cappadocia in mid-southern Anatolia. It makes crisp refreshing straw-colored wines, with notes of pineapple, kiwi, lemon, orange, rose, limestone and minerality. It rarely sees oak.

Turkey's very general (and informal) wine regions include:

Marmara spreads over three countries: southern Bulgaria (Northern Thrace), northeastern Greece (Western Thrace), and northwestern Turkey. It touches the Black Sea, the Aegean Sea and the Sea of Marmara. Climate is Mediterranean with hot summers and mild winters. Soils range from lime to gravelly loam and dense clays. Marmara produces 15% of all Turkish wine. Major wine grapes are Adakarası, Cabernet Franc, Cabernet Sauvignon, Chardonnay, Cinsault, Gamay, Kalecik Karası, Merlot, Papazkarası, Riesling, Sauvignon Blanc, Sémillon, Syrah, and Viognier.

The **Aegean** region is the western part of Turkey facing the Aegean Sea and Greek Islands, with a hub in the coastal city of Izmir. Climate ranges from maritime near the coast to continental inland. Soils range from clay loam in the lower elevations to calcareous chalks at elevation. The region accounts for more than half of all Turkish wine. Grapes include Alicante Bouschet, Boğazkere, Bornova Misketi, Cabernet Franc, Cabernet Sauvignon, Carignan, Chardonnay, Çalkarası, Çavuş, Dimrit, Grenache, Kalecik Karası, Karalahna, Kuntra, Malbec, Merlot, Mourvedre, Narince, Öküzgözü, Petit Verdot, Pinot Noir, Sangiovese, Sauvignon Blanc, Syrah, Sultaniye, Tempranillo, Vasilaki, and Viognier.

The **Mediterranean** region is the southern part of Turkey on the Mediterranean Sea. Climate is Mediterranean. Soils range from pebbly clay loam to calcareous chalks. The region accounts for less than one percent of Turkey's wines, with plantings of Boğazkere, Cabernet Sauvignon, Chardonnay, Kalecik Karas, Malbec, Merlot, Öküzgözü, Pinot Noir, Sauvignon Blanc, and Syrah.

Central Anatolia has a continental climate, with cold winters and hot summers. Soils are red clay and decomposed granite. Accounting for about 15% of all Turkish wine, the region produces the indigenous grapes Boğazkere, Narince, and Öküzgözü. **Eastern Anatolia** has similar soils and produces the same grapes. **Southeastern Anatolia** borders Iraq and Syria. Climate is harsh. The region accounts for three percent of Turkey's wine, mainly from Boğazkere.

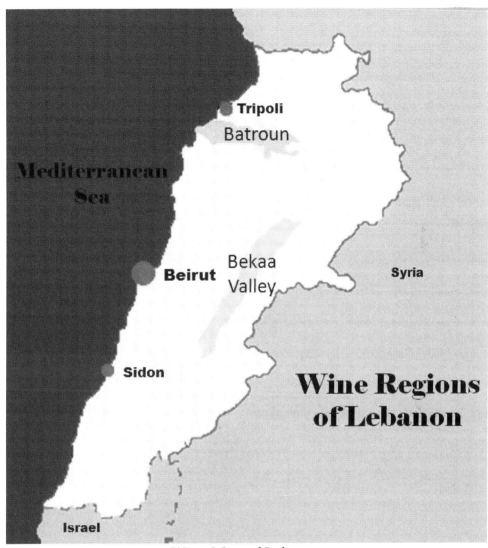

Wine Map of Lebanon

One fortunate thing happened to Lebanon after the breakup of the Ottoman Empire with its defeat in the First World War. A League of Nations mandate gave administration of the country to France, so the influence of that wine arbiter is strong. A fifth of the Lebanese population uses French on a daily basis. The language is used alongside Arabic on bank notes, public buildings, and vehicle license plates. It is also the language of, and the inspiration for, much Lebanese wine. French oenologists know Lebanon well.

Lebanon is hot and dry, with 300 days of sunshine a year. Viticulture becomes possible in the country because of high elevations. Wine is usually strong and red. Château Musar in the **Bekaa Valley** is Lebanon's most well known producer, creating distinctive age-worthy red blends of Cabernet Sauvignon, Cinsault, and Carignan. The country in general is moving away from Bordeaux varieties, however, in favor of a southern French and Spanish configuration of Syrah, Grenache, Mourvèdre, Carignan, and Tempranillo.

In the north, the region of **Batroun** (named after that city, one of the world's oldest) is known for wine from a number of Maronite Monasteries as well as commercial wineries like Neila al-Bitar, producing Syrah, Mourvèdre and the whites Marsanne and Chardonnay—all nicely French.

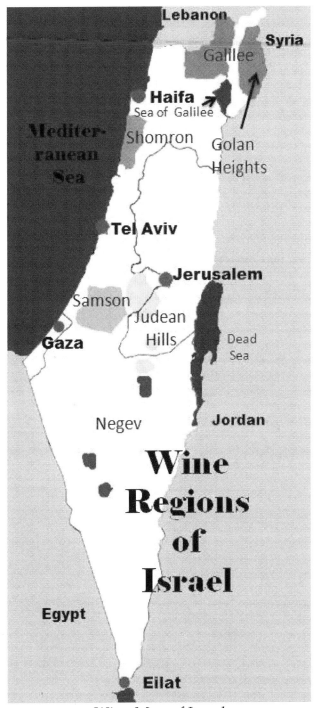

Wine Map of Israel

The wines of the Bible, if they survived the expulsion of the Jews from Israel at all, did not survive the Arab conquest of the seventh century. In the late 19th century Jewish French Baron Edmond de Rothschild, owner Château Lafite-Rothschild, began importing French grape varieties and technical expertise to the region, but a viable industry did not begin until the 1970s. All grapes are international. Cabernet Sauvignon, Merlot, Chardonnay, and Sauvignon Blanc are the leaders, but above all Cabernet Franc is making itself Israel's signature wine. Many of Israel's exports are of rapidly-improving Kosher wines.

Latitude-challenged Israel depends on altitude to grow quality grapes for wine. The best wines come from several thousand feet up in **Galilee** and from up to four thousand feet in elevation in the disputed **Golan Heights**. Here are planted 40% of Israel's vines. South and east of Jerusalem, the **Judean Hills** produce about 8% of the wines, but vines grow improbably in the **Negev** desert in the south. Throughout this sun-baked region, maintaining grape acidity is the challenge. Drip irrigation is essential.

Chapter Twenty-Two

World Wine Regions
Asia

India

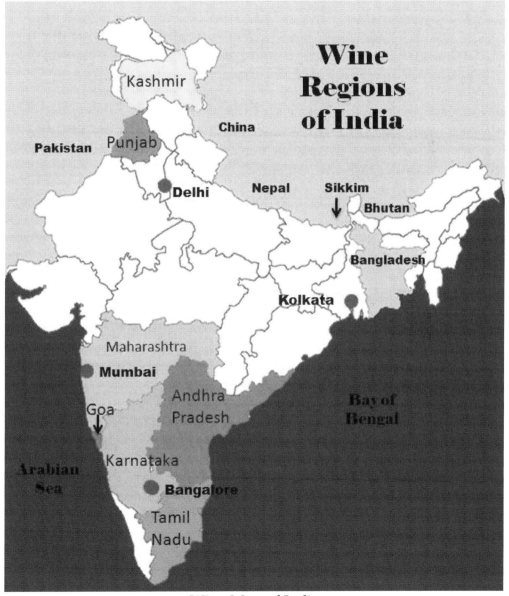

Wine Map of India

India's large and expanding middle class, combined with high taxes on wine imports, have acted as a real impetus for the Indian wine industry. In 2001, Mumbai's state of **Maharashtra** created financial incentives for wine investment, and now produces two-thirds of India's wines, primarily in the high altitude Nashik district on the Deccan Plateau. The Sula winery, flush with Silicon Valley investment, has become India's number one producer, making red wines from Shiraz, Cabernet Sauvignon, Zinfandel, Merlot and Malbec, rosé from Zin, whites from Sauvignon Blanc and Chenin Blanc, and a late harvest dessert wine from Chenin Blanc. In the Nandi Hills near Bangalore in the Indian state of **Karnataka**, Grover Vineyards, with the help of renowned French winemaker Michel Rolland, has been producing whites from Sauvignon Blanc and Viognier and reds and rosés from Cabernet Sauvignon and Shiraz. In this tropical climate, vines never go into dormancy, but precise pruning tames them appropriately, allowing the vines to repose as they would otherwise do in winter. **Goa**, with its Portuguese heritage, has long produced a Port-like fortified wine.

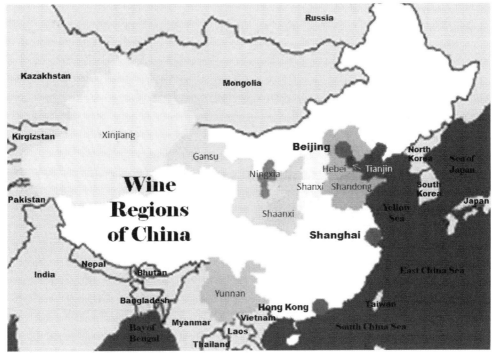

Wine Map of China

Wine consumption is on the rise in China to such an extent that the market for top quality Bordeaux classed growths is going through the ceiling. Not content with buying all the imported wine they can get their hands on, the newly affluent Chinese are planting many a vine. Despite being in temperate latitudes, much of China is climatically hostile to the grapevine. Like the United States, whose latitudes are similar, the center of the country sees vast temperature extremes, vine-killing frost in winter and too much heat in summer, Similarly, the east coast sees humidity and over-eager monsoons. Unlike the US, China does not have the equivalent of California in its west—Tibet is hardly wine country. The Chinese use ingenuity to get around all this. **Shandong** and **Hebei**, near the capital of Beijing, work with a favorable maritime climate to produce vinifera grapes. Shandong's Yantai-Penglai, with over 140 wineries, produces 40% of China's wine. Entrepreneurial wine producers have begun to move due west, to **Shanxi**, and **Ningxia** (which recently beat Bordeaux wines in a blind Cabernet tasting). **Yunnan**, with help from Australian winemakers, is beating its low latitude with the usual antidote, altitude.

The grapevine in China's northwest Central Asian region of **Xinjiang** dates back to Greek settlers who followed the conquests of Alexander the Great in the fourth century BC. Marco Polo mentions Xinjiang's wine in his *Travels*. Today Xinjiang is a careful producer of Cabernet Sauvignon.

Reliable statistics are hard to come by where China is concerned, but Cabernet Sauvignon, Merlot, Chardonnay, Cabernet Franc, and Syrah appear to be the most widely planted wine grapes. To cohabit with the international grapes, investment from abroad might account for up to half of Chinese vineyard and winery development.

Japan's
Major Wine-
Producing
Prefectures

Hokkaido

Yamagata

Nagano

Hyogo

Yamanashi
Tokyo
Yokohama

Osaka

Ōita

Kumamoto

Miyazaki

Wine Map of Japan

Take the humidity and temperature extremes of the US east coast, the similar difficulties of China's east coast, and add a few typhoons, score the country with crags and precipitous mountains, and you get Japan—veritably a terrible place to try to grow European winegrapes. To this dire scenario one must add an extreme level of refinement when it comes to all things food and drink—Japan has more sommeliers than any other country. Add a pragmatic streak, and what do you get? Grapes that work in Japan, rather than the usual international crowd. Japan adapted the pink-skinned **Koshu**, originally a table grape, for its signature wines. These wines are a pale straw, quite delicate, and as such a match for the delicate nature of Japanese cuisine. Koshu has vinifera genes, and might be of central Asian origin. The Japanese also developed a hybrid, **Muscat Bailey-A**, which has been used for sweet wines, but is coming into greater prominence as a component in dry white blends.

Japan's primarily vine growing areas are those that tend to have less rainfall, or are otherwise shielded from the elements, often by mountains and ridgelines. The northern island of **Hokkaidō** and **Yamanashi Prefecture** near Tokyo are the best known regions, followed by **Nagano** and **Yamagata**. On the southern island of Kyushu, the three prefectures of **Ōita**, **Kumomoto**, and **Miyazaki** take advantage of warmer conditions to produce Chardonnay and sweet rosés from the American-bred Campbell Early grape.

1. Agiorgitiko (I-your-yee'-tee-ko)
2. Aglianico (Ahl-yan'-ee-co)
3. Airen (Air'-in)
4. Alicante Bouschet (Al-uh-con'tay Boo-shay')
5. Albarino (Al-ba-reen'-yo)
6. Aleatico (Ahl-yah'-tee-co)
7. Arneis (Ar-nayss')
8. Assyrtiko (Ahs'-sir-teeko)
9. Amarone (Ah-ma-roe'-nay)
10. Barbaresco (Bar-ba-ress'-co)
11. Barbera (Bar-bear'-ah)
12. Barolo (Ba-roll'-lo)
13. Brachetto (Bra-ket'-to)
14. Beaujolais (Bo'-zho-lay)
15. Blaufränkisch (Blau-frenk'-ish)
16. Burger (Ber'-gur)
17. Cabernet Franc (Cab'-air-nay Fronc)
18. Brunello (Brew-nel'-lo)
19. Cabernet Pfeffer   (Cab'-er-nay Fef-fur')
20. Cabernet Sauvignon (Cab'-er-nay Sow'-vin-yaw (n))
21. Canaiolo (Kah'-nay-Yo'-loh)
22. Catarratto (Ca-ta-rat'-toe)
23. Carignane (Cah'-reen-nyahn)
24. Carmenere (Car-meuh-nair')
25. Chablis (Shab-lee')
26. Champagne (Sham-payn)
27. Cava (Kah'-va)
28. Charbono (Shar'-bo-no)
29. Chardonnay (Shar'don-nay)
30. Chasselas (Shass'-la)
31. Chianti (Key-ahn'-tee)
32. Chelois   (Shel'- Wah)
33. Chenin Blanc   (Shay'-nan Blawn)
34. Colombard(Coll'-um-bar)
35. Cortese   (Cor-tay'-zay)
36. Cinsaut / Cinsault (San'-so)
37. Counoise (Coon-wahz)
38. Dafni (Daf- Nee)
39. Étraire de la Dui / Étraire (Ay-trair' duh lah Dwee)
40. Dolcetto (Dole-chet'-toe)
41. Ederena (Ed'- her-rayna)
42. Gamay (Gam'-may)
43. Gewürztraminer (Geh-verts'-tra-min-er)

44. Folle Blanche (Fall Blawnsh)
45. Grechetto (Greh-keh'-toh)
46. Grenache (Gren-nash')
47. Grenache Blanc (Gren-nash' Blawnk)
48. Kerner   (Kair'-ner)
49. Gruner Veltliner (Groo'-ner Velt-leen'-eer)
50. Kadarka / Kadarka Blau (Kah-dark'-Ah)
51. Madeira (Mad-deer'-ah)
52. Malbec (Mal'-beck)
53. Lacrima (La'-Creem-ah)
54. Marsanne (Mar'-sahn)
55. Merlot (Mair-lo')
56. Montepulciano d'Abruzzo (Mawn-tay-pool-chon'-no Dah Broot'-zo)
57. Muscadet (Moos'cah-day)
58. Moscato d'Asti / Moscato (Mos-caht'-toe)
59. Mourvedre / Mataro / Monastrell (Moor-ved'-ruh)
60. Nero d'Avola (Ne'roh dee-Ahv' -ol - lah)
61. Petite Sirah / Durif (Puh-teet' Seer-rah')
62. Nebbiolo (Neb-be-oh'-lo)
63. Pinot Blanc (Pee'-no Blawnk)
64. Pinot Gris / Pinot Grigio (Pee'no Gree)
65. Pinot Noir (Pee'-no Nwahr)
66. Ramandolo   (Rah-mahn'-doe-lo)
67. Pinotage (Pee'-no-tazh)
68. Port
69. Retsina (Ret-zeena')
70. Ribolla Gialla   (Ree-boh'-lah Jah'lah)
71. Recioto (Ray-chaw'-toe)
72. Riesling (Rees'-ling)
73. Rosso Conero (Roh'-so Coh'-nae-ro)
74. Rosso di Montalcino (Ross'-so dee Mawn-tal-chee'-no)
75. Sagrantino (Sah-grahn-tee'-no)
76. Rousanne (Roo-sahn')
77. Rousette (Roe'-set)
78. Sauternes - Eng(Saw'-turn) - Fre(So-tairn')
79. Sauvignon Blanc (Sow'-vin-yaw(n) Blawnk)
80. Sangiovese (San-gee-oh-vay'say)
81. Scheurebe (Shoy'-ray-buh)
82. Schiava   (Ski-ah'-va)
83. Semillon (Say'-me-yawn)
84. St. Laurent (Sonkt Louw-rohn)
85. Seyval Blanc (Say-Vuhl' Blawnk)
86. Shiraz / Syrah (Sir-rah')
87. Tempranillo (Tem-pran-nee'-yo)
88. Terret Blanc (Tair-Ray Blawnk)
89. Sylvaner / Silvaner / Gruner Silvaner   (Sil-von'-ner)

90. Terret Gris (Tair-Ray Gree)
91. Terret Noir (Tair-Ray Nwahr)
92. Torrontes (Tor-on'-tyez)
93. Verdelho / Verdejo (Vair-dayl'-yo)
94. Ulavino   (Oo-lah-veen'-oh)
95. Valpolicella (Val-po-Lee-chel'-la)
96. Viognier (Vee'-oh-nyay)
97. Vouvray (Voo'-vray)
98. Vinho Verde (Veen'-yo Vair'-day)
99. Zinfandel (Zin-Fan-dell)

Acknowledgements

My name is Alma and I'm the Founder of **BuyWine.com** a Website that truly works to connect wine lovers with the world of wine in an easy and uncomplicated fashion. I love wine and I love travel and I just think that they should be accessible to all. There is no secret to wine, at the end of the day it is just grapes and hard work put together to create something we all love. I'm an Entrepreneur that came to America in 1988 from Ireland. I'm a very courageous, fearless, confident, positively unique woman who loves to inspire everyone I come in contact with. My Dream has come true out of hard work, dedication and never giving up, and doing the right thing.

But this Book could not come to **FRUITION** without having an incredibly awesome team. **Elliott Essman, Zeke Quezada** and **Joe Filutze** for allowing me to indulge them with my dream of **BuyWine.com**

Elliott, I used to think I knew a lot about Wine, but I really didn't until getting to know you, for that I'm so appreciative. **BuyWine.com** has the best Wine Academy and that's because of you and your knowledge, thank you so very much.

Zeke, where do I start, you've been by my side since I requested 12 minutes and 17 seconds of your time a few years ago. Understanding you didn't know me; you gave me the time anyway. Wonderfully you've been here everyday helping me with my crazy dream. **BuyWine.com** could not be possible without all YOU do for me and for that, no words can describe how important you are to me.

My Darling Joe, there is not one word that I can actually say of how I feel about you. In a lifetime, I never thought I'd find someone who could put up with my crazy ideas, and me but I did, YOU. Thank you for always being there, supporting me on this journey and pushing me to new greatness every day. When we met, I told you **"I'd never make it boring",** and that is so true, life has been so marvelous with you by my side. Joe, you said, **"I've always wanted to do something big, and when I met you Alma, I knew it was You and BuyWine.com "** Joe, Thank You, I Love you more and more every day!

Lastly, to my exceptionally brilliant daughter Miss Victoria, I'm so proud of you for being such an incredible young adult. Thank you for sharing your time with my Business for all these years. You are my treasure; God gave me you as the most precious thing ever! **"Stay Blessed Always"!**

Elliott, Zeke, Joe and Miss Victoria, my heart is so filled with respect and I truly admire all of you. Thank you for making **BuyWine.com** and this Book a reality.

Dreams do come to a reality, Thank you God for allowing me to stay focused and be where I am today.

Alma Callan, Founder of BuyWine.com